Cleveland Fishing Guide

John Barbo

GRAY & COMPANY, PUBLISHERS
CLEVELAND

Photographs by the author except where noted.

Fish illustrations from *Fishes of Ohio* by Milton Trautman
(reprinted with permission of the Ohio State University Press)

Gray & Company, Publishers
1588 E. 40th St., Cleveland, OH 44103
(216) 431-2665
www.grayco.com

Library of Congress Cataloging-in-Publication Data
Barbo, John
Cleveland fishing guide / by John Barbo.
Includes bibliographical references and index.
1. Fishing—Ohio—Cleveland—Guidebooks. 2.
Fishing—Ohio—Cleveland—Directories. I. Title.
SH535.B37 1998
799.1'1'0977132—ddc21   98-25347   CIP

ISBN 1-886228-13-2

Printed in the United States of America

Second printing

This book is dedicated to my parents, John and Mary Barbo, who always found the time to take me fishing. Little did they know that they were introducing me to a lifelong pursuit.

I would also like thank my wife, Nancy, for her patience while I completed the research for this book and for occasionally humoring me by joining me on a fishing excursion. She may not understand this crazy sport, but at least she tolerates it. I could not have completed this project without her support and encouragement.

And lastly, thank you to the dedicated men and women of our local park districts and conservation agencies who work tirelessly to conserve Ohio's natural resources and to provide first-class recreational opportunities for the citizens of this beautiful state. Job well done.

Acknowledgments

This book would not have been possible without generous and knowledgeable help from the following individuals and groups: Vince LaConte, Phil Hillman, and Kevin Kayle from the Ohio Division of Wildlife District Three; the Ohio Environmental Protection Agency; the Ohio Department of Health; Kim Coy at the City of Akron Water Supply; Frank Meyerholtz, Dave Cartee, Dan Urbania—all local fishermen who shared a wealth of knowledge with me; representatives from Geauga Park District; Steve Madewell from Lake Metroparks; Ken Halko, Fisheries Specialist at Cleveland Metroparks; Chris Gram of Lorain County Park District; Kevin Durkin, Dave Bernert, and John Barbo Sr.—all of whom accompanied me on several fishing trips; Nancy Barbo and Paige Hosier for reviewing the manuscript; and John Tidyman for hooking me up with Gray & Company, Publishers. And lastly, thank you to all the polite, generous, and colorful fishermen who supplied me with vast amounts of worthwhile information while I researched this book. They made the research a lot of fun.

Contents

West

Farther West

South

Farther South

Worth the Drive

Introduction

The first time I visit a lake, pond, or river, certain things tend to happen. I will generally get lost on the way, taking at least twice as long to get there as I had planned and using twice as much gas. Upon arrival, I will discover that the water is too low to launch a boat, a special permit is required to launch, or there are no motors allowed on the lake. Then, if the "stocked lake" bragged about in the park's pamphlet hasn't turned out to be a half-acre pond with fish barely large enough to use for bait, I will probably spend half the time I had allocated for the trip trying to decide where to fish, what to fish for, and what bait or lures to use. On the ride home, I may get lost again.

My second visit normally runs a little smoother, and I might actually spend most of my time fishing. But I will have already sacrificed one day trying to figure the place out. And that's a shame.

Maybe you've had a similar experience, when an outing you hoped would be a fun and productive day of fishing turned into a disaster just because you overlooked a few seemingly insignificant variables, like how to get there, what to bring, or even when to go.

If so, then this book is for you.

It introduces 55 fishing destinations—51 within an hour's drive of downtown Cleveland, 4 a little farther away—and tells you everything you'll need to know in order to make your first trip to each a productive, safe, and enjoyable outing.

It will also open your eyes to exciting fishing opportunities you might not have known existed in Northeast Ohio and help you discover the variety of natural resources that make our part of the Buckeye State such a wonderful place to fish.

This guide includes fishing spots for a broad range of fishermen.

Some are perfectly suited for an afternoon of family fishing, where the main quarry is bluegill and the fishing gets no more complicated than a hook and bobber. These are ideal destinations for beginners or families whose goal is not to catch the maximum number of fish but to have the maximum amount of fun.

Others present more challenging opportunities for experienced fishermen. These more complex fisheries are capable of giving up some very large fish and offering a wider variety of fishing.

For times when the travel bug hits and you might be in the mood for a short two- or three-day adventure, I've also included several weekend getaway ideas. These destinations provide the chance to experience some beautiful areas in other parts of Ohio and in surrounding states and will give you the opportunity to catch species of fish that might not be available locally.

How to Use This Book

For catfish, soak entire book in chicken blood, firmly impale on no. 2 hook, and fish at or near the bottom. For bass, impale through cover, then jerk through the water like a wounded fish. For all other purposes, just keep reading.

How the Fishing Sites Were Selected

I have tried to give a fair representation of the best nearby fishing destinations for a wide variety of Cleveland anglers, something for everyone regardless of your fishing ability or your level of passion for the sport.

Several criteria guided me in choosing the destinations. First, I wanted the book to be versatile, and to contain information that would be valuable to the remarkably diverse population of fishermen in this area. Therefore, I tried to balance the locations with regard to skill level needed to fish them, availability of access, and species of fish found at each one. Whether your fish of choice is largemouth bass, walleye, bluegill, or steelhead, whether your favorite way to fish is from the shore, from a boat, or wading, this book will provide you with numerous locations that suit your style of fishing.

Second, I tried to include locations throughout the Cleveland area, so that no matter where you live or might be visiting, you can page through the book and find several near you. Some locations may not be the most productive in terms of lunker bass or skillet-sized panfish, but as a group they do offer a range of exciting fishing opportunities throughout Greater Cleveland. For a short fishing trip or a summer evening on the water, most of us desire a location that is close to home. Hopefully this book will provide you with several destinations that fit the bill.

Third, every location had to offer the opportunity to actually catch fish. Regardless of how accessible or close a location might be, if it provided little in the way of fishing excitement, it was not included in this book. After all, while scenery, wildlife, and relaxation are certainly reasons to fish, the thrill of feeling the tug of a fish on the other end of the line is what keeps us coming back.

What About Lake Erie?

This guide covers rivers, streams, inland lakes, ponds, and the Lake Erie shoreline. It does not cover open-water fishing on Lake Erie. There are two main reasons for this.

First, I want this to be a guide for most Cleveland-area anglers, not just those lucky enough to own boats. This is why all locations covered have access for shoreline fishing, albeit limited access at certain places.

Second, Lake Erie is a rapidly changing fishery. Zebra mussels and round gobies, for example, are having a dramatic effect on the Lake's ecosystem. Water clarity, the presence of extended weed beds, and the makeup of the fish populations seem to be changing very rapidly. Information that may have been accurate last year might be out of date already. A book of this sort just can't do the subject justice. Better to rely on frequently updated sources, such the very good fishing columns in local newspapers (most notably D'Arcy Egan's in *The Plain Dealer* and Jeff Frischkorn's in the *News-Herald*) or fishing reports from local bait shops.

Area Covered

I have included fishing destinations that are roughly within an hour's drive of downtown Cleveland. There are some exceptions, such as Pymatuning, that are important enough to warrant relaxing the one-hour rule. These places might require more of a drive, but they offer fishing opportunities that more than make up for the added travel. See the map at the beginning of the "Locations" section on pages 42–43.

Difficulty Rating

Each location in this guide is rated by level of fishing difficulty, as summarized by the following three categories: *Recreational, Intermediate*, and *Challenging*. Every location fits at least one of these categories, and many fit more than one because they offer a variety of fishing challenges.

Locations listed as *Recreational* are ideal for family fishing adventures, for young anglers, and for those fishermen who want to wet their lines without wading rivers, launching boats, or covering hundreds of acres of shoreline in search of a prime fishing spot. Despite the heavy fishing pressure these smaller locations receive, rest assured you can still hook into some surprisingly large fish. Usually, these locations have other activities and resources for all members of the family, such as picnic areas, swimming beaches, and hiking trails.

A rating of *Intermediate* indicates that a location offers a somewhat greater challenge in terms of access and of required fishing techniques. Novice anglers can do well at these locations, and even the most advanced fishermen can enjoy them, too.

Lastly, the *Challenging* listings indicate that even the most advanced anglers will at times scratch their heads and wonder, "Where in the hell are the fish?" These are the locations that offer new challenges seasonally and also produce some trophy-sized fish. Their locale is likely to be more remote, and access can present some serious tests of angling ability.

I considered several factors when deciding on these ratings, including the following:

Size. Experienced anglers may not find a three-acre pond challenging, but that same pond provides a perfect fishing environment for the novice or the recreational fisherman. Similarly, expansive Pymatuning Reservoir, at 14,000 acres, provides an extremely challenging fishery for those who take the sport a bit more seriously, but is probably not the best choice for the novice.

Access. Is there shoreline access, or is the access primarily by boat? Is a long hike required to reach the fishing hole? Is there a possibility of dangerous river wading?

Complexity of the fishery. Is the location a small pond with large-mouth bass and panfish, or a larger body of water with a diverse population of fish that migrate seasonally? Are experience and know-how required in order to be consistently successful, or are advanced angling tactics not a necessity?

Amenities. Are there restrooms, playgrounds, or other amenities that make it appropriate for family outings?

Remember, these ratings are provided only as a rough guide to help you decide if a certain location is appropriate for the type of fishing you choose to take part in and for your skill level. They are not meant to scare you away from destinations that may offer more challenge than you are used to.

Water Type
Water Type gives an idea of what to expect from these destinations in terms of size. Anything under about 10 acres I considered a pond; anything over I listed as a lake. Many of the entries I listed as inland lakes are technically reservoirs constructed earlier in this century for flood control and water supply. Lake Erie entries are restricted to shoreline fishing and, other than listing boat launches that provide access to the lake, do not go into detail regarding boat fishing.

Access
You'll want to know what kind of access there is to the water so you can plan what kind of gear to bring. I list the major kinds of access: shoreline, wading, piers, breakwalls, and boating. (I make a distinction between piers and breakwalls. Piers are generally elevated platforms extending into the body of water. Breakwalls are barriers, usually made of large boulders or concrete, that may extend into the water or follow the shoreline. Both provide excellent fishing access, though piers usually offer more convenient, easier fishing.)

What's Biting
This list of what you can generally expect to catch at a given location was gathered through anecdotal research and by consulting EPA electroshocking surveys. I did not list the occasional rare catches. A king salmon and lake trout were reportedly caught out of the Rocky River while I researched this book, but I have not included them in the "What's Biting?" section because they are the exception, not the norm. Most of the fisheries I visited are dynamic and complex, and there is always the possibility of catching an introduced species, a survivor from

a remnant population once stocked locally, or a misguided member of a species stocked in one of the other Great Lakes that somehow found itself on the shores of Lake Erie.

I have also categorized some subspecies under a single heading. "Catfish," for example, might include channel catfish and bullheads. When I list "Crappie" as being present in a body of water, I do not distinguish between black and white crappie, and I do not make distinctions between the several varieties of sunfish that one might catch locally. Fishing techniques for closely related fish are usually very similar, and combining them into one listing makes the entry easier to read.

Season and Hours

Generally, I have listed most of the entries as being suitable for fishing year round, which includes, of course, winter. This time of year can be a confusing time for anglers, as temperatures vary from subzero to above freezing. As long as the water remains free of ice, all of the local rivers can be fished. In fact, they can be very productive for steelhead, with the added bonus of providing the brave angler with a quiet, often isolated fishing experience. The winter beauty of the Grand, Chagrin, and Rocky rivers is breathtaking.

Reservoirs and lakes can also be fished throughout the year. When these are not frozen over, shore anglers can do quite well for walleye and rainbow trout where they are stocked. When a cold snap hits and temperatures remain below freezing long enough for lakes to freeze, it's ice fishing time. Ice fishing is a wonderful way to extend the fishing season clear through the winter, but caution is mandatory. Cleveland Metroparks does a good job of providing anglers with ice condition information. For most other lakes and reservoirs, however, ice safety determination is left up to the individual angler.

Facilities

This listing tells you what facilities to expect, including concessions, bait shops, restrooms, picnic facilities, hiking trails, playgrounds, and rangers. (When I have indicated that a location is patrolled by a ranger, it is not a guarantee that the ranger is on duty at the park full time. It does mean that a ranger drives through the park as part of his or her rounds but most likely is not on the premises at all times. Keep this in mind if you have concerns regarding safety.)

Maps

I have included maps for many locations to provide important information fishermen need to be aware of, such as the location of off limits, boat launches and fishing piers, the areas where shoreline fishing is allowed, and other pertinent details that will make your outing more enjoyable. They are not drawn to exact scale and should not be used for navigational or off-trail hiking purposes.

Directions

I have given basic directions to each site's main parking area from the closest major highway. These directions will get you there as long as you can find the main interstate or state route. But you may need to consult a road map if you're coming from across town. And it's possible there might be a shorter route from your location. Play it safe and always take a good road map along.

Other Information Provided in This Guide . . .

The Fish

This section introduces our cast of characters: the different species of fish that are commonly caught in our area. Each entry describes the physical characteristics of the fish, their habitat preferences, and some tips on how to catch them. It also gives the average weight and length of the species along with the current Ohio record. Illustrations are provided to help you identify your catch.

Directory of Local Fishing Resources

This book also provides a directory of fishing-related resources available in Greater Cleveland and Northeast Ohio that can help you when planning and outfitting for your next trip. It includes *Charter services* that can take you or a group on a guided outing; *Suppliers*—such as bait-and-tackle shops, sporting goods stores, and specialty retailers—that can help you choose the right gear for the trip or replace whatever it is you lost on the last trip; and *Fishing Organizations* that provide opportunities to learn more about local fishing and meet knowledgeable anglers who share your passion for the sport, as well as promote the interests of fishermen and conservationists.

* * *

I have tried to do as much of the legwork as possible so that your first trip to a new destination can be fun, not frustrating. While I can't be so detailed as to make you an expert on all fifty-five locations (that would require more than a single book), the information offered here should get you started in the right direction. Then, learning all about the intricate details at each fishing spot is your job. And what a fun and exciting job it is!

Good luck, and happy fishing!

Getting Started

Why Fish?

An interesting question. Why spend countless hours sitting in an aluminum boat getting pelted with rain, or wading chest-deep in river water hovering just a few degrees above freezing? Why tromp through woods and brush, tolerating swarms of mosquitoes and deerflies buzzing around your head and biting your skin? Why spend large amounts of money, time, and effort in pursuit of an animal that we often release unharmed once we catch it? It has been said that some anglers fish for an entire lifetime without realizing that it was not the fish they were after, but something else. What? Here are just a few of the things we gain from fishing:

Family Togetherness

Fishing can be a wholesome, fun experience in a setting that is conducive to communication and exploration. The cost of a single trip to Disney World could buy complete fishing outfits for an entire family, including licenses, rods and reels, polarized sunglasses, lures, and bait—and you'd still have enough money left over for a pair of funny-looking mouse ears. Besides, the make-believe of amusement parks hardly compares to the real-life wonders one encounters in nature.

"Quality time" may be a trendy term, spawned by the hectic lifestyles we lead, but nonetheless it refers to something we all seek. A morning spent fishing with the entire family, or just a dad and son or mother and daughter, provides the quality time necessary to build and maintain healthy, strong relationships.

Physical and Mental Health

Fishing is also a great way to stay healthy—both mentally and physically. Although the stereotypical fisherman is often shown sitting on a fishing pier contemplating a bobber, the sport of fishing can be just that—a sport. Fishing can involve wading in a river for several hours, constantly fighting to maintain your balance against the current's flow. Or it can mean hiking through difficult terrain to reach your "secret spot." It might mean lugging several pounds of fishing gear, and, if you are lucky, struggling to reel in and land a large fish.

It is hard to avoid getting at least some exercise from fishing. More often than not, I am physically drained, yet spiritually refreshed, after a morning or afternoon of fishing. And I have fun doing it.

But fishing is much more than exercise for the body—it is both exercise and relaxation for the mind. Norman MacLean wrote, "One great thing about fly-fishing is that after a while nothing exists of the world but thoughts about fly-fishing." This observation is true not only for fly-fishing but for all types of angling. We get an opportunity to completely forget about work, money, and the rest of the turmoil and stress we deal with daily and focus instead on the single act of catching fish.

Deeper Appreciation of Nature

Fishing also exposes us to many of Greater Cleveland's natural resources that we might not otherwise become familiar with. In the spring and fall keep your eyes open for songbirds and waterfowl that fly through on their migration routes. At several of the destinations listed, you might be lucky enough to catch a glimpse of a bald eagle soaring high above. I have shared a riverbank with deer, and a woodland trail with a red fox and black squirrels, and I've fished under the watchful eye of an osprey. I have tracked the seasons by the species of wildflowers currently in bloom and watched as clouds of mayflies hatched from the Grand River into a summer evening sky. Being outdoors puts me more in touch with the changing of the seasons and the cycles of the natural world. Sometimes I think I fish just as an excuse to get out into the beatiful natural settings found in this area.

Good Eating

Need more reasons to fish? Well, it should come as no surprise that fish can be a healthy addition to any diet. It is low in fat and provides plenty of protein. And let's face it, them fish taste good! Fresh Lake Erie walleye, pan-fried to a golden brown, is certainly one of the most delicious meals you can eat. And you get the satisfaction of knowing that the meal before you is a direct result of your efforts. There are, of course, health risks related to eating fish caught from many local waterways, and these are presented in more detail later in the book.

Just Plain Fun

And hey, let's admit it—catching fish always has been and always will be a whole lot of fun. The thrill I get from the muscled pull of a fish on the other end of my line has not diminished from when I was a child. This seems to be true for most fishermen. I have seen both middle-aged men and children shout with the same delight after fighting and landing a fish. That alone is reason enough to keep at it.

Rules and Regulations

If you're ready to start fishing and are over the age of 16, the first thing to do is purchase a fishing license. You may not enjoy parting with the money, but take heart, because fishing and hunting licenses constitute a large part of the Ohio Division of Wildlife's annual budget. License fees go toward land preservation, fish stocking, education, wildlife management and research, and a host of other tasks that the division carries out in order to maintain high-quality outdoor recreation for Ohio residents. There are places listed in this book that do not require a fishing license, but this is uncommon. Your best bet is to purchase a license and always carry it with you whenever you are out on the water.

Next, familiarize yourself with Ohio fishing regulations, which include restrictions on the size and number of fish you may harvest. Many lakes and rivers have special restrictions with which you must be familiar if you fish them. Remember, ignorance of the law is no excuse if you get into trouble.

Equipment

"The difference between men and boys is the price of their toys" is an adage that certainly rings true with fishermen. The options are endless and will depend largely on the type of fishing you see yourself doing. There are four main types of fishing outfits you can equip yourself with—spinning, spin casting, bait casting, and fly-fishing.

Spinning reels and and spin-cast reels are perhaps the easiest to master and the most versatile, and can be used in almost any fishing situation.

Bait-casting reels are a little more difficult to become proficient with but are very effective in the right circumstance, such as casting a heavy spinnerbait or crankbait for largemouth bass.

Fly-fishing has become quite popular in recent years for catching not only trout but panfish, bass, steelhead, and almost any other species of fish found in our local waters. Catching any of these species on a fly rod is a sure prescription for exciting and challenging fishing.

The most versatile all-around setup for Northeast Ohio would be a spinning reel balanced with a 5 ½- to 7-foot medium-action rod. This rig would be appropriate for just about every entry in this book. A spinning reel is very easy to learn how to operate, making it ideal for young anglers or newcomers to the sport. Yet despite its simplicity, it can be used for some of the most sophisticated fishing techniques.

As you learn more about the sport, and perhaps gravitate toward pursuing one species or another, you can then purchase more appropriate equipment. Rest assured, there is no shortage of specialized gear regardless of the type of fishing you prefer.

When purchasing your gear, a good rule of thumb is to buy the best you can reasonably afford. This does not mean plunging into your kid's college fund. But the quality of a reel or rod is, up to a point, directly related to the cost. A fishing rod in the $50 to $100 price range will outperform one in the $20 to $50 price range. The same can be said for reels, lures, and almost any other piece of fishing equipment. Of course, there is such a thing as overkill.

Of equal importance to the quality of your gear is its proper maintenance. Take good care of it. Equipment that functions properly and performs reliably is essential to enjoyable fishing. Nothing can ruin a trip faster than frequent line tangles or other rod and reel malfunctions.

Perhaps the best piece of advice I can give is that your equipment should never become the focus of why you fish. There is nothing wrong with developing a love for your favorite fishing rig, or longingly scanning the pages of a fishing gear catalog, drooling over a graphite rod with gold-plated eyelets and a titanium ball-bearing reel. Just remember why you got into the sport. It was not because you wanted to blow insane amounts of money on equipment. It was because you loved to catch fish. That is what got you into the sport, and it should always be the reason you stay in it. Since Stone Age man first threw his primitive hook and line into the unseen depths, fishing has provided humans not only with a means of physical subsistence, but also with sustenance for our souls.

Other Useful Gear

Other than actual fishing gear, there are several items I like to carry that might also make your fishing trip a little better.

Sunblock. Few anglers equate fishing with a day at the beach; however, with respect to the amount of exposure to bright morning and afternoon sun, they're not much different. Sunblock is an essential addition to your tackle box. Apply it to the backs of your hands, and to your face (especially the nose), ears, and any other exposed body parts.

Sunglasses. When you go to set the hook into a fish and miss, sending the lure sailing back at you with barbed treble hooks flying, you'll be glad you had these babies on your face. They'll also protect your eyes from the harmful effects of the sun. And the polarized lenses on fishing glasses greatly reduce glare on the water, making underwater structure and fish much easier to see.

Hat. A hat can keep the sun out of your eyes, helping you spot fish and reducing fatigue caused by squinting. It can also be an effective sunblock, keeping the harmful rays off your neck, face, and—for those who are hair-impaired—cranium.

Binoculars and bird book. Perhaps this is just the amateur ornithologist in me, but riparian (river) and pond and lake habitats attract a diversity of avian life that can be fascinating. Bird identification is a hidden pleasure of fishing, and being able to identify a rare species is quite a thrill.

First-aid kit. A small kit, with band-aids, antibacterial ointment, and perhaps an insect sting kit is a good idea. It really helps out in emergencies. Learning basic first-aid techniques is important, too.

Insect repellent. Mosquitoes, deerflies, and horseflies are the bane of fishing and can ruin a trip through sheer annoyance. Bring insect repellent to keep these bothersome little biters at bay.

Food and drink. Normally, I'm so focused on catching fish that I forget about nourishment and hydration. Bring some snacks to keep your energy levels up and try to drink water to keep your body properly hydrated. This is true during both the heat of summer and cold of winter, when your body must be properly hydrated to maintain a healthy temperature. Subnormal body temperature, or hypothermia, can potentially cut short any fishing trip if you aren't careful.

Responsibilities of the Angler

One afternoon, I was walking with a non-fishing friend along the causeway of a local reservoir. Noticing the considerable amount of trash that was strewn along the shoreline, she remarked that it was shocking that fishermen could be so ignorant as to litter and abuse the very places they rely on for their sport.

It is a sad fact that many members of the angling community see our natural resources merely as something to abuse or exploit, with no regard to how their inconsiderate actions might be impacting the very resources that give them pleasure.

When you make the decision to fish, you should understand the importance of being a responsible, ethical angler. This means acting with true respect both for our natural resources and other fishermen. Proper conduct makes fishing a much more enjoyable experience for you as well as your fellow anglers. And it helps maintain the health of the very resources we rely on for our sport. Here are some guidelines:

Don't litter. This includes pop cans, bait containers, food wrappers, lure packaging, cigarette butts, and monofilament, which poses a health threat to wildlife. If you bring it in, take it out.

"Probably the number one complaint we get about fishermen is litter," explained a representative from the Ohio Division of Wildlife. "As a matter of fact, when we do surveys, the reason a lot of people say they leave the sport of fishing is because of litter."

You might want go one step further by carrying a small plastic bag and picking up any litter you find, leaving the area even cleaner than you found it.

Limit your kill, don't kill your limit. Keeping a few fish to eat is fine, but make sure that you do not keep more than you will be able to clean or eat. Throwing fish out because you got tired of cleaning them or they became freezer burned is a shameful waste of a valuable resource.

Respect property boundaries. Do not fish on someone else's property without first receiving permission.

Respect other anglers' rights.

Respect the resources that make our sport possible.

Support local conservation efforts.

Provide a good example by being a responsible angler. Others might learn from you and follow your example.

Advanced Angling Ethics

If everybody followed the rules mentioned above, our sport would certainly be better for it. But today, serious anglers need to do more than simply avoid harming the environment. To protect our valuable resources from increased pressures, today's anglers must make themselves aware of the dangers facing our fisheries and become involved in local and national conservation efforts to fight them.

Somehow, we have let our guard down. It is now common knowledge that many of the fish caught in Northeast Ohio waters test positive for PCBs, lead, mercury, and other toxic chemicals. It is sinful that, as a society, we have so polluted our surroundings that fish taken from public waters are no longer safe to eat, and that harmful chemicals have entwined themselves in the fabric of local food webs. Raw sewage continues to flow into Lake Erie after heavy rainfalls. Unchecked development, especially that occurring close to rivers, continues to funnel runoff directly into waterways, increasing siltation, erosion, and flooding, and decimating the populations of aquatic organisms that live there. And industrial chemicals continue to find their way into our local waterways.

As fishermen, we rely on clean water and undisturbed habitats. It is up to us to act as watchdogs for these resources to guarantee that future generations can enjoy not only the same angling opportunities we currently are blessed with, but perhaps even better ones. Being able to catch and eat a fish from a public waterway without fear of PCBs or heavy metal contamination, and wading in Northeast Ohio rivers without subjecting ourselves to dangerous levels of coliform bacteria, are rights we should be able to enjoy without question. Learn about some of the issues that affect the health of our lakes and rivers and, most importantly, become involved. You'll enjoy the results.

Boating Safety

Many of the fishing spots listed in this book have boat launches for anglers who own boats and boat rentals for those who do not. Fishing from a boat allows you to access coves, deep water, and other places inaccessible to shore fishermen. It is also tremendously relaxing and enjoyable.

But nothing can end a fishing trip faster than a boating accident. If you lose your head out on the water and become careless, you risk not only sending your tackle and equipment to the bottom of the lake for good, but also serious bodily injury or death. You owe it to yourself and anyone else who is in the boat with you to practice safe boating habits anytime you are on the water—regardless of water conditions, distance from shore, or water depth.

Before you venture out into the open water for your next fishing excursion, take some time to become familiar with the following safety guidelines:

Read the Ohio Boat Operator's Guide, which will give you a detailed summary of Ohio's laws and rules regarding boating. (Get a copy by calling the Ohio Department of Natural Resources Division of Wildlife at 614-265-6480.) Ignorance of the law is no excuse for breaking it.

Be certain there is a life jacket for every person on the boat, that they are easily accessible, and that everybody knows their location.

Familiarize yourself with the boat radio and ask the captain to show you how to make an emergency call should the situation arise. Also inquire about the whereabouts of other signal devices, such as flares, smoke, and horns.

Locate the first-aid box and fire extinguisher of any boat you will be riding on.

If an emergency situation did arise, could you stop, start, and steer the boat? The situation may be unlikely, but if something did happen to the captain of the boat, it would be up to you to get yourself and anyone else on the boat back to safety.

In small boats, be sure to follow the load capacity limits listed on the boat, and center your gear both from side to side and bow to stern.

Keep at least three points of contact while moving around in a small boat in order to maintain your balance. An Ohio watercraft safety pamphlet states, "Small boats aren't unstable—people are!" Don't be reckless, and you should not have a problem.

If a small boat capsizes, stick with the boat. Modern small craft are required to have level flotation built in, which means that in the event of a capsize, the boat will float level with the water's surface.

Learn at least the most rudimentary swimming strokes.

And finally, *never mix alcohol and boat piloting*, regardless of your swimming, boating, or drinking experience. There is no denying the strong correlation between boating fatalities and alcohol consumption. Therefore, it is vital for you to make sure that the skipper of the boat refrains from consuming any alcohol. Furthermore, any passengers who are drinking should wear life jackets in case of an unexpected slip overboard.

For you and everyone on your boat, take the time to do it safely.

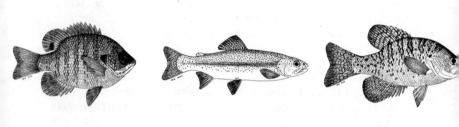

The Fish

Bluegill

Family: Sunfish Family (Centrarchidae)

Scientific Name: *Lepomis macrochirus*

Average Length: 6–10 in.

Average Weight: Under 1 lb.

Ohio Record: 3 lbs. 4 ½ oz. Caught by Willis D. Nicholas on April 28, 1990, at Salt Fork Lake.

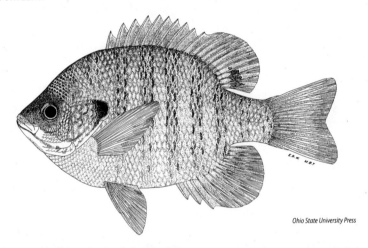

Ohio State University Press

Identification: Bluegill are pan-shaped fish with a small mouth, a long pectoral fin, and a big appetite. The ear flap is always black.

Habitat: Bluegill can be found almost everywhere, from small ponds to large reservoirs and rivers. They prefer clear ponds and lakes with rooted vegetation.

How to Catch: Bluegill will often hit anything that falls in the water, which makes them ideal quarry for beginning anglers. They prefer live bait such as worms, maggots, or terrestrial insects (like crickets, grasshoppers, and ants), but will take small spinners and jigs. Fly fishermen can be successful with a nymph or terrestrial pattern.

Where to Find:

Found at most locations

Bullhead (Yellow, Brown, and Black)

Family: Catfish Family (Ictaluridae)

Scientific Name: *Ameiurus spp.*

Average Length: 10–12 in.

Average Weight: Under 1 lb.

Ohio Record: 4 lbs. 4 oz., 18 ½ in. Caught in farm pond by Hugh Lawrence Jr. on May 20, 1986.

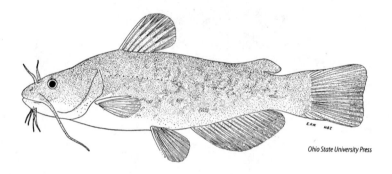

Ohio State University Press

Identification: It is often difficult to distinguish between these catfish. They all have scaleless bodies and color varying from yellow-olive-brown to brownish-black.

Habitat: Bullheads are common throughout the state and can live in a variety of habitats. Brown bullheads are commonly found in habitats with little or no vegetation and having relatively clean, clear water. Black bullheads are able to tolerate more turbid water than brown or yellow bullheads. Yellow bullheads are most numerous in areas with heavy vegetation.

How to Catch: Bullheads will bite a number of baits, including chicken livers, red worms, night crawlers, or any commercially prepared catfish baits. Use a sinker to keep the bait right near the bottom.

Where to Find:
36. Mill Stream Run Reservation
38. Rocky River Reservation
39. Rocky River Reservation
45. Hinckley Reservation
52. American Electric Power ReCreation Land

Common Carp

Family: Carp and Minnow Family (Cyprinidae)

Scientific Name: *Cyprinus carpio*

Average Length: n/a

Average Weight: 1–10 lbs.

Ohio Record: 50 lbs., 40 in. long. Caught by Judson Holton on May 24, 1967, from Paint Creek.

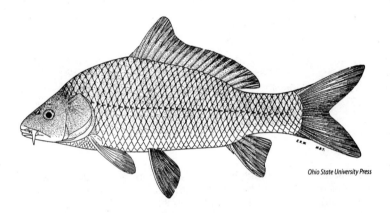

Ohio State University Press

Identification: Carp are bronze-gold to golden-yellow with a yellowish belly and two barbels on each side of the upper jaw.

Habitat: Carp are very common in many lakes, rivers, streams, and ponds throughout Ohio. They prefer water rich in organic matter.

How to Catch: Fish for carp on the bottom using worms, crayfish tails, dough-balls, or most other types of bait. They can grow very large and put up a strong fight, so stout tackle is a good idea.

Where to Find:

1. CEI Breakwall
3. Daniels Park
4. East 55th Street Marina
5. Gilson Park
6. Gordon Park
8. South Chagrin Reservation
9. Todd Field
10. Wildwood/Villa Angela State Park
11. Arcola Creek Metropark
14. Conneaut Creek
16. Fairport Harbor
17. Geneva State Park
18. Harpersfield Covered Bridge
19. Headlands Beach State Park
20. Headwaters Park
21. Helen Hazen Wyman Park
23. Indian Point Park
24. LaDue Reservoir
25. Mosquito Lake State Park
26. Painesville Kiwanis Park
28. Pymatuning State Park
33. Bradstreet's Landing
34. Edgewater Park. Cleveland Lakefront State Park
35. Huntington Reservation
36. Mill Stream Run Reservation
37. Rocky River Reservation
38. Rocky River Reservation
42. Lakeside Landing
43. Vermilion River Reservation
44. Cuyahoga River Dam/Ohio & Erie Canal Towpath. CVNRA

The Fish

Channel Catfish

Family: Catfish Family (Ictaluridae)

Scientific Name: *Ictalurus punctatus*

Average Length: 12–14 in.

Average Weight: n/a

Ohio Record: 37 lbs. 10.4 oz. Caught by Gus Gonowski on August 15, 1992, from LaDue Reservoir.

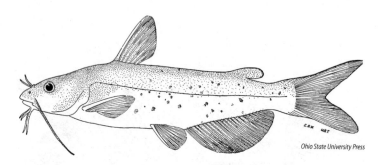

Ohio State University Press

Identification: Channel catfish are generally bluish-silver on their upper half and silver to white on the lower half. Bodies are slender and scaleless, with barbels around the mouth. They have extremely sharp spines in the dorsal and pectoral fins.

Habitat: These fish are found in most rivers and lakes in Ohio and extensively stocked in several local lakes. They prefer deep water, clean gravel, and low to moderate current.

How to Catch: Fish for channel catfish on or near the bottom with night crawlers, crayfish, chicken liver, minnows, or any of the commercially prepared catfish baits. Channel cats are very tasty fish. One very effective method for catching channel catfish is to put a ¼- to 1-ounce egg-sinker on your line, with a barrel swivel tied on immediately in front of it. Attach an 18- to 24-inch length of 10- to 20-pound monofilament to the other end of the barrel swivel. A number 4 hook is appropriate for most baits. Catfish have very poor eyesight, relying instead on very sensitive taste buds located on the barbels and often mistaken for whiskers; therefore, when it comes to bait, the stinkier the better for catfish. Commercially prepared stink baits are very effective.

Where to Find:
Found at most locations

Flathead Catfish

Family: Catfish Family (Ictaluridae)

Scientific Name: *Pylodictis olivaris*

Average Length: 15–30 in.

Average Weight: 5–40 lbs.

Ohio Record: 76 lbs. 8 oz., 53 5/8 in. Caught from Clendening Lake by Richard Affolter on July 28, 1979.

Ohio State University Press

Identification: As its name implies, the flathead catfish's head is flattened between the eyes. Also, its lower jaw is longer than its upper jaw, and it has a square tail. Coloration is usually olive or dark brown with brown blotches and a yellow belly.

Habitat: Flathead catfish are common in large river systems and a few inland lakes. They tend to hang out in deep pools with slow currents and like to have nearby cover. Look for them near submerged logs or other underwater structure.

How to Catch: These fish are often very large, and anglers have the most success fishing for them using very large live bait, such as suckers, creek chubs, bluegills, or other panfish. Present the bait in or around underwater structures such as drift piles or downed trees. Heavy tackle is an absolute necessity when fishing for these brutes, which can grow to frightening proportions and can put up unbelievable fights.

Where to Find:
Found at most locations

The Fish

Black Crappie

Family: Sunfish Family (Centrarchidae)

Scientific Name: *Pomoxis nigromaculatus*

Average Length: 6–12 in.

Average Weight: 1–2 lbs.; seldom over 2 lbs.

Ohio Record: 4 lbs. 8 oz., 18 ⅛ in. Caught from private lake by Ronald Stone on May 24, 1981.

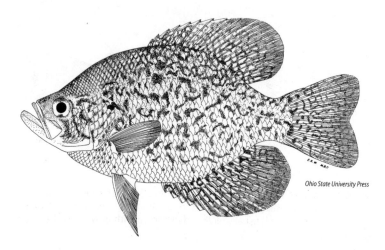

Ohio State University Press

Identification: The black crappie is darker and chunkier than the white crappie. It has seven or eight spines in its dorsal fin, while its relative the white crappie has five or six.

Habitat: The black crappie is not as tolerant of various water conditions as the white crappie, preferring clear water, underwater vegetation, and a sand or muck bottom. This fish does not do well in lakes with heavy concentrations of white crappie.

How to Catch: Black crappies feed primarily on minnows, making this an excellent bait. Small jigs and spinners are also effective. Concentrate on areas around weed beds or other vegetation. As with the white crappie, take care when landing these fish; they have tender mouths.

Where to Find:

15. Eldon Russell Park
17. Geneva State Park
18. Harpersfield Covered Bridge
20. Headwaters Park
24. LaDue Reservoir
25. Mosquito Lake State Park
28. Pymatuning State Park
32. Bradley Woods Reservation
36. Mill Stream Run Reservation
39. Rocky River Reservation
41. Findley State Park
42. Lakeside Landing
43. Vermilion River Reservation
45. Hinckley Reservation
46. Hinckley Reservation
48. Hubbard Valley Park

White Crappie

Family: Sunfish Family (Centrarchidae)   **Scientific Name:** *Pomoxis annularis*

Average Length: 6–12 in.

Average Weight: 1–2 lbs.

Ohio Record: 3.904 lbs., 18 ½ in. Caught from private farm pond by Kyle Rock on April 25, 1995.

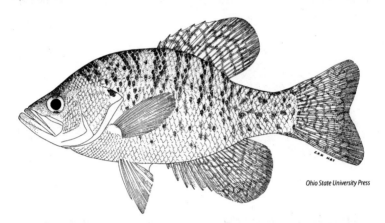

Ohio State University Press

Identification: White crappie have very thin mouths, earning them the nickname "papermouth." They have olive or brownish-green backs with silvery-white sides. Back and sides have 5–10 vertical black bands. Dorsal fin contains five or six spines (the black crappie has seven or eight spines in the dorsal fin).

Habitat: White crappie are prevalent throughout Ohio and can tolerate a wide variety of habitats and water conditions. They are commonly found near structure, such as fallen trees, rock piles, docks, stumps, and vegetation. There are healthy populations of crappie in most local reservoirs, lakes, and ponds.

How to Catch: Successful anglers know to look for underwater structure if they want to find white crappie. In spring and fall, fish near shore, concentrating on areas with brush, downed trees, and other structure. In the summer and early fall, white crappie move to deeper water, locating themselves along old creek channels, roadbeds, and other deepwater structure. Crappies readily fall for minnows suspended from a bobber, but small jigs and spinners can also take fish. Once hooked, crappie should be landed carefully; their tender mouths are prone to tearing. Crappie have a very mild flavor and are best battered and fried.

Where to Find:

15. Eldon Russell Park
17. Geneva State Park
18. Harpersfield Covered Bridge
20. Headwaters Park
24. LaDue Reservoir
25. Mosquito Lake State Park

28. Pymatuning State Park
32. Bradley Woods Reservation
36. Mill Stream Run Reservation
39. Rocky River Reservation
41. Findley State Park
42. Lakeside Landing

43. Vermilion River Reservation
45. Hinckley Reservation
46. Hinckley Reservation
48. Hubbard Valley Park

Sheephead (Freshwater Drum)

Family: Drum Family (Sciaenidae)

Scientific Name: *Aplodinotus grunniens*

Average Length: 12–30 in.

Average Weight: Up to 20 lbs.

Ohio Record: 22 lbs. 4 oz., 33 ½ in. Caught from the Muskingum River by Jerry Stack on May 12, 1980.

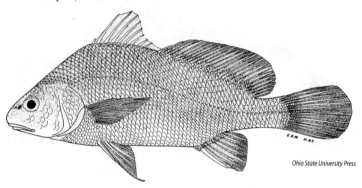

Ohio State University Press

Identification: Sheephead are silver-gray in color and have a rounded tail. They have earned the nickname "grunter" because of their tendency to grunt when landed and unhooked.

Habitat: Sheephead are very common throughout Lake Erie, much to the dismay of anglers hoping to catch walleye and perch. They can also be caught in large rivers.

How to Catch: These fish can be caught using most live baits and lures. They are not very particular in their food selection. Although the majority of fishermen do not intentionally fish for sheephead, these fish do grow quite large and do put up a very good fight when hooked.

Where to Find:

1. CEI Breakwall	17. Geneva State Park	38. Rocky River Reservation
6. Gordon Park	19. Headlands Beach State Park	42. Lakeside Landing
11. Arcola Creek Metropark	33. Bradstreet's Landing	
14. Conneaut Creek	35. Huntington Reservation	
16. Fairport Harbor	37. Rocky River Reservation	

7. Holden Arboretum	31. Walter C. Best Wildlife Preserve	45. Hinckley Reservation
12. Beartown Lakes Reservation	32. Bradley Woods Reservation	46. Hinckley Reservation
13. Big Creek Park	36. Mill Stream Run Reservation	47. Hinckley Reservation
15. Eldon Russell Park	37. Rocky River Reservation: Ford Tour	48. Hubbard Valley Park
18. Harpersfield Covered Bridge	38. Rocky River Reservation: Scenic Park and Marina	50. Plum Creek Park
20. Headwaters Park		51. River Styx Park
24. LaDue Reservoir	39. Rocky River Reservation	52. American Electric Power ReCreation Land
28. Pymatuning State Park	40. Carlisle Reservation	53. Chapman State Park
29. Swine Creek Reservation	41. Findley State Park	54. Lake La Su An
30. Veterans Park		

Largemouth bass

Family: Sunfish Family (Centrarchidae)

Scientific Name: *Micropterus salmoides*

Average Length: 12–15 in.

Average Weight: 1–3 lbs.

Ohio Record: 13 lbs. 2 oz., farm pond, by Roy Landsberger on May 26, 1976.

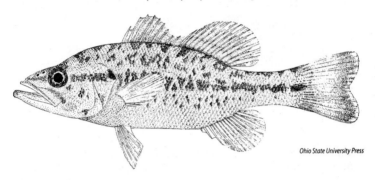

Ohio State University Press

Identification: The largemouth bass's most telling feature is, of course, its large mouth, which, unlike that of the smallmouth bass, extends past the eye. A dark lateral band extends from head to tail.

Habitat: Largemouth bass prefer shallow ponds and lakes with plenty of vegetation and also can be found in sluggish streams. They prefer structure, such as rocks, downed trees, and weed beds, where they wait to ambush passing prey.

How to Catch: Largemouth bass can be caught using live bait or lures. The wide range of possible techniques and types of lure is staggering, and the proper choice depends on the water conditions and the preferences of the fish in a given lake. Thick, weedy lakes are favorite hangouts for largemouths, so you can't be afraid to fish weedy water. A Texas-rigged rubber worm is a proven favorite and can be fished in weedy situations. In lakes where the surface is covered by weeds, try working a rubber mouse or other weedless lure very slowly across the top. Bass sense the vibrations and nail it right through the weeds. Spinner baits also can get a bass to strike. Largemouth bass often feed in seemingly impossibly shallow water, so work the edges of lakes thoroughly. Always try to look for structure when bass fishing, be it weeds, shoreline structure, or deepwater structure, such as tree stumps or brush piles. Largemouth bass provide exciting action for fly fishermen. Use at least a 6-weight outfit and a fairly stout leader, as these fish must often be muscled from weeds. Baitfish imitations can work well, as will surface poppers.

Where to Find:

The Fish

Smallmouth Bass

Family: Sunfish Family (Centrarchidae)

Scientific Name: *Micropterus dolomieui*

Average Length: 12–15 in.

Average Weight: 1–2 lbs.

Ohio Record: 9 lbs. 8 oz. Caught in Lake Erie by Randy Van Dam on June 16, 1993.

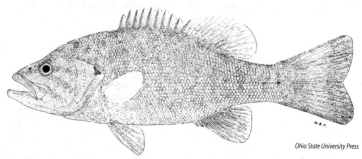

Ohio State University Press

Identification: Also known as bronzebacks because they often have a deep bronze color, smallmouth bass are usually dark greenish on top, lightening up near the belly. The lower part of the jaw does not extend past the eye.

Habitat: Smallmouth bass prefer deep lakes and rivers with gravel or rock bottoms and plenty of structure. In rivers, look for them primarily in the deeper pools, especially near a riffle area. Smallmouth bass fishing is gaining notoriety in Lake Erie and its tributaries because of changing water conditions—thanks to zebra mussels and round gobies, two exotic species from European waters. Zebra mussels, now found in Lake Erie in the trillions, act like miniature filters. The result is much clearer water, exactly the way smallmouth like it. Round gobies and their penchant for stealing bait may be the bane of anglers, but they are an important food source for smallmouth. More food means more and bigger smallmouth, too.

How to Catch: Smallmouth bass just love crayfish, which make very effective live bait. They can also be caught using hellgrammites and minnows. Crayfish-colored jigs fished along the bottom work well. The annoying buzz of a buzzbait is often too much for smallmouth. If you fly fish, a Woolly Bugger, Muddler Minnow, or crayfish pattern will take smallmouth. Lake Erie boaters should focus exclusively on areas with plenty of structure—rock piles, humps, downed trees, and drop-offs. Shore anglers can do well at any of the access points with breakwalls extending into the lake. Smallmouth bass favor the rocky habitat found in these harbors and especially along the breakwalls. Wise anglers will not overlook the weed beds that are present in ever-increasing numbers in Lake Erie, as these attract not only smallmouth bass but also northern pike, largemouth bass, and other species. Crankbaits work well in rivers and on Lake Erie.

Where to Find: ——————————————————

The Fish

Rock Bass

Family: Sunfish Family (Centrarchidae)

Scientific Name: *Ambloplites rupestris*

Average Length: 7–10 in.

Average Weight: 1 lb.

Ohio Record: 1 lb. 15 ½ oz., 14 3/4 in. Caught from Deer Creek by George A. Keller on September 3, 1962.

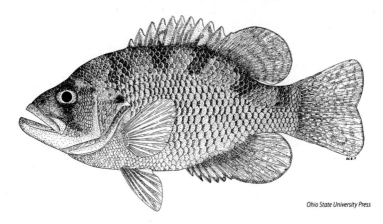

Ohio State University Press

Identification: Rock bass are thick fish, usually with a dark slate or olive-green color with bronze and coppery iridescence. Their mouths are large, with the upper jaw extending past the middle of the eye. They sometimes have noticeably red eyes.

Habitat: These fish are relatively common throughout Ohio and are especially abundant in clearer streams with a course gravel substrate. They are common in Lake Erie near reefs, large boulders, and around docks.

How to Catch: Rock bass are often caught using the same techniques used for smallmouth bass, including small spinners and live bait, such as crayfish, worms, hellgrammites, and minnows.

Where to Find:

2. Chagrin River Park	21. Helen Hazen Wyman Park	26. Painesville Kiwanis Park
8. South Chagrin Reservation	22. Hogback Ridge Park	43. Vermilion River Reservation
18. Harpersfield Covered Bridge	23. Indian Point Park	

1. CEI Breakwall	14. Conneaut Creek	34. Edgewater Park. Cleveland Lakefront State Park
2. Chagrin River Park	16. Fairport Harbor	
3. Daniels Park	17. Geneva State Park	35. Huntington Reservation
4. East 55th Street Marina	18. Harpersfield Covered Bridge	37. Rocky River Reservation
5. Gilson Park	19. Headlands Beach State Park	38. Rocky River Reservation
6. Gordon Park	21. Helen Hazen Wyman Park	42. Lakeside Landing
8. South Chagrin Reservation	22. Hogback Ridge Park	43. Vermilion River Reservation
9. Todd Field	23. Indian Point Park	44. Cuyahoga River Dam/Ohio & Erie Canal Towpath. CVNRA
10. Wildwood/Villa Angela State Park	26. Painesville Kiwanis Park	53. Chapman State Park
11. Arcola Creek Metropark	27. Punderson State Park	55. Oak Orchard Creek
	28. Pymatuning State Park	
	33. Bradstreet's Landing	

White Bass

Family: Temperate Basses Family (Percichthyidae)

Scientific Name: *Morone chrysops*

Average Length: 10–14 in.

Average Weight: 1 to 3 lbs.

Ohio Record: 4 lbs. Caught from a gravel pit by Ira Sizemore on July 1, 1983.

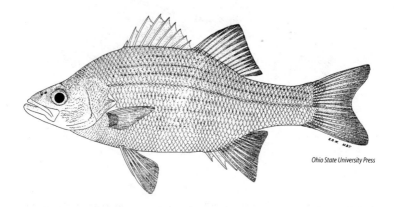

Ohio State University Press

Identification: The white bass has a bluish-silvery overall color with a milk-white belly and six or more dark lateral lines on the sides and back. It has two dorsal fins, the front one with nine spines.

Habitat: White bass are found primarily in Lake Erie and its tributaries. Schools can often be found near shore, especially during late April and May. They prefer depths of less than 30 feet.

How to Catch: White bass gather in large schools in May and June, attacking anything within their sight. Minnows are effective, as are small spinners or plugs. A school of white bass displays true feeding-frenzy behavior; if you cast into one, your lure will be hit repeatedly until a fish is hooked. Gulls and terns frequently follow schools of white bass, feeding on minnows that the bass have driven to the surface. They have ravenous appetites, weighing one pound or more at two years. If you stumble upon a school of white bass, be prepared for fast, exciting action.

Where to Find:

1. CEI Breakwall
4. East 55th Street Marina
10. Wildwood/Villa Angela State Park
14. Conneaut Creek
17. Geneva State Park
25. Mosquito Lake State Park
28. Pymatuning State Park
35. Huntington Reservation

Muskie (Muskellunge)

Family: Pike Family (Esocidae)

Scientific Name: *Esox masquinongy ohioensis*

Average Length: 22–39 in.

Average Weight: 3–21 lbs.

Ohio Record: 55 lbs. 2 oz. Caught in Piedmont Lake by Joe D. Lykins on April 12, 1972.

Ohio State University Press

Identification: Muskellunge have a long body with dorsal and ventral fins occurring far back, close to the tail. They are similar in appearance to northern pike and have sharp teeth that can shred a careless angler's fingers.

Habitat: Muskie prefer lakes with heavy cover and structure, and clear water. They are found primarily in local reservoirs but are also occasionally taken from Lake Erie.

How to Catch: Cast or troll near weed beds, using a variety of lures, including spoons, spinners, jerk baits, and anything else that imitates a wounded baitfish. Heavy-duty tackle is necessity for muskie fishing. Muskie are ferociously predatory. Bass, bluegill, mice, ducklings—if it's in the water, a muskie will attack it. Fishing for muskie is truly a case of quality over quantity—you may not catch a whole lot of them, but the ones you catch can be frighteningly large.

Where to Find:
18. Harpersfield Covered Bridge
21. Helen Hazen Wyman Park
22. Hogback Ridge Park
23. Indian Point Park
28. Pymatuning State Park

Northern Pike

Family: Pike Family (Esocidae)

Scientific Name: *Esox lucius*

Average Length: 20–32 in.

Average Weight: 2–10 lbs.

Ohio Record: 22 lbs. 6 oz. Caught by Chris Campbell on October 3, 1988, on Lyre Lake.

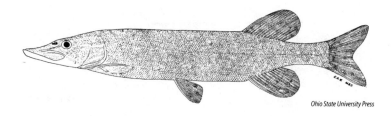

Ohio State University Press

Identification: Long, slender body. The lower half of the gill cover is scaleless with a fully scaled cheek. Northern pike have very sharp teeth.

Habitat: Northern pike, though once abundant throughout Lake Erie, are now mostly found in the marshes and bays of the Western Basin, although they are occasionally caught by shore anglers in the Central Basin. There is a decent population in the Cuyahoga River close to its headwaters.

How to Catch: The most productive way to catch northern pike is with minnows or chubs, although Rapala-type lures can also produce. Concentrate on weedy areas and structure.

Where to Find:

15. Eldon Russell Park
18. Harpersfield Covered Bridge
20. Headwaters Park
25. Mosquito Lake State Park
31. Walter C. Best Wildlife Preserve
42. Lakeside Landing
45. Hinckley Reservation
48. Hubbard Valley Park
49. Medina Fish Hatchery

The Fish

Pumpkinseed Sunfish

Family: Sunfish Family (Centrarchidae)

Scientific Name: *Lepomis gibbosus*

Average Length: 5–8 in.

Average Weight: Under 1 lb.

Ohio Record: No entry. New category.

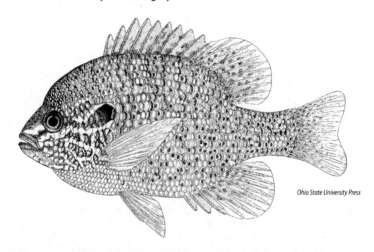

Ohio State University Press

Identification: Sunfish are very colorful, slab-bodied fish with a small mouth. The ear flap is black, bordered with an orange-red spot.

Habitat: Sunfish are common throughout the ponds and lakes of Ohio. They prefer still water with dense, submerged vegetation. They are often found with bluegill.

How to Catch: As with bluegill, sunfish can readily be taken with live bait, such as worms, maggots, or terrestrial insects. They will also take small spinners and jigs. Fly fishermen can be successful with a nymph or terrestrial pattern.

Where to Find:
Found at most locations.

The Fish

Rainbow Trout

Family: Trout Family (Salmonidae)

Scientific Name: *Salmo gairdneri*

Average Length: 7–20 in.

Average Weight: ½–1 lb.

Ohio Record: N/A

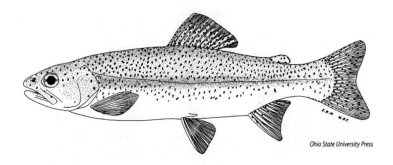

Ohio State University Press

Identification: Rainbow trout are easily distinguished by the rainbow-colored lateral band along the middle of each side. The dorsal fin and tail are spotted. When rainbow trout migrate to Lake Erie, they experience very rapid weight and length increases and return to the river where they were originally stocked as steelhead. (See separate steelhead listing.)

Habitat: Rainbows require cold, clear water and swift currents. Most waters in Ohio become too warm for trout during the summer months, so natural repro-duction is basically nonexistent except in a few isolated areas. Rainbow trout are frequently stocked in local lakes and rivers by the Ohio Division of Wildlife and by county park districts. They are stocked extensively in several northeast-ern Ohio rivers as part of the state's steelhead stocking program.

How to Catch: Rainbow can be taken on natural baits, such as live insects, worms, and salmon eggs. Small spinners and Rapalas can also be effective. Small Mepps spinners can be particularly effective. Fly anglers should focus on nymph and terrestrial patterns, and baitfish imitations such as Woolly Buggers and Minnows.

Where to Find:

8. South Chagrin Reservation
27. Punderson State Park
30. Veterans Park
32. Bradley Woods Reservation
36. Mill Stream Run Reservation
45. Hinckley Reservation
46. Hinckley Reservation
47. Hinckley Reservation
49. Medina Fish Hatchery
51. River Styx Park
53. Chapman State Park
55. Oak Orchard

Steelhead

Family: Trout Family (Salmonidae)

Scientific Name: *Oncorhynchus mykiss*

Average Length: 20–23 in.

Average Weight:

Ohio Record: 20.97 lbs., 36 ½ in. Caught by Mike Shane on October 2, 1996, from Lake Erie.

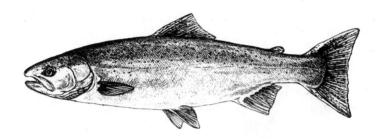

Identification: Steelhead, which are actually lake-run trout, are bright silver with a bright pink band, black spots, and a squarish to rounded tail. Males develop a hooked jaw during the spawning season.

Habitat: Steelhead prefer coldwater streams with rocky bottoms and plenty of cover. They are stocked in these streams but migrate into Lake Erie for two to three years, and then migrate back to the stream to spawn.

How to Catch: Anglers catch steelhead in Lake Erie using spoons and deep running crankbaits. Shore anglers primarily use spoons and maggot-tipped jigs. When steelhead enter the rivers, spawn bags, salmon eggs, maggots, and worms can produce. Woolly Buggers, egg patterns, and nymph imitations can prove successful for the fly fisherman. Rooster Tails and Rapalas can also be very effective. Lake Erie fishermen are catching increasing numbers of steelhead while trolling for walleye.

Where to Find:

1. CEI Breakwall
2. Chagrin River Park
3. Daniels Park
5. Gilson Park
6. Gordon Park
9. Todd Field
10. Wildwood/Villa Angela State Park
11. Arcola Creek Metropark
14. Conneaut Creek
16. Fairport Harbor
17. Geneva State Park
18. Harpersfield Covered Bridge
19. Headlands Beach State Park
21. Helen Hazen Wyman Park
22. Hogback Ridge Park
23. Indian Point Park
26. Painesville Kiwanis Park
34. Edgewater Park. Cleveland Lakefront State Park
35. Huntington Reservation
37. Rocky River Reservation
38. Rocky River Reservation
42. Lakeside Landing
43. Vermilion River Reservation
44. Cuyahoga River Dam/Ohio & Erie Canal Towpath, CVNRA
55. Oak Orchard Creek

The Fish

Walleye

Family: Perch Family (Percidae)

Scientific Name: *Stizostedion vitreum*

Average Length: 14–22 in.

Average Weight: 2–4 lbs.

Ohio Record: 15.95 lbs., 33 in. Caught by Mike Baidel on March 24, 1995, from Lake Erie.

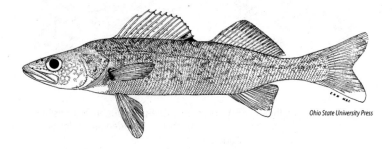

Ohio State University Press

Identification: Walleye are yellow-olive with a milky white belly. Their eyes are large and cloudy, and they have a mouthful of sharp teeth.

Habitat: Walleye are found throughout Lake Erie and are stocked in several inland reservoirs. They like slightly turbid waters, and prefer rocky bottoms with structure.

How to Catch: Bouncing jigs tipped with minnows or weight forward spinners tipped with night crawlers off the bottom are effective for catching walleye. Crankbaits also produce well. Predawn and dusk are the most productive times for shore fishing.

Where to Find:

1. CEI Breakwall	16. Fairport Harbor	28. Pymatuning State Park
4. East 55th Street Marina	17. Geneva State Park	34. Edgewater Park. Cleveland
6. Gordon Park	18. Harpersfield Covered Bridge	Lakefront State Park
10. Wildwood/Villa Angela State	19. Headlands Beach State Park	35. Huntington Reservation
Park	24. LaDue Reservoir	37. Rocky River Reservation
11. Arcola Creek Metropark	25. Mosquito Lake State Park	38. Rocky River Reservation
14. Conneaut Creek	26. Painesville Kiwanis Park	42. Lakeside Landing

Yellow Perch

Family: Perch Family (Percidae)

Scientific Name: *Perca flavescens*

Average Length: 5–12 in.

Average Weight: ¼ to 1 lb.

Ohio Record: 2 lbs. 12 oz., 14 ½ in. Caught by Charles Thomas on April 17, 1984, on Lake Erie.

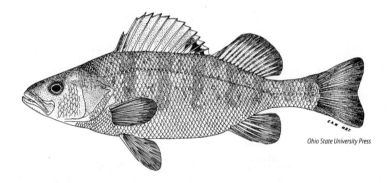

Ohio State University Press

Identification: Perch are golden yellow and have six to eight broad, dark, vertical bands and a white to yellow belly.

Habitat: Perch are common throughout Lake Erie but also found in reservoirs, ponds, and slow-moving rivers. They prefer clear water with moderate vegetation and a sand or gravel bottom.

How to Catch: Using spreaders with worms, minnows, or shiners is the most effective method for catching these tasty fish. Perch will often suspend just above the bottom, so keep bait in that strike zone. Spring is the most productive time for shore anglers, as perch move out into deeper water during the summer. With the arrival of fall, perch move in closer, usually within two to three miles of shore.

Where to Find:

1. CEI Breakwall
4. East 55th Street Marina
6. Gordon Park
10. Wildwood/Villa Angela State Park
11. Arcola Creek Metropark
14. Conneaut Creek
16. Fairport Harbor

17. Geneva State Park
19. Headlands Beach State Park
24. LaDue Reservoir
25. Mosquito Lake State Park
28. Pymatuning State Park
31. Walter C. Best Wildlife Preserve
33. Bradstreet's Landing

34. Edgewater Park. Cleveland Lakefront State Park
35. Huntington Reservation
38. Rocky River Reservation
42. Lakeside Landing

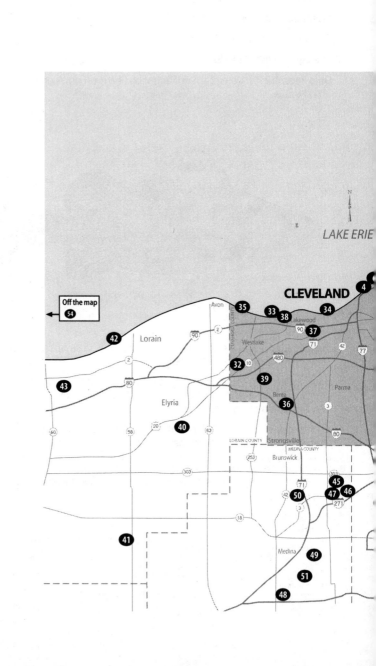

LAKE ERIE

CLEVELAND

Off the map
54

The Places

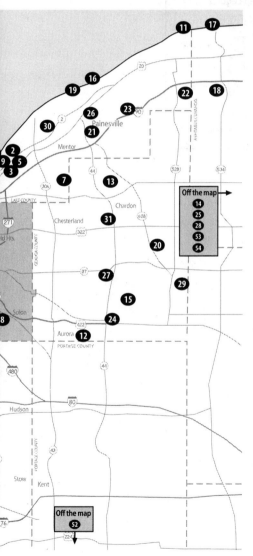

1 CEI Breakwall
2 Chagrin River Park
3 Daniels Park
4 E. 55th Street Marina
5 Gilson Park
6 Gordon Park
7 Holden Arboretum
8 South Chagrin Reservation
9 Todd Field
10 Wildwood/Villa Angela State Park
11 Arcola Creek Metropark
12 Beartown Lakes Reservation
13 Big Creek Park
14 Conneaut Creek *
15 Eldon Russell Park
16 Fairport Harbor
17 Geneva State Park
18 Harpersfield Covered Bridge
19 Headlands Beach State Park
20 Headwaters Park
21 Helen Hazen Wyman Park
22 Hogback Ridge Park
23 Indian Point Park
24 LaDue Reservoir
25 Mosquito Lake State Park *
26 Painesville Kiwanis Park
27 Punderson State Park
28 Pymatuning State Park *
29 Swine Creek Reservation
30 Veterans Park
31 Walter C. Best Wildlife Preserve
32 Bradley Woods Reservation
33 Bradstreet's Landing
34 Edgewater Park, Cleveland Lakefront
    State Park
35 Huntington Reservation
36 Mill Stream Run Reservation
37 Rocky River Res., Ford Tour
38 Rocky River Res., Scenic Park
39 Rocky River Res., Oxbow Lagoon
40 Carlisle Reservation
41 Findley State Park
42 Lakeside Landing
43 Vermilion River Reservation
44 Cuyahoga River Dam/Ohio & Erie Canal
    Towpath, CVNRA
45 Hinckley Res., Hinckley Lake
46 Hinckley Res., Judges Lake
47 Hinckley Res., Ledge Lake
48 Hubbard Valley Park
49 Medina Fish Hatchery
50 Plum Creek Park
51 River Styx Park
52 American Electric Power
    ReCreation Land *
53 Chapman State Park *
54 Lake La Su An *
55 Oak Orchard Creek*

* = Beyond map boundaries

Map Legend

 Parking

 Boat launch

 Fishing area

 Restrooms

Building

•••• Trail

East

1

CEI Breakwall
Lake Erie Shoreline
Erie Rd., Eastlake

> Recreational | Intermediate | Challenging
>
> **Water Type:** Lake Erie
> **Access:** Breakwall, pier
> **What's Biting:** Bluegill, smallmouth bass, carp, catfish, sheephead, perch, steelhead, suckers, sunfish, walleye, white bass
> **Season:** Year-round **Hours:** N/A
> **Fee:** $4 adults; $1 seniors; free for Eastlake residents **Permission:** Not required
> **Facilities:** Bait shop, restrooms
> **Administered by:** Port Authority
> **Directions:** SR 2 to exit for SR 91 (S.O.M. Center Rd.); north on SR 91; right (east) on Lake Shore Blvd.; left (north) on Erie Rd.; look for the smokestacks.

Description If you're looking to fish in a pristine wilderness setting, the CEI Breakwall, located under the towering smokestacks of the Cleveland Electric Illuminating Company, might not be your best bet. If, however, you're looking for convenient, safe access to Lake Erie, then it would certainly be worth your while to include this site on your fishing destination list.

The breakwall is a popular spot for Lake Erie anglers hoping to hook into the standard fare of shoreline fishing: catfish, perch, carp, walleye, white bass, and steelhead. The breakwall is close to the mouth of the Chagrin River, so when the steelhead are staging to migrate in the spring and fall, an occasional steelie is caught. This spot is also a popular winter fishing destination. The warm-water discharge from the power plant keeps the lake ice-free throughout the winter, and anglers have been known to do quite well during the frigid Cleveland winters.

Occasionally a school of white bass will move within casting distance of the breakwall, and for a short period of time the fishing can be fast and furious. White bass are ravenous eaters, and a spinner thrown into the middle of a school will be repeatedly hit until a fish is hooked.

There is no boat launch at the CEI Breakwall, but the waters around the plant are a popular spot for boat fishermen. The warm-water discharge attracts large schools of bait fish, which in turn attract a good number of predatory fish. According to several anglers who regularly anchor their boats here, smallmouth bass and steelhead fishing in these waters can be enormously productive.

For years I fished the breakwall, never quite sure if I was allowed to be there or if there was a fee. A little investigation answered many of my questions. The land itself is owned by CEI and was leased to Eastlake for a very small sum. Eastlake then enlisted the help of the Port Authority, which has operated it as an agent of the city for the past few years.

A concessionaire, Civitarese's, sells hot dogs, sandwiches, candy, bait, and fishing tackle. They are also willing to dispense valuable information about the day's hottest lure, bait, or fishing technique. You can also stop at Erieshore Bait & Tackle, located at the corner of Lake Shore and Erie Rd., to purchase live bait, fishing tackle, and food and beverages.

The fishing area is open to accommodate Eastlake residents, who can use it at no cost. Don't fret if you live outside of the city, however, because for four dollars anyone can take advantage of this great fishing opportunity. And if you're a senior (citizen, not high school), the price is just one dollar.

Nearby bait shop(s): Civitarese's, Erieshore Bait & Tackle. (See Directory section for details.)

2

Chagrin River Park
Chagrin River
Reeves Rd., Willoughby

Recreational | Intermediate | Challenging

Water Type: River **Acreage:** N/A

Access: Shoreline, wading, canoe

What's Biting: Bluegill, rock bass, smallmouth bass, steelhead, sunfish, suckers

Season: Year-round **Hours:** Dawn–dusk

Fee: Free **Permission:** Not required

Facilities: Restrooms, picnic area, hiking trails, ranger

Administered by: Lake Metroparks

Directions: SR 2 to Lost Nation Rd.; north on Lost Nation; left (west) on Reeves Rd. to Chagrin River Park, on left.

Description The Chagrin River Park, located in Willoughby close to State Route 2, provides hassle-free opportunities for anglers to take advantage of the productive fishing opportunities on the Chagrin River.

A short trail from the parking lot leads down to the river, and from there you can wade or hike up- or downstream. The Chagrin River, as it flows through this park, is relatively flat and featureless, and it offers few of the deep pools, riffles, and runs characteristic of other sections of the river. The shallower holes and flats are basically devoid of fish, especially in the summer, when the water level is at its lowest. There are a few deep holes, however, and chances are that there are some catchable fish lurking there.

Lake Metroparks

On one summer trip, I had fished several small holes and some flat, boring water without success. A short distance downstream from the parking lot, I stumbled across a deep hole and, to my amazement, saw several smallmouth bass, some bluegill, suckers, and a couple very large carp. A rock outcropping created an ideal habitat for the bass, which were snugly hidden underneath this precipice. It was a veritable fish smorgasbord! I was able to hook and land two 12-inch smallmouth bass on an olive Woolly Bugger dragged along the bottom in crayfish fashion. The water in this hole flowed faster and was at least several degrees cooler than elsewhere; apparently the fish prized this small oasis in the stagnant water of the flats.

These same holes are also worth fishing during steelhead season. The Chagrin River receives some very nice runs of steelhead and is one of the more heavily fished of the local rivers. Chagrin River Park provides a great deal of access to the river and can be a productive fishing destination during the spring or fall.

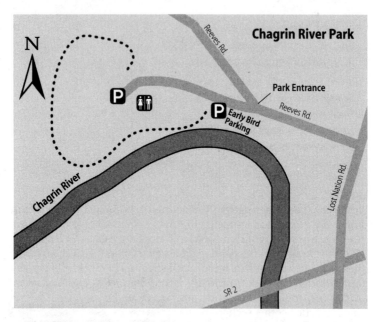

The Chagrin River can be fished as long as the river is free of ice. In fact, not only can the fishing be productive during the colder months, but those anglers who brave the frigid temperatures will often find that they have the river to themselves, a situation much harder to come by in the spring, summer, and fall.

A canoe launch is available at the park, although the water level of the Chagrin River may force canoeists to do more portaging than rowing. Ample parking, picnic areas, and restrooms make the park a very comfortable place to visit and fish.

Chagrin River Park is open from sunrise to one-half hour after sunset. An Ohio fishing license is required to fish on the Chagrin River.

Nearby bait shop(s): Erieshore Bait & Tackle (See Directory section for details.)

3

Daniels Park
Chagrin River
Ridge Rd., Willoughby

East

Recreational | **Intermediate** | Challenging

Water Type: River **Acreage:** N/A

Access: Shoreline

What's Biting: Bluegill, smallmouth bass, carp, catfish, steelhead, suckers, sunfish

Season: Year-round **Hours:** N/A

Fee: Free **Permission:** Not required

Facilities: Restrooms, picnic area, food nearby

Administered by: Willoughby Parks and Recreation

Directions: SR 2 to Vine St. (east) exit; east on Vine; right (south) on Erie St.; left on River St. just past the city hall; left on Ridge Rd. (SR 84); park is on left.

Description On both my trips to Daniels Park during the summer there were a handful of anglers fishing from the concrete walkway adjacent to the dam. When they were asked what they were fishing for, the initial answer was usually, "anything that will bite." Upon further prodding, they revealed that they were primarily expecting to catch carp and suckers, which hang out in the deeper water below the dam.

"What's the best bait for the carp?" I asked one gentleman. "Dough-balls" was all I could get out of him before he reached down, grabbed his rod, and jerked it like he was setting his hook into a 200-pound tuna. He reeled his line in, and I half expected to see a set of carp lips—minus the carp—dangling from his hook, ripped off from the force of his hook-setting technique.

Smallmouth bass also lurk below the dam and can be caught with jigs, spinnerbaits or buzzbaits. Be warned, however, that if you are bouncing a jig off the bottom there are numerous lure-eating snags. Expect to lose a couple. Crayfish are in abundance here, with a few under every rock I turned over. These are not only very effective for catching smallmouth, they are also fun to catch as they dart from rock to rock in their backwards style. It's just not summer without at least one finger pinch from a crawdad's claw.

Most of the river here is flat and shallow during the summer months, with few deep holes in the area just downstream from the dam. The action occurs in the deep water directly below the dam and in the calm waters above it.

Daniels Park is a popular steelhead location, perhaps the most heavily fished on the river. The dam provides a barrier to the migrating fish, so there tends to be a slightly higher concentration of steelhead here. The standard fare—jigs tipped with maggots or spawn, Rapalas, or Rooster Tails—can all catch fish. After heavy rains, the raised water level makes it possible for steelhead to get past the dam and continue on their migration route upstream, and I've even seen fishermen land a steelhead below the dam and release it above.

Despite its popularity, Daniels Park is not my favorite spot on the Chagrin River. The noise from State Route 84, combined with its high use, usually sends me searching for quieter waters downstream at Todd Field or Gilson Park. But it is one of the most popular fishing destinations on the river, and certainly worth a visit. Just don't forget the doughballs.

Nearby bait shop(s): Erieshore Bait & Tackle (See Directory section for details.)

4

East

East 55th Street Marina
Lake Erie Shoreline
North Marginal Rd., Cleveland

Recreational | Intermediate | Challenging

Water Type: Lake Erie **Acreage:** N/A

Access: Shoreline, pier

What's Biting: Bluegill, smallmouth bass, carp, catfish, perch, sunfish, walleye, white bass

Season: Year-round **Hours:** Dawn–11 p.m.

Fee: Free **Permission:** Not required

Facilities: Bait shop, restrooms, picnic area, food onsite

Administered by: Ohio Department of Natural Resources

Directions: I-90/SR 2 (East Shoreway) to Exit 175 (E. 55th St.); north on E. 55th; follow signs to marina.

Description I must have driven past Cleveland Lakefront State Park's East 55th Street Marina hundreds of times in my life, but it was researching this book that made me finally pay a visit. It's nothing fancy in terms of amenities, but it does provide easy access to Lake Erie.

There is substantial fishing access from the breakwall near the restrooms and the far parking lot. Anglers can also fish along the breakwall that runs parallel to the freeway. For your comfort, be sure to bring a bucket or lawn chair to sit on.

Michael McElroy/Cleveland Lakefront State Park

Perch rigs baited with minnows and still fishing with worms are two popular fishing methods used along the lake. Common catches include perch, catfish, sheephead, and the occasional walleye. If a school of white bass is close by, minnows or spinners tipped with jigs fished near the surface, where the white bass typically feed, can provide some very exciting fishing.

Walleye fishing can be decent in the fall, typically from late September through December, as water temperatures drop and schools of walleye begin to move back in near shore. Night fishing is the best approach. Often, fishermen line the breakwall well into the small hours of the morning, braving the elements in the hope of hooking into a lunker walleye. Large Rapalas and Rat-L-Traps are very effective for this frigid nighttime fishing. I have seen some very large walleye caught from the shore in this area.

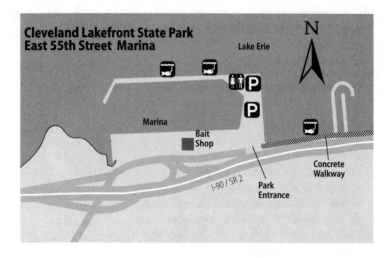

On my visit to this location, I saw a small school of smallmouth bass chasing minnows along the shoreline in the calm waters of the harbor, immediately to the left of the entrance road. I was able to coax a nice 12-incher into striking a floating Rapala. The weed beds and rocky outcroppings of the harbor's breakwall are worth checking out if smallmouth is your game. A bait shop on the premises is open during the regular boating and fishing season, usually starting sometime in March. The park is open all night for fishermen. Shine's Live Bait, Tackle and Beverage is a good nearby source for fishing supplies and information. Shine's (216-431-9090) is located on E. 55th St., not far from the park.

There is no public boat launch available at the park, but boaters can use the Gordon Park Boat Launch, located on the North Marginal a short distance east of the East 55th Park. There are six free boat launches and restrooms available. The park closes at 11 p.m.

The East 55th Park provides a clean, comfortable location for Lake Erie shore fishing. On a clear morning or evening, the Cleveland skyline provides the perfect backdrop, especially with a picture-perfect Lake Erie sunset reflecting off the buildings.

Nearby bait shop(s): E. 55th St. Marina Bait Shop; Shine's Live Bait (See Directory section for details.)

5

Gilson Park
Chagrin River
Pelton Rd., Willoughby

Recreational | Intermediate | Challenging

Water Type: River **Acreage:** N/A
Access: Shoreline, wading
What's Biting: Bluegill, smallmouth bass, carp, catfish, steelhead, suckers, sunfish
Season: Year-round **Hours:** Open 24 hrs.
Fee: Free **Permission:** Not required
Facilities: Restrooms, food nearby
Administered by: Willoughby Parks and Recreation
Directions: SR 2 to Lost Nation Rd.; south on Lost Nation; right on Pelton Rd.; on right.

Description It had been many years since I wet a line at Gilson Park. It was researching this book that finally brought me back. Why had it taken so long to return to this scenic locale along the Chagrin River? Chalk it up to that part of every angler's psyche that keeps him away from a place where his youthful dreams have been dashed, or in my case, where my equipment was swiped by an underwater thief.

It all started many years ago when I was knee-high to a grasshopper, just getting my feet wet—literally—in the sport of fishing. My older brother was playing baseball at Gilson Park, and while my parents took in the game I enjoyed the river. I had my father's new rod and reel with me, rigged with a sinker the size of a grapefruit, a hook the size of a gaff, and a night crawler. Finesse fishing was something I had yet to learn. The whole ensemble was propped up with a Y-shaped branch stuck in the soil next to the riverbank. The line, cast about 20 feet into the murky depths, was reeled tight, and I anxiously awaited my first strike.

After 15 minutes without so much as a nibble, I started to explore the river a bit, slowly meandering farther and farther away from the fishing rod. I was a good distance away when I heard a noise—the sound of my rod breaking free of its perch and hitting the ground. Then, as I watched, horrified, the rod took off toward the water. Before I could move, it was gone, dragged into the Chagrin by a fish the size of which I could only imagine. I can vividly remember the way the rod slowly slipped out of sight, never to be seen again.

Luckily, Dad seemed not to care that his new rod and reel were being dragged up and down the river by some monstrous carp or sucker. Much to my relief, he and my mom (and just about every other adult in the bleachers) thought the whole thing was so damn funny that the thought of being angry never occurred to them.

But I haven't forgotten. I can still hear the scraping of the fiberglass rod being dragged across the rocky shoreline. I can still see the rod and reel combo (a Shakespeare, I think) sliding slowly into the Chagrin River.

On my return visit, some two decades later, I left with all the equipment I had brought along. And I found a very accessible section of the Chagrin River that can provide an exciting fishing experience. One can land a variety of fish, depending on the season. A fair amount of the shoreline is accessible for fishermen, and much of the river is open for wading. But be aware: depending on the river level, there are spots that can submerge even the tallest of anglers. Exercise caution when wading here.

Deep pools, riffles, and runs provide excellent habitat for smallmouth bass. Crayfish-colored jigs or, if you can catch some, live crayfish, can be effective. Regardless of what you use, you will have the most success by retrieving the lure or bait right along the river bottom, where smallmouth are accustomed to seeing crayfish. Hook the crayfish through the tail and watch your line very carefully. At the slightest hesitation, set the hook. Smallmouth bass strikes can often be violent and aggressive, but just as often they can be soft and subtle. If you use a buzzbait, which spins annoyingly at the surface during the retrieve, you will have no problem detecting strikes. In fact, strikes on buzzbaits can be very acrobatic and frenzied. It's great fun. Fly fishermen should try olive, brown, or black Woolly Buggers, Muddler Minnows, or any other fly that resembles crayfish. Again, remember to keep it deep.

Because the park is open 24 hours, it is also a favorite stop for steelhead fishermen, many of whom believe the best times to catch these silver missiles is early in the morning or late in the evening. If you are going after steelhead, wear polarized glasses and look very carefully for the dark shadows that indicate deep holes, ideal holding spots. Drift some spawn or a maggot-tipped jig through the holes, keeping the bait as close to the bottom as possible. Of course, other standard steelhead lures will work, including Rapalas and spinners. Woolly Buggers, spawn patterns, and nymph imitations can be very effective if your weapon of choice is the fly rod.

Anglers are allowed in the park 24 hours a day. Restrooms, however, are open only during the summer baseball season. Fall, winter, and spring anglers will have to find other accommodations. A current Ohio fishing license is required to fish at Gilson Park.

By the way, if you should happen to be fishing at Gilson Park and land a really big fish with a rod and reel still attached to it, give me a call.

Nearby bait shop(s): Erieshore Bait & Tackle (See Directory section for details.)

6

Gordon Park
Lake Erie Shoreline
North Marginal Rd., Cleveland

Recreational | **Intermediate** | Challenging

Water Type: Lake Erie

Access: Breakwall, boat

What's Biting: Bluegill, smallmouth bass, carp, catfish, sheephead, perch, steelhead, sunfish, walleye

Season: Year-round   **Hours:** Fishing areas open 24 hours; boat launch closes 11 p.m.

Fee: Free   **Permission:** Not required

Facilities: Bait shop, boat launch, restrooms, picnic area, ranger

Administered by: Ohio Department of Natural Resources

Directions: I-90/SR 2 (East Shoreway) to Exit 177 (Martin Luther King, Jr., Blvd.); follow signs to N. Marginal Rd.; entrance on N. Marginal west of MLK.

Description It is not hard to question the sanity of some fishermen. On a late November night, with the temperature hovering around 35 degrees and snow blowing in on a westerly wind, the fishing breakwall at Gordon Park is lined with fishermen. Bundled up in winter jackets, long johns, hats, scarves, and gloves, it's amazing they can move enough to cast their lures out into the nearly frozen water of Lake Erie. But they do.

What is it that drives people to tolerate such inclement weather and fish into the early hours of the morning? An incredible love of the sport of fishing? Or is it a macho thing, enabling them to later brag to their friends about the conditions they endured to catch a trophy-sized walleye? Or are they just a few bricks shy of a load? Well, it's probably a combination of all three, but the jealous excitement felt by anglers when you hook and land a jumbo-sized

Michael McElroy/Cleveland Lakefront State Park

walleye makes it worth the frozen fingers and toes.

Located near the northern end of Martin Luther King, Jr., Blvd., Gordon Park is a nice place to spend a summer morning or winter night fishing. Massive boulders line the lakeshore, with an occasional concrete path breaking through and leading to a concrete fishing area at the

East

very edge of the lake. The breakwalls are just a couple of feet above the water level; on rough days waves tumble over the wall.

Gordon Park is actually connected via a sidewalk to the E. 55th Street Marina, which also offers great Lake Erie access and a baitshop/concession stand. Breakwalls between the two offer numerous places to fish, some with relatively quieter waters. This area used to be very popular during the colder months of the year because the warm-water discharge from the Cleveland Electric Illuminating plant attracted large numbers of baitfish and, consequently, large schools of walleye and other predatory fish. Unfortunately, the plant currently operates on a seasonal basis, with most discharges occurring during the summer.

Anglers can still do well here, however, pulling in perch, walleye, carp, catfish, sheephead, white bass, and smallmouth bass. Fishing minnows or night crawlers off the bottom is effective for most species. Spinners and Rapalas work well for smallmouth and white bass during the warmer months and walleye in the spring and fall.

The Gordon Park breakwall is also popular for fall and winter walleye fishing. Through rain, sleet, or snow, hardy anglers pound the lake's waters for walleye, usually beginning around 8 p.m. and fishing until about 2 a.m. or until their fingers freeze—whichever comes first.

There is a public boat launch available, with six free boat launches and restrooms. Enter the park through the entranceway closest to Martin Luther King. The boat launch closes at 11 p.m.

Shine's Live Bait, Tackle and Beverage on E. 55th St. (216-431-9090) is a good nearby source for fishing supplies and information.

Anglers have 24-hour access to the fishing areas.

Nearby bait shop(s): E. 55th St. Marina Bait Shop; Shine's Live Bait. (See Directory section for details.)

7

Holden Arboretum
Foster Pond, Corning Lake, Fisherman's Ponds
9500 Sperry Rd., Kirtland

Recreational | Intermediate | Challenging

Water Type: Inland lake **Acreage:** 28 acres total
Access: Shoreline
What's Biting: Bluegill, largemouth bass, sunfish
Season: Spring/Summer/Fall **Hours:** Tue–Sun 10 a.m.–5 p.m.; closed Mon
Fee: Daily: $4 adults, $3 seniors, $2 children; Annual membership $40
Permission: Required
Facilities: Restrooms, picnic area, food nearby, hiking trails, ranger
Administered by: Holden Arboretum
Directions: I-90 to Exit 193 (SR 306); south on SR 306; left on Kirtland/Chardon Rd.; left on Sperry Rd.; entrance on left.

Description The Holden Arboretum, located in the rural setting of Kirtland, just 25 miles east of downtown Cleveland, is the largest arboretum in the country. It encompasses more than 3,100 acres of plant collections, gardens, woods, fields, and ravines. There are also several ponds and lakes dotting the Arboretum's holdings; these offer decent to good shoreline fishing for largemouth bass and bluegill.

I hold a special place in my heart for the Holden Arboretum. As a youngster, I spent countless afternoons probing its shores for bluegill and the occasional bass, while my mom stayed back at the picnic blanket crocheting an afghan and undoubtedly enjoying the peace created by my absence.

By parking in the main lot located near the nature center, fishermen can reach Foster Pond (3 acres) and Corning Lake (15 acres), both of which offer plenty of shoreline fishing access. There are plenty of weeds

Holden Arboretum

and lily pads in Corning Lake that attract bass. A weedless rubber worm or Sluggo in and around these weeds might pull out a bass or two.

The Fisherman's Ponds (10 acres) are located off Kirtland-Chardon Rd. just west of Sperry Rd. A locked gate blocks the entrance to the parking area, but Arboretum members (see below) are given the lock's combination. These ponds offer good fishing for panfish and large-mouth bass. A great amount of the land in this area is undisturbed woodland and prairie habitat, so keep your eyes open for deer, hawk, and other exciting wildlife-viewing opportunities.

The ponds and lakes at the Holden Arboretum all provide plenty of easy shoreline access around their perimeters and are ideal places to bring youngsters who have yet to perfect their casting technique.

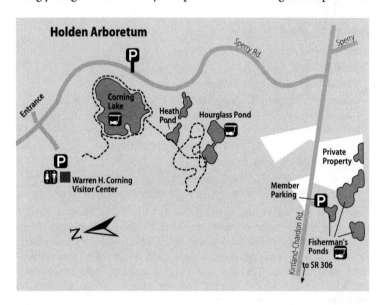

There is no stocking program in place for Holden's lakes and ponds. Catch-and-release is encouraged and widely practiced by its members to help keep the fish populations at a catchable level. Most of the fish, especially bass, will be on the smaller side. Still, given the rather large size of some of the lakes, the abundance of shoreline structure, and the decent populations of bluegill, it is entirely possible to catch some larger bass.

Membership is required to fish at or visit the Holden Arboretum, with a general membership for an individual or family costing $40 ($25 for seniors). You can also pay a daily visitor fee of $4 for adults and $2 for children (ages 6 to 15). Kids under 6 are admitted free. A fishing license is not required to fish at the Holden Arboretum.

Membership does have its privileges, including use of the Arboretum's interpretive trails for hiking and cross-country skiing. Members are also allowed access to the fishing lakes before and after regular Arboretum hours. Advance notice of programs, merchandise discounts, and a quarterly magazine are a few more of the perks members enjoy. It truly is a wonderful facility rich in natural beauty and outdoor recreation opportunities.

8

South Chagrin Reservation
Shadow Lake and Chagrin River
Hawthorne Pkwy., Solon

Recreational | Intermediate | Challenging

Water Type: River, pond **Acreage:** 3.3 acres

Access: Shoreline

What's Biting: Bluegill, smallmouth bass, rock bass, carp, catfish, suckers, sunfish, trout

Season: Year-round **Hours:** 6 a.m.–11 p.m.

Fee: Free **Permission:** Not required

Facilities: Restrooms, picnic area, food nearby, hiking trails, ranger, guides

Administered by: Cleveland Metroparks

Directions: I-271 to Exit 23 (Forbes Rd.); east on Forbes; left (north) on Richmond Rd.; right (east) on Hawthorne Pkwy.; Shadow Lake on right.

Description The Cleveland Metroparks' annual Spring Fishing Derbies successfully lure many young anglers to the sport. If you have a youngster you would like to encourage, one of these (such as the annual Children's Spring Fishing Derby) is a great start. Shadow Lake, located in the South Chagrin Reservation, is the East Side site for Cleveland Metroparks' annual Children's Spring Fishing Derby, which is held on the third weekend in May. For more information on the derby, call the Natural Resources Office (440-234-9597).

Located among the hemlock, white oak, red oak, and shagbark hickory trees of the South Chagrin Reservation, Shadow Lake is a 3.3-acre pond that was created in 1968. This easily accessible pond continues to offer productive fishing to this day.

Fishermen can do well here thanks to the efforts of the Cleveland Metroparks Natural Resources personnel, who conduct an active fish management program that includes habitat improvement and stocking. Anglers can catch the usual array of pond fish species, including largemouth bass, bluegill, and channel catfish. Adult rainbow trout are stocked in the winter to bolster the ice fishing.

Be advised of the special fishing regulations at Shadow Lake. The minimum legal size for largemouth bass is 12 inches, and the daily harvest limit is two bass per angler. For rainbow trout, the daily limit is three fish per angler. Also located in the South Chagrin Reservation is a section of the West Branch of the Chagrin River, a stream fishery that is surprisingly undisturbed. (See map.) Considering its close proximity to Cleveland and the effect that urbanization has on most waterways, this spot is truly an angling jewel worth visiting.

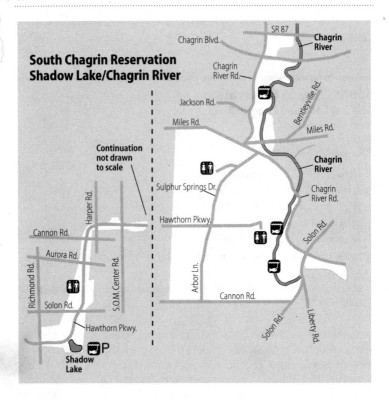

Bridle trails and access trails along the west side of the stream provide excellent access for anglers. In the summer, it is a pleasure to wade this section of the stream in shorts and an old pair of sneakers, with the bare essentials in terms of tackle, probing its deeper holes for smallmouth and rock bass, crappie, and other river denizens. Be sure to take a few moments, especially if you are with a youngster, to catch some crayfish. Lift up a few rocks and observe the hellgramites, stonefly nymphs, and other fascinating creatures that rely on the stream's clean water for life.

Light tippets are the order for fly fishermen; light line, such as 4- to 6-pound test, will help spin fishermen hook into some fish. Anything resembling those foods normally found in the river (minnows, crayfish, and hellgramites) will catch fish, although live versions of these will prove even more delectable to smallmouth and rock bass. Worms and maggots can also prove effective, especially for panfish.

Anglers are asked to please stay within the park boundaries when fishing the West Branch of the Chagrin River, and to avoid trespassing on neighboring properties.

9

Todd Field
Chagrin River
Glenn St., Willoughby

Recreational | Intermediate | Challenging

Water Type: River **Acreage:** N/A
Access: Shoreline
What's Biting: Bluegill, smallmouth bass, carp, catfish, steelhead, suckers, sunfish
Season: Year-round **Hours:** Dawn–dusk
Fee: Free **Permission:** Not required
Facilities: Picnic area, food nearby
Administered by: Willoughby Parks and Recreation
Directions: SR 2 to Vine St. (east) exit; east on Vine; right at Erie St.; left on Glenn St.; Todd Field is at bottom of hill.

Description Todd Field is actually a collection of several baseball fields and a football field managed by the City of Willoughby. During game days a concession shop and restrooms are available. It's a beautiful park, made even more beautiful by the Chagrin River, which flows along it. Todd Field offers a tremendous amount of shoreline access for anglers hoping to hook into the smallmouth bass, carp, steelhead, and suckers found in this section of the river.

Park in the upper lots and take any of a number of short trails that lead to the Chagrin River. The Vine Street bridge spans the river just downstream from the parking lot. Upstream from the bridge for at least a quarter-mile the river is primarily flat and slow. I have never done very well on this stretch of the river for smallmouth bass or steelhead, nor have any of my fishing friends. There are, however, some hog-sized carp scrounging along the bottom.

Past this stretch, though, things get more interesting. Riffles and deep pools provide great habitat for smallmouth bass, which often fall for buzzbaits, spinnerbaits, and jigs. There are several ways to fish this section. Often buzzbait or spinnerbait retrieved over the deeper holes successfully lure smallmouth up from the depths, the annoying buzz of a buzzbait irritating the fish enough to spur them into striking it out of anger. Be careful when wading this section of the Chagrin River, as some of the deep holes here are seriously deep. At certain water levels, they are certainly shoulder deep or over your head.

For more of a finesse approach, try working a lure through the riffles, always ready for quick, strong strikes of smallmouth bass. I have had good luck by working a crayfish-colored jig through the deeper tail sections of a pool right before it enters a fast run. Tick it along the bottom like a crayfish and wait for a smally to suck it up. Small spinners tipped with rubber grubs—retrieved just fast enough to get the spinner moving—also work very well.

Lastly, it's tough to beat a live crayfish drifted through the deeper pools. Crayfish are plentiful along the river bottom, and make up a decent portion of the smallmouth bass's diet.

Todd Field is also a fine place for fall and spring steelhead fishing. The deeper pools make ideal resting spots for the migrating steelhead, and a maggot-tipped jig or spawn drifted through them is often a successful approach, as are most other steelhead techniques. You'll want to concentrate on the sections downstream from the bridge, and the riffles and pools upriver. Avoid the slow, flat section closest to the open field.

Todd Field is open from dawn to dusk. A current Ohio fishing license is required to fish the Chagrin River. Nearby attractions include downtown Willoughby, which boasts a neat assortment of shops, restaurants, coffee shops, and a microbrewery. It is an easy walk to downtown Willoughby.

Nearby bait shop(s): Erieshore Bait & Tackle. (See Directory section for details.)

10

Wildwood/Villa Angela State Park
Lake Erie Shoreline and Euclid Creek
Lake Shore Blvd., Cleveland

East

Recreational | **Intermediate** | Challenging

Water Type: Lake Erie, river **Acreage:** N/A

Access: Shoreline, breakwall, canoe, boat

What's Biting: Bluegill, smallmouth bass, carp, catfish, perch, sheepshead, steelhead, sunfish, walleye, white bass

Season: Year-round **Hours:** 6 a.m.–11 p.m., but anglers may stay in park all night

Fee: Free **Permission:** Not required

Facilities: Bait shop, boat launch, restrooms, picnic area, food onsite, food nearby, hiking trails, ranger

Administered by: Ohio Department of Natural Resources

Directions: I-90 to Exit 182A (E. 185 St.); north on E. 185; left (northwest) on Neff Rd.; left (west) on Lake Shore Blvd.; on right.

Description I was lucky to visit Wildwood State Park on the same day an official from the Division of Wildlife was doing a creel survey there. I had never seen this done, so I watched over his shoulder as he quickly weighed and measured the walleye he had taken from an angler's cooler, and then, using a knife, scraped a few scales from the side of the fish. These he placed in a numbered envelope. Through the scale sample, biologists can determine the age of the fish. Comparing the fish's age with its length and weight provides insight into the health of Lake Erie's fish population. It may have been premature to say at the time, but that plump, tasty-looking walleye appeared pretty healthy to me.

Wildwood State Park has recently undergone an extensive renovation, shifting the entrance from Neff Rd. to directly off Lake Shore Blvd. Two breakwalls extend into Lake Erie and provide great access to the lake. Anglers can fish the quieter waters of the harbor or the rougher waters of Lake Erie. The majority of fishermen here still fish with minnows and worms and catch standard Lake Erie fare, including perch, catfish, carp, sheephead, and walleye. Artificial lures are also effective, especially on white bass, and on walleye and steelhead when they come in close to shore.

There are usually very few people fishing for smallmouth bass, and this day I saw none, despite the fact that several were lurking around the breakwall rocks, driftwood, and docks. Wear your polarized fishing glasses and take a look around any structure you see for the football-shaped profile of smallmouth bass. You might be surprised.

If you are going after walleye, your best bet is spring (late April to early June), and fall (November to ice-over). Nighttime is most productive, and Rat-L-Traps and Rapalas have proven to be very effective.

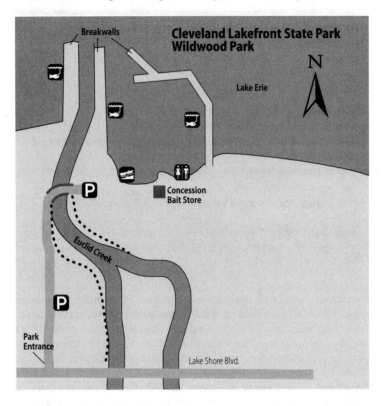

During fall and spring, it is also possible to pick up a steelhead or two. During early fall, try going off the breakwall next to the mouth of Euclid Creek with spinners, spoons, or spawn. Although it is not stocked, Euclid Creek does get a decent steelhead run. Rooster tails work well, and drifting spawn and maggot-tipped jigs on the slow current of Euclid Creek can produce.

During the summer, perch fishing can be quite slow along the lake shore as these tasty fish move several miles out into deeper water. If you are determined to have that perch dinner, be sure to check out Linda Mae, a head boat that departs from Wildwood State Park. It is open to the public on a walk-on basis, and for a modest price it will take you to where the fish are. For more information on the Linda Mae, or any of the other charter services provided by One Stop Charters, call (216) 481-5771. To hear their 24-hour recorded message detailing fishing conditions and angling success, call (440) 942-1909.

Perch fishing can be fantastic just a few miles offshore, making this a great destination for small-boat fishermen. The free boat launch can get you in the water and out into a school of perch without much hassle, and without having to go too far out on the lake. Any experienced boater can attest to the quickness with which Lake Erie can go from calm to crazy, and being close to shore provides peace of mind for small-boat anglers.

A well-stocked bait shop (216-481-5771) is open from May through early November and is a great source of angling information. The park is open from 6 a.m. to 11 p.m.; anglers, however, can stay in the park all night.

Nearby bait shop(s): Wildwood Marina; Sonny Shore's Live Bait. (See Directory section for details.)

East

11

East

Arcola Creek Metropark
Beach and Stream Fishing
Dock Rd., Madison

Recreational | **Intermediate** | **Challenging**

Water Type: Lake Erie, river **Acreage:** N/A

Access: Shoreline

What's Biting: Bluegill, smallmouth bass, carp, catfish, sheephead, perch, steelhead, suckers, sunfish, walleye

Season: Year-round **Hours:** N/A

Fee: Free **Permission:** Not required

Facilities: Restrooms, picnic area, food nearby

Administered by: Lake Metroparks

Directions: SR 2 east to US 20; east on US 20; left (north) on Dock Rd. for 3.5 miles; entrance on right (east) side.

Description Exploring a new fishing destination can lead to more than just a great place to fish. Sometimes, it leads to the discovery of a fascinating piece of local history. Such was the case when I journeyed to Arcola Creek Metropark in Madison for a morning of fishing.

At the beginning of the 1800s, a town by the name of Ellensburg was built at the junction of Arcola Creek and Lake Erie. The sheltered waters of Arcola Creek formed a natural harbor, and Lake Erie provided a great means of transporting goods. Arcola Iron Works prospered at this time, using bog iron, which was discovered in Madison in 1812, as its raw material and the area's abundant timber to fuel its fires. A thriving community of shipbuilders, fisher-

Lake Metroparks

men, and merchants developed in the area. During the early 1800s more ships were built in and launched from this port than any other on Lake Erie. By 1840, however, supplies dwindled and shifting sandbars made it difficult to bring goods into the harbor. The last ship was built in 1863, and Ellensburg was soon abandoned. The short, productive history of Ellensburg had drawn to a close.

There's not much sign left of Ellensburg anymore. In fact, it seems impossible that anything along the lines of a shipbuilding industry could have ever existed at the tranquil shoreline setting of what has since become Arcola Creek Metropark. To me, the park represents the impermanence of human endeavors.

Arcola Creek Metropark still provides great access for fishing the shores of Lake Erie and Arcola Creek. From the parking lot, you can take the trail heading north to get to the lakeshore. Surf fishing is popular from the beach and especially around the mouth of the creek. Smallmouth bass, sheephead, and steelhead are just some of the species you might hook into. If you are going to still fish, minnows and worms are a good bet. If smallmouth bass are your quarry, try lead-head jigs or twister-tails.

Steelhead fishermen can be successful using plugs, spinners, and spoons for steelies. PowerBait fished on the bottom is an especially effective shore-fishing method at Arcola Creek. Attach a small to medium-sized short-shanked bait hook about a foot below a sinker. The sinker gets the whole rig down deep, while the buoyancy of the PowerBait elevates it off the lake bottom, putting it right in the strike zone.

Fishing access is limited on Arcola Creek. Most of the creek in this stretch is swampy as it flows through the estuary. There is a trail leading south out of the parking lot that will take you to the creek, just upstream from where it separates itself and begins flowing freely through wooded terrain. Expect to get muddy, and be sure to stay within the boundaries of the park. (Most of the upstream sections of the river run through private property.)

Upstream from the park Arcola Creek winds through mostly private property, and although there are several points on the creek that anglers can fish from without harassment, the legality of fishing there is questionable. Suffice it to say that the inquisitive angler can still locate access points on Arcola Creek. Unfortunately, wooded, quiet areas that were open for fishing a year or two ago have since fallen victim to residential development, decreasing access to this natural resource.

Arcola Creek has earned a reputation as a potential hot spot during the steelhead season. It's not a huge waterway, but it reportedly gets very good runs in the spring and fall. Indeed, some stories I've heard from fellow anglers tell of steelhead catches that would seem almost unbelievable (except that I know fishermen don't lie or exaggerate). You can't go wrong with maggot-tipped jigs or spawn sacs drifted freely near the bottom. The shoreline can be tight, making this a very challenging fishing location for fly fishermen. Arcola Creek's shoreline is a popular place for Lake Erie surf fishermen, who cast plugs, spinners, and spoons for steelies. PowerBait fished on the bottom can be effective. Attach a small to medium-sized short-shanked bait hook about a foot past a sinker. The sinker gets the whole rig deep; the buoyancy of the PowerBait elevates it off the lake bottom, putting it right in the strike zone.

Arcola Creek is one of the last remaining natural estuaries along the Great Lakes. A freshwater estuary is defined as a place where creek or river water mixes with the waters of the Great Lakes, creating a separate habitat. It is truly an unusual park, and the great variety of birds it attracts is worth a visit in itself. An observation deck overlooking the estuary affords the observant a chance at glimpsing a host of songbirds, including the migratories that make this a rest stop on their way to winter or summer grounds north and south of Ohio.

Catch and Release

The decision to keep a fish or practice catch-and-release fishing is a personal one. It can also be a controversial subject. I have known fishermen at both extremes on this issue. Some argue vehemently against keeping any fish, forgetting that fishing, whether we like to believe it or not, is often a blood sport. Others insist that there is no sense at all in fishing if you plan to release everything and come home with an empty creel.

But to me, it comes down to one simple question: "Will this fish serve more value harvested or released back into its habitat?"

Too often anglers err on the side of believing that no fish should ever be harvested, to the point where those who do keep fish may be looked down upon. This is unfortunate because in the right situations, harvesting fish is perfectly acceptable and may even be an important component of a management plan for a given pond, lake, or river. Lake Erie walleye and perch are certainly sustainable and renewable resources, and with sound management they are not negatively affected by controlled harvesting.

There are also fisheries that are considered "put-and-take," in which fish literally are stocked in order that they may be caught and kept. Local stockings of trout are one example. The trout are put in a lake, river, or pond with the sole intention that they be harvested. Because of water conditions, the trout will usually not even survive longer than a year. Obviously, these are situations where harvesting fish is perfectly acceptable and encouraged.

Panfish especially can be harvested to some extent without a detrimental impact on overall fish populations. The rapid reproduction rate of these fish makes them vulnerable to overpopulation, which can result in a pond or lake filled with undersized fish.

There is also a romantic quality to ending a fishing trip with a dinner of fresh fish that you caught yourself. Many anglers consider it a ceremonial end to a successful day.

In many situations, though, I find it difficult to justify keeping the catch, especially with regard to the major sport fish, such as muskie, largemouth and smallmouth bass, and northern pike, to name a few. The role these fish play in their environment and in the sport of fishing outweighs their value as a single meal or a decoration above the mantelpiece.

If the fish is released it can return to its important function in its ecosystem. And it will live to fight another day, helping to maintain catchable populations for your fellow anglers. After all, how many fish do you think you have caught that were previously released by considerate fishermen? For some fishing locations, I would guess the vast majority of them. Consider that when making your decision.

Too often fishermen keep only the large ones and "let the little ones go," in the belief that they will become next year's lunkers. This is an admirable thought, but unfortunately it is not always correct.

Let's look at just a few advantages of releasing the larger fish. First off, these larger fish eat smaller ones, helping to control fish populations and prevent size stunting. Second, large fish carry in their genes the survival instincts that enabled them to outlive the others. These are the genes we want to have passed on to future fish, and they are therefore important breeders. Last, when we release a large fish, we are giving somebody else the pleasure of catching it another day.

If you choose to practice catch-and-release, it is a wasted effort if the fish dies soon after being placed back in the water. The following are steps you can take to help decrease the mortality rate of released fish:

Land the fish quickly. Use tackle that will let you land the fish without having to fight it for too long. Catching a lunker bass on ultralight gear may be fun, but it normally involves playing the fish to the point of exhaustion, thereby decreasing its chance for survival after release. Some may consider this sporting, but it too often results in a dead fish.

Handle the fish with care. This includes wetting your hands before touching it in order to preserve the protective slime (the fish's, not yours). Cradle the fish gently, without squeezing it. Also, do not let the fish flop around on land or in the bottom of your boat, and keep it in the water as long as possible. Keep your fingers away from the gills and eyes.

Remove the hook as quickly as possible. If the fish is hooked deeply, cut the line and release it. If there is blood coming from its gill, keep it and count it against your legal limit, as it will most likely die anyway.

Keep the fish in the water as long as possible. Take it out only for a quick photograph.

Revive the fish by pointing it into a slow current, or by gently moving it back and forth. When it has recovered, let it swim away under its own power.

By taking these precautions you can help ensure that the fish are caught and released with a minimum of stress and increase their survival rate. After all, isn't that exactly why you decided to practice catch-and-release?

Farther East

12

Beartown Lakes Reservation
Lower and Middle Bear lakes, Minnow Pond
18870 Quinn Rd., Auburn Township

Recreational | Intermediate | Challenging

Water Type: Inland lake **Acreage:** 22 acres total

Access: Shoreline, pier

What's Biting: Bluegill, largemouth bass, sunfish

Season: Spring/Summer/Fall **Hours:** 6 a.m.–11 p.m.

Fee: Free **Permission:** Not required

Facilities: Restrooms, picnic area, food nearby, hiking trails, ranger

Administered by: Geauga Park District

Directions: I-480/I-271 to US 422; east on US 422; exit at SR 306; south on SR 306; left (east) on Taylor May Rd.; right (south) on Quinn Rd. to park entrance.

Description Al and Jocie Bieger purchased land in Auburn Township in 1950, and by the end of the decade they had opened a private fishing club, creating three interconnecting lakes, a trout raceway, and a minnow pond. Members could fish for trout, catfish, and northern pike. Anglers enjoyed fishing there until the club closed in the early 1970s.

Today you don't need to belong to a fishing club to take advantage of the largemouth bass and panfish found in the lakes. In January 1993, the Geauga Park District purchased the land, and because of the large number of black bears that had historically roamed the area, it was renamed Beartown Lakes Reserva-

Geauga Park District

tion. The necessary improvements were made, creating a beautiful park that offers a great fishing opportunity for shore anglers. Four fishing piers provide good access to both Middle Bear Lake (5 acres) and Lower Bear Lake (10 acres), the deepest of all the lakes. Beartown Lakes Reservation is angler-friendly because of the large amount of shoreline fishing permitted on Lower and Middle Bear lakes and the smaller Minnow Pond (0.5 acres).

Lure fishermen can do well at Beartown, but natural bait is still the bait du jour for panfish. Suspending small red worms and maggots from a light bobber is a proven technique. Don't forget, if the fishing for panfish is slow, scale down the size of your offering and try to present it in as natural a way as possible. Smaller hooks and lighter line can improve your chances for success.

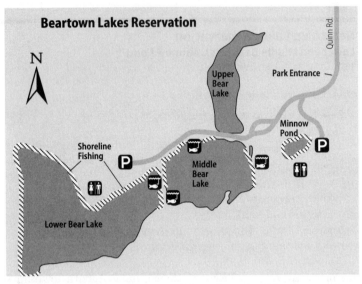

Fishing pressure is moderate at this park, so the fish are not quite as skittish as at more heavily fished lakes. There are good populations of bass and panfish, and although I have never witnessed one being caught, there are rumored to be some northern pike swimming these waters.

The park district does not have a stocking program in place, so they encourage a catch-and-release policy to maintain healthy fish populations. Please remember that collection of live bait is not permitted. Due to safety concerns, fishing from the causeway is also prohibited. A current Ohio fishing license is required when fishing Beartown Lakes Reservation.

Three covered shelters are available within the park, making it a good place to enjoy a picnic after a morning of fishing. For the hiking enthusiast, three well-maintained hiking trails wind their way through the park and give visitors a firsthand look at the wildflowers, songbirds, trees, and other natural features of the park.

Beartown Lakes Reservation is just several miles from the quaint shops and restaurants of downtown Chagrin Falls. There are fast-food purveyors close to the US Route 422 and State Route 306 intersection.

Nearby bait shop(s): One Stop Fishing Shop Ltd. (See Directory section for details.)

13

Big Creek Park
Chestnut, Tupelo, and Wild Goose Ponds
9160 Robinson Rd., Chardon

Recreational | Intermediate | Challenging

Water Type: Pond **Acreage:** 6.5 acres total

Access: Shoreline

What's Biting: Bluegill, largemouth bass, catfish, sunfish

Season: Spring/Summer/Fall **Hours:** 6 a.m.–11 p.m.

Fee: Free **Permission:** Not required

Facilities: Restrooms, picnic area, food nearby, hiking trails, camping, ranger

Administered by: Geauga Park District

Directions: I-90 to Exit 200 (SR 44); south on SR 44; left (east) on Clark to Robinson Rd.; right on Robinson to park entrance.

Farther East

Description There are three ponds located in Geauga Park District's Big Creek Park. Chestnut Pond (2 acres) and Wild Goose Pond (2.5 acres) are both located by the Donald W. Meyer Center, which you can get to by following the directions above. Both of these ponds are heavily fished. Combine this with a small amount of cover and the absence of any type of stocking program, and you can get some pretty slow fishing. Access is good, however, making it an ideal spot for youngsters.

Geauga Park District

That's not to say it's a lost cause. There are some decent-sized bluegill and bass in these ponds. The problem is that with the fishing pressure these ponds receive, the fish have become quite lure-wary, and do not take easily to artificial baits. For the bass, small spinnerbaits or twister-tails can produce, as will rubber worms. Surface lures at dusk can also be an effective technique. For the bluegill, try using either live bait—for example small worms, maggots, or crickets—or a small nymph pattern on a fly rod. Morning and evening are the most productive times for these fish.

The third fishing hole, called Tupelo Pond (2 acres), is located on the other side of the park and can be found by taking Robinson Rd. back to Clark Rd., and turning left (west). When you get to Ravenna Rd., go left (south). Tupelo Pond sneaks up on your left.

Fewer fishermen pound these waters, and in the summer the pond is heavily covered with weeds. If you want bass, catfish, or larger panfish, this is your best bet. Work the edges of the weed beds with a spinnerbait or rubber worm, or drop a Texas-rigged rubber worm in any opening in the weed canopy. Another good technique is to work something weedless, like a Rat or Sluggo, over the weeds. Bass pick up these slight vibrations as the lure pushes down on the weed mat, and they will often take it violently right through this seemingly impenetrable layer.

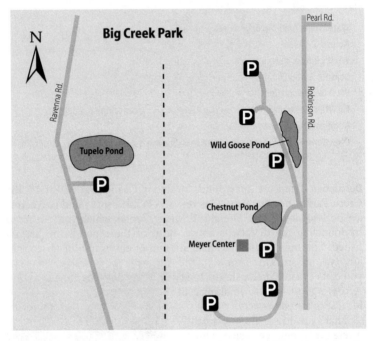

Big Creek Park is a great place to spend an entire day with the family. A 6.4-mile network of trails winds through the park's 640 acres of beech and maple woods. Picnic shelters and grills are available. The Donald W. Meyer Center offers educational displays and is definitely worth visiting. Limited primitive camping is available, but you must call at least 10 days in advance to reserve a camping space.

Because of the fishing pressure on these ponds and the lack of a stocking program, catch-and-release is strongly encouraged. Collection of live bait within the park is prohibited.

Nearby attractions include historic Chardon Square, a quaint town center with plenty of unique and interesting shops. The Red Hawk Grill, located on Auburn Rd. near I-90, offers good food and cold beverages in a casual setting.

14

Conneaut Creek
Conneaut

Farther East

> Recreational | Intermediate | Challenging
>
> **Water Type:** Lake Erie, river **Acreage:** N/A
> **Access:** Wading
> **What's Biting:** Bluegill, smallmouth bass, carp, catfish, sheephead, perch, sheephead, steelhead, suckers, sunfish, walleye, white bass
> **Season:** Year-round **Hours:** N/A
> **Fee:** Free; boat launch $5 per day, $80 per season **Permission:** Not required
> **Facilities:** Bait shop, boat launch, restrooms, food onsite, food nearby
> **Administered by:** N/A
> **Directions:** I-90 east to Exit 241 (SR 7); left (north) on SR 7. See description for specific location directions.

Description People have their own ideas of what heaven might be like. For some, it might be sitting in a major-league ballpark on a sunny summer day watching the home team bat its way to victory. For others, a comfortable blanket, warm beach, and gently lapping waves might be their version of Nirvana.

As I pulled off the side of Keefus Rd., watching a small dust cloud catch up with me in the rearview mirror, I anxiously scanned the rest of the area for other fishermen or cars. Nothing. Opening the door, I was greeted with the faraway sounds of rushing water emanating from Conneaut Creek. When I closed my eyes, I could have sworn that I heard the splashing of several steelhead thrusting their way through the currents. El Niño had exerted its influence on our weather patterns, and at a time when we should have had snow and subzero temperatures, we were instead experiencing sunny days with the mercury easily reaching into the 40s. This, I thought, is heaven as I visualize it. And I am sure there are more than a handful of fishermen out there who share my belief that the pearly gates must open up to a river like the Conneaut, and that instead of holding a harp, Saint Peter will be handing out spawn patterns, maggots, and fly rods.

The highway sign on State Route 7 indicated that the distance from Conneaut to Cleveland was 68 miles as the crow flies. Quite a drive, especially if you want to be on the river at first light. But the fishing opportunities and sheer natural beauty of Conneaut Creek make it more than worth the drive.

Conneaut Creek is unique locally in that, unlike the Grand, Chagrin, and Rocky rivers, public parks are few and far between. Most of the land through which Conneaut Creek flows is private. But, luckily for area anglers, most of it is also open for fishing.

To get you started, I have listed six locations worth visiting on your next trip to this far northeast section of the Buckeye State. These locations will give you a taste of this dynamic creek; as you become more familiar with the area and talk to fellow anglers, you will learn about other access points and fishing holes.

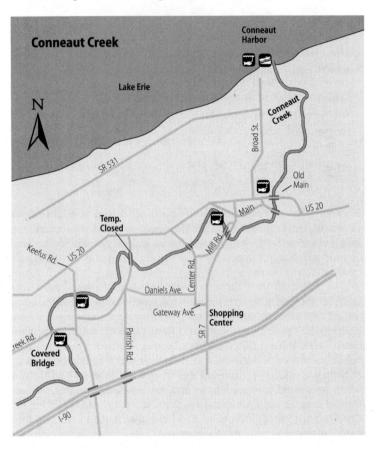

West Breakwall/Conneaut Harbor. Located at the north end of Broad St. is Conneaut Harbor, a Lake Erie access point offering a decent amount of breakwall fishing action. Enter off Broad St., park, and walk west to the west breakwall. In the spring, the breakwall is a hot spot for smallmouth bass. In the fall, steelhead are the order of the day. At the public boat launch, ramp passes cost $5 per day, or $80 seasonally. There is also a wildlife viewing platform. A bait and concession store is open seasonally at the harbor, and Snug Harbor Sports, located almost adjacent to the harbor, is open year round. They offer a good supply of fishing tackle and bait, and the employees provide up-to-date information about the current fishing situation both on Lake Erie and on Conneaut Creek. The harbor is managed by the Conneaut Port Authority (440-593-1300).

The following locations offer fishing a little farther upstream. There is parking at all of them, but it is very limited, usually consisting of a few spots just off the road. There are no restrooms, picnic shelters, or other amenities at any of them. There is, however, enough fishing access to attract even the most seasoned anglers. And to make things even better, most stretches of Conneaut Creek flow through countryside that is isloated and beautiful—perfect settings for a morning of fishing.

Much of the shoreline is suitable for fishing, and at normal water levels most of the river is open for wading fishermen. Steelhead are perhaps the most sought-after fish here, but Conneaut Creek is also a good smallmouth bass fishery. On one trip, a friend hooked into a two-pound fish at the beginning of February using spawn. On the same trip, I hooked and landed a respectable-sized white sucker. They weren't steelhead, but they were still fun to catch.

Old Main Street Bridge. Take Old Main St. off US Route 20 in downtown Conneaut. The downstream side of the bridge is posted no trespassing, so anglers should concentrate on the upstream sections. There are concrete remnants of something, perhaps an old dam, and a good assortment of riffles and pools. A very interesting stretch of river that does produce fish.

Mill Road Bridge. Mill Rd. is located off State Route 7 just about a mile from I-90. There is an island underneath the bridge that, at low water, funnels the river to either side, creating fast, fairly deep runs. Anglers can hike either up- or downstream from this point. Fishermen I spoke with claim that this, too, can be an excellent location for steelhead when they are running.

Keefus Road Bridge. Take Daniels Rd. to get to Keefus Rd., or take US Route 20. The land on either side of the creek at this location, owned by the Conneaut Fish and Game Club and by Monroe Athletic, is open for fishing. There are several parking spots just before the bridge when heading north on Keefus Rd. Although it is fairly close to US Route 20, the bridge is quiet and offers a strong sense of isolation, making it an enjoyable place to explore. The river offers a good number of deep pools perfect for holding steelhead.

Creek Road Covered Bridge. Located on Creek Rd., off Keefus Rd. There is something wonderfully nostalgic about fishing near a covered bridge. The Creek Road Covered Bridge, located in the hinterlands of Con-

Farther East

neaut, offers great fishing opportunities in the shadow of a relic from Ashtabula County's history. There are very deep pools located underneath the bridge and just downstream, so be sure to use enough weight to get your offering down to the fish. The river is open for wading up- and downstream, with plenty of fish-holding water for the adventurous angler.

There is no denying that Conneaut is quite a hike from Cleveland. That, combined with the vast amounts of river to explore, might make it advisable to spend a night or two in Conneaut. There is a Days Inn (800-325-2525) located close to I-90, along with quite an assortment of bed and breakfasts. For a complete list of places to stay, call the Conneaut Chamber of Commerce (440-593-2402).

Farther East

15

Eldon Russell Park
Upper Cuyahoga River
16315 Rapids Rd., Troy Township

Recreational | Intermediate | Challenging

Water Type: River **Acreage:** N/A
Access: Shoreline, canoe, boat
What's Biting: Bluegill, largemouth bass, catfish, crappies, pike, sunfish
Season: Spring/Summer/Fall **Hours:** 6 a.m.–11 p.m.
Fee: Free **Permission:** Not required
Facilities: Boat launch, restrooms, picnic area, food nearby, hiking trails, ranger
Administered by: Geauga Park District
Directions: I-480/I-271 to US 422; east on US 422 through Auburn Corners; left (north) on Rapids Rd., just past LaDue Reservoir, to park entrance on right.

Description When most people think about the Cuyahoga River, they probably envision the river that was historically so polluted it caught fire. Take time to explore the river closer to its headwaters, however, and you might change your mind. The upper reaches of the Cuyahoga bear no resemblance to the muddy stretch that flows through Cleveland's Flats. For fishermen, the Upper Cuyahoga is definitely worth exploring. A great place to do this is at Eldon Russell Park, located in Troy Township in Geauga County.

Eldon Russell Park has a very rich history. In 1901, Pace Latham of Burton attempted to deepen and straighten the Cuyahoga River in order to drain the rich muck soil of the surrounding wetland. His eventual aim was to establish large-scale onion farming. Well into the dredg-

Geauga Park District

ing project, it was realized that a natural rock dam at Hiram Rapids would still impede the flow of water. Hired ruffians twice attempted to dynamite the dam but were greeted by local townspeople armed with shotguns loaded with rock salt. The ill-advised scheme was abandoned, and the events surrounding it have since become known as the Onion Wars. Anglers, hikers, and canoeists who visit Eldon Russell Park today will see spoil banks that still remain from Latham's devious plan.

Shoreline anglers can have decent success at Eldon Russell Park by fishing from the canoe landing area right next to the parking lot, or by taking the trail following the section of the river that flows through the park. Buzzbaits and spinnerbaits can be effective, as can small spinners or twister-tail type jigs.

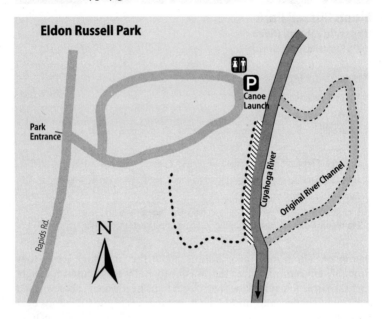

Eldon Russell Park

The Upper Cuyahoga does have a population of northern pike, or "waterwolves" as some call them, and Eldon Russell Park has produced some large fish. Live bait, such as shiners and minnows, can work well, as will Rapala-type crankbaits and spoons. These fish are not stocked in the river, but rather maintain their precarious populations through natural reproduction. Therefore, catch-and-release is highly encouraged to help keep their numbers up.

Many people enjoy fishing this section of the river from small boats and canoes. It flows lazy and slow, so even novices can navigate it easily. A canoe has the advantage of getting you into the more remote stretches of the river. The canoe landing, which is located just off the parking lot, is not suitable for trailered boats.

Eldon Russell Park is composed mostly of wetlands, which provide a perfect breeding habitat for mosquitoes. Insect repellent is a must during the summer, when these annoying bloodsuckers are at their worst. Please remember that collection of live bait within the park is prohibited. Nearby attractions include quaint, comfortable Burton Square, which offers good food and pleasant window-shopping.

16

Fairport Harbor
Lake Erie and Lake Erie Shoreline
High St., Fairport

Recreational | **Intermediate** | **Challenging**

Water Type: Lake Erie, harbor

Access: Shoreline, breakwall, canoe, boat

What's Biting: Bluegill, smallmouth bass, carp, catfish, sheephead, perch, steelhead, sunfish, walleye

Season: Year-round   **Hours:** Dawn–dusk

Fee: Free; fee for boat launch   **Permission:** Not required

Facilities: Boat launch, restrooms, picnic area, food nearby

Administered by: Lake Metroparks

Directions: SR 2 to Fairport Harbor/Richmond St. exit; north on Richmond past SR 283 intersection (Richmond becomes High St.); follow High to park entrance.

Description Fairport Harbor, for the purposes of this book, consists of two parts: the park, which is managed and maintained by Lake Metroparks, and the breakwall and boat launch, which fall under the jurisdiction of the Fairport Harbor Port Authority.

The park is typical of most lakefront parks—stunning sunsets and scenic views of the lake. It also has a sandy beach, walking trails, restrooms, and ample parking. From the park it is a very short walk to the fishing area. Hours are from sunrise to one-half hour after sunset.

The fishing breakwall and boat launch are located just to the west of the park. During the regular boating season there is a $5 launching fee. There is some paid parking by the boat launch, but not as much as at the Metropark.

During the spring and summer, breakwall anglers might hook into perch, sheephead, smallmouth bass, and the occasional walleye. I have heard reports of impressive schools—both in size and number—of smallmouth bass in this section of the Grand. With the large and steady increase in smallmouth bass populations, stumbling upon a school of these hard-fighting fish is becoming more and more common.

Steelhead normally start showing up around the middle of September as they get ready to migrate up the Grand River. Spoons are effective, as are Rooster Tails. Maggot- and minnow-tipped jigs floated beneath a bobber are both popular methods, and of course you can't go wrong drifting spawn.

During the summer I researched this book, I talked to several boaters who had done very well for perch straight out of Fairport Harbor about three miles out. If the lake's waters are too rough, boaters can explore the Grand River or harbor instead, trolling for steelhead or casting for smallmouth bass. The harbor and the rocky ledges of the breakwall have become a hot area for anglers in search of smallmouth bass.

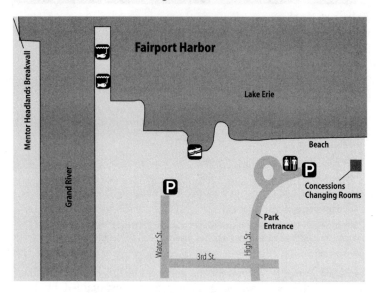

There are two bait shops close by. D & W Bait is located on Richmond St. in Painesville, one block north of the State Route 2 Painesville exit. Grand River Tackle is located on High St. in Fairport Harbor, 500 feet north of the Richmond Street Bridge. They've both got a great selection of tackle, refreshments, and live bait, and provide a reliable source of information.

Nearby attractions: The Fairport Marine Museum is located on Second St. in downtown Fairport Harbor. A National Historic Landmark, the Fairport Marine Museum was the first Great Lakes lighthouse marine museum in the United States. It's a neat place to visit to learn more about the fascinating nautical history of the area. It is open from the Saturday before Memorial Day through Labor Day. Hours are 1 p.m. to 6 p.m. Wednesdays, Saturdays, Sundays, and most holidays.

Nearby bait shop(s): D&W Bait & Tackle; Grand River Tackle. (See Directory section for details.)

17

Geneva State Park
Lake Erie Shoreline, Wheeler Creek and Cowles Creek
Padanarum Rd., Geneva

Recreational | Intermediate | Challenging

Water Type: Lake Erie, river **Acreage:** N/A

Access: Shoreline, breakwall, canoe, boat

What's Biting: Bluegill, smallmouth bass, carp, catfish, crappies, sheephead, perch, sheephead, steelhead, sunfish, walleye, white bass

Season: Year-round **Hours:**

Fee: Free; fee for boat rental and camping **Permission:** Not required

Facilities: Bait shop, boat launch, restrooms, picnic area, food onsite, food nearby, hiking trails, camping, ranger

Administered by: Ohio Department of Natural Resources

Directions: I-90 to Exit 218 (SR 534/Geneva); north on SR 534 through Geneva; continue for several miles; park on left side before the bend (leads into Geneva-on-the-Lake).

Description There are times when I'm surprised at the beauty of Lake Erie. I have lived close to this dynamic body of water my entire life, but I tend to take this immensely valuable resource for granted.

I reflected on this one beautiful summer morning while fishing from the shoreline at Geneva State Park. The temperature was a mild 78 degrees, and the sun floated in a cloudless sky. American goldfinches flitted around; seagulls soared above. If it weren't for the incessant, high-pitched wailing of the jet skis, it would have been perfect.

The fishing wasn't too bad, either. As with any lakeshore fishing, action tends to slow down a bit for perch, smallmouth bass, and walleye during the summer. In fact, on that day, the charters were going several miles out before they hit any fish. Spring and fall are the best times for shore fishing, when the schools of walleye and perch move in closer, and the steelhead start staging for their migration upriver.

But shoreline fishermen can still do well even after the walleye and perch have moved to deeper water. I talked to about 10 people that day, and at least 6 of them had caught fish. My informal creel census showed that smallmouth bass, perch, sheepshead, and catfish made up the

Farther East

species caught. I personally caught two smallmouth bass, about 12 inches each, on a yellow twister-tail retrieved just fast enough to keep the spinner moving. If I were to bottom fish here, minnows would be my first choice, fished on a perch spreader.

In the spring and fall, however, start thinking steelhead. Anglers can cast from the beach areas around the mouths of Wheeler and Cowles Creek in late September and early October, when the steelhead are cruising the shoreline in preparation for their migratory runs. Although they are not stocked in these streams, both receive a decent run. Access is decent along the shores of these creeks, although you might have to do a little hiking. To get to Wheeler Creek, take Lake Rd. west off State Route 534 and continue through the park. Turn right on the dirt just east of the creek, where you can access the mouth of the creek.

According to the park manager, the levels of these two creeks have risen with the rising level of Lake Erie, to the point where he believes it has affected the steelhead fishing. Areas where the river used to be shallower are now bank to bank with water. Fishing has gotten tougher, and the number of fishermen has decreased. Less fishing pressure, of course, can mean greater success to those who do fish here. Try locating some of the deeper potholes along the upper stretches of the creeks within park boundaries, where anglers sometimes have success.

The marina, completed in 1989, is clean, well run, and accommodates both seasonal dockers and daily visitors. A six-lane boat ramp provides free launching opportunities, and there are 383 docks available to seasonal renters. The Geneva State Park Marina, which opens from May 1 through October 31, sells gasoline, boating essentials, bait, and food and drink, and has a very small selection of fishing and boating gear. It is also a good resource for fishing information. Hours are limited during the beginning and end of the boating season, so give them a call at (440) 466-7565 to check on their hours.

Other sources of fishing gear and information are Geneva Bait and Tackle, located on State Route 534 about one-half mile from the Geneva State Park, and Karran's, located closer to the freeway on State Route 84, about one-half mile east of State Route 534.

As a vacation spot, Geneva State Park can't be beat. A full-facility campground with electricity, showers, and flush toilets is available during the summer months, as are 12 cabins equipped with cooking utensils and dishes for six people. There are hiking trails, picnic areas, naturalist-led interpretive programs, a 300-foot guarded swimming beach, and rentable jet skis. Charter services depart from the state park, offering great fishing for perch, smallmouth bass, steelhead, or walleye. (See the directory section for more information.)

Area attractions include the historic community of Geneva-on-the-Lake, 12 local covered bridges, and several local wineries. Firehouse Winery is located within walking distance, which is always a bonus.

Nearby bait shop(s): Geneva State Park Marina; Geneva Bait & Tackle; Karran Shop. (See Directory section for details.)

18

Harpersfield Covered Bridge
Grand River
County Rd. 154, Harpersfield Township

Recreational | Intermediate | Challenging

Water Type: River **Acreage:** N/A

Access: Shoreline, wading, canoe, boat

What's Biting: Bluegill, rock bass, smallmouth bass, largemouth bass, carp, catfish, crappies, muskie, pike, steelhead, suckers, sunfish, walleye

Season: Year-round **Hours:** N/A

Fee: Free **Permission:** Not required

Facilities: Bait shop, boat launch, restrooms, picnic area, food nearby

Administered by: Harpersfield Metro Park

Directions: I-90 to Exit 218 (SR 534/Geneva); right (south) on SR 534 bear right on Harpersfield Rd. through one intersection and down a hill to park entrance.

Farther East

Description Ashtabula County takes great pride in the 15 covered bridges that span the rivers flowing through the county. The Harpersfield Covered Bridge is certainly one of its most handsome. Constructed in 1868, this two-span Howe Truss bridge stretches 234 feet above the mighty Grand River, making it the longest covered bridge in Ohio.

In addition to its beauty, the Harpersfield Covered Bridge is also a great place to fish for some of Ohio's most vicious, acrobatic fish, including smallmouth bass, steelhead, walleye, and muskie, to name but a few. Anglers can fish above and below the dam, or hike downstream quite a distance to get away from the crowd and try out some of the riffle and pool areas.

Electroshocking surveys done on the tailwater under the dam have recorded an amazing variety of fish, and the photos tacked to the wall of the bait shop located next to the river provide anecdotal evidence to back up these findings. When you are casting your line into this section of the Grand, there's no telling what you'll hook into.

From the spring through fall, nice-sized smallmouth and largemouth bass can be caught on live bait, spinners, or flies above and below the dam. The largemouth are primarily caught above the dam, where the water is slower. The smallmouth inhabit the water below the dam, which is broken up by rapids, runs, and deep pools, habitat much more suitable for these denizens of fast, gravel-bottomed rivers. I've had good luck with Muddler Minnows and black Woolly Buggers when I fly fish, and twister-tail jigs below small spinners if I opt for the spin-casting outfit. Crayfish and hellgramites can be absolutely deadly when drifted along the bottom. Concentrate on the deeper pools, and let your lure sink deep. About a quarter-mile downstream from the dam there is a deep pool just upstream from a set of riffles that always seems to hold smallmouth. This section is best approached by hiking along the southern side of the river.

According to the ODNR and fishermen I have talked to, there is a naturally reproducing population of muskie above the dam, where the water is slower, has more structure, and provides more suitable habitat. They can, however, also be caught below the dam and further downstream at various locations on the Grand River. Spinnerbaits and very large jerkbaits can be productive for muskie.

In the fall and spring the covered bridge is a hot spot for spawning steelhead, which, after a long trip up the Grand River, reach the dam and can go no farther. Anglers working the river just below the dam can find some very productive fishing, as can those who hike a little downstream and fish the pockets. Spawn sacs and maggot-tipped jigs floated through the pocket water are favorite techniques. Many anglers do well with chartreuse Rapalas and Rooster Tails. Each fisherman, it seems, has his or her own lure of choice. This is also a wide-open section of the Grand River, and it is an ideal location for fly fishermen not wanting to battle too much streamside vegetation.

The boat ramp is suitable for launching canoes or small boats, but not larger boats from trailers. Two picnic shelters, restrooms, and a small playground make it ideal for a family outing. The Covered Bridge Bait & Tackle is open from March to November and is a great place to inquire about what's biting and on what type of lure or bait. I highly recommend stopping in there for a fishing report and, usually, lively conversation before hitting the river.

Nearby points of interest: What better way to relax after a day on the water than by visiting one of the area's several wineries? Chalet Debonne (440-466-3485), Ferrante Wineries (440-466-8466), and Cantwell's Old Mill Winery (440-466-5560) are all located within a few miles of the covered bridge and offer some of the area's finest wines. Hours vary, so call ahead to check on when they're open.

Nearby bait shop(s): Covered Bridge Bait & Tackle; Karran Shop. (See Directory section for details.)

19

Headlands Beach State Park
Lake Erie Shoreline and Fairport Harbor
9601 Headlands Rd., Mentor

Recreational | Intermediate | Challenging

Water Type: Lake Erie, harbor

Access: Breakwall

What's Biting: Bluegill, smallmouth bass, carp, catfish, sheephead, perch, steelhead, suckers, sunfish, walleye

Season: Year-round **Hours:** Open 24 hrs.

Fee: Free **Permission:** Not required

Facilities: Restrooms, picnic area, food onsite, ranger

Administered by: Ohio Department of Natural Resources

Directions: SR 2 east to SR 44 north/Heisley Rd. exit; north on SR 44/Heisley Rd. to park entrance.

Farther East

Description Long ago in the geological history of this area, Lake Erie was a much larger body of water than it is now. The Niagara River opened, however, and the lake drained down to its present size. Sand beaches, remnants from the former lake, can still be found along the northern shore. Headlands Beach, which is the largest natural sand beach in Ohio, is one of them. Most people visit Headlands Beach State Park to enjoy the beautiful beach, swim in the cool waters of Lake Erie, have a picnic, or lie out in the sun. Add one more activity to this list—fishing.

It was for the fishing that I found myself visiting the park on a windy, frigid fall day. The swimmers and sunbathers had long since shaken the sand from their towels, and the beach was eerily silent. Strong westerly winds had stirred up the lake, and waves crashed over the top of the fishing breakwall at its eastern end. The only souls joining me were two duck hunters silently waiting amid the driftwood on the beach, and their decoys, bobbing several feet offshore.

Unfortunately, neither the hunters nor myself were successful that day. But with Lake Erie fishing, you either learn to accept the fruitless days or give up the sport altogether. It is often hit-or-miss.

To get to the fishing breakwall at Mentor Headlands, enter the park through the main entrance off Heisley Rd. and continue following the road to the right, where it will dead-end in a 24-hour parking lot for fishermen and hunters. Follow the signs to a trail that heads north from this point. It is a short, sandy walk to the breakwall.

The federal breakwall is located at the eastern end of the park, away from the volleyball courts and bathing beauties. The breakwall provides great access to both Lake Erie and Fairport Harbor. Even if the lake is too rough to fish, the waters of the harbor are normally calm enough. Anglers here can catch many species of Lake Erie fish, including walleye, smallmouth, largemouth, and rock bass, yellow perch, carp, sheephead, sucker, and catfish. During the spring and fall the steelhead start making their appearance as they prepare to migrate up the Grand River, which enters the lake at Fairport Harbor.

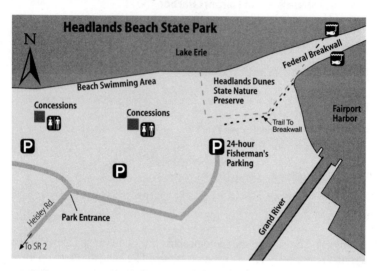

Anglers primarily still fish minnows, shiners, and night crawlers off the bottom. Spinners and spoons, along with spawn and maggots, drifted below a bobber can be effective for steelhead.

During the summer months the concessions on the beach sell food and drinks, but during the off-season they are closed. The restrooms are quite a walk from the breakwall, so you might want to take care of business before making the trek out there.

As mentioned above, hunting is allowed off the breakwall and the beach to the east of it during duck hunting season. If guys dressed in camouflage and carrying shotguns make you nervous, you might want to skip the area during this time.

Nearby attractions include the Mentor Marsh State Nature Preserve, located at the south side of the park. This 644-acre preserve, composed mostly of a marsh swamp forest, is home to varied plant and animal life and can be enjoyed by hiking the five-mile Zimmerman Trail. On the east side of the park is the Headlands Dunes State Nature Preserve, one of the last and finest remaining examples of Lake Erie beach and dune areas in Ohio. Both sites provide wonderful examples of what some of Lake Erie's beaches looked like before human impact.

Nearby bait shop(s): The Minnow Bucket; D&W Bait & Tackle; Grand River Tackle. (See Directory section for details.)

20

Headwaters Park
East Branch Reservoir
13365 Old State Rd., Claridon/Huntsburg

Recreational | Intermediate | Challenging

Water Type: Inland lake **Acreage:** 425 acres

Access: Shoreline, pier, canoe, boat

What's Biting: Bluegill, largemouth bass, carp, catfish, crappies, pike, sunfish

Season: Spring/Summer/Fall **Hours:** 6 a.m.–11 p.m.

Fee: Free **Permission:** Not required

Facilities: Bait shop, boat launch, restrooms, picnic area, food nearby, hiking trails, ranger

Administered by: Geauga Park District

Directions: I-90 to Exit 193 (SR 306); south on SR 306; left (east) on US 322; right (south) on SR 608 to entrance, on left.

Description I've had some great fishing partners in my time, but the majestic bald eagle soaring above me, searching the water for its breakfast, is certainly one of the most beautiful. Our nation's symbol, the bald eagle, a shining example of an endangered species success story—and a damn good angler—is just one of the many natural beauties that make Headwaters Park a favorite fishing destination for area anglers. The fishing, of course, is what draws me back time and again.

Located in Claridon and Huntsburg townships in Geauga County, Headwaters Park consists of the 425-acre East Branch Reservoir and the 500-plus acres of forest, meadow, and wetland that surround it.

The City of Akron actually owns East Branch Reservoir, along with the surrounding land, and maintains it as a component of their water supply system. For 35 years the city managed East Branch Reservoir as a public facility, and during that time it was an immensely popular fishing and camping spot. It was not uncommon for most of its 112 campsites to be filled. In 1991, however, Akron was forced to close East Branch to the public due to a loud sucking sound coming from the area—the sound of the city's coffers being drained from the expenses of operating the camping and boat rentals.

East Branch Reservoir is still owned and managed by the City of Akron Water Supply, but as of May 1996, management of the reservoir and surrounding land was transferred to Geauga Park District, which reopened it as Headwaters Park. Improvements were made to the west side of the park for the public's enjoyment, including hiking trails, picnic areas, fishing piers, and restrooms. The east side was designated as a preserve and as such is off-limits to the public. Access can be gained only through park programs.

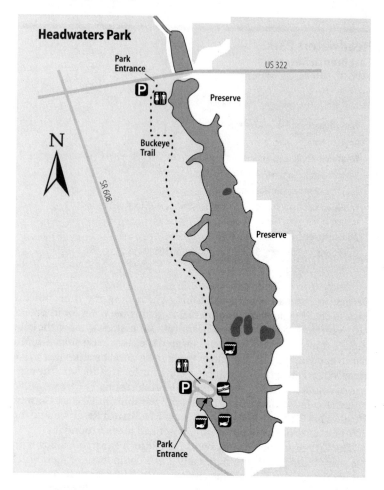

The reservoir received very little fishing pressure during the five years it was closed to the public, allowing a good-sized population of fish to develop. Largemouth bass are in good supply, with many big boys lurking in the numerous inlets that surround the lake. Several islands dot the reservoir's interior, providing decent action around their perimeter. Keep in mind, however, that these islands are considered part of the preserve and as such are off-limits.

The reservoir is relatively shallow; the deepest section is located along the original stream corridor that existed before the area was flooded by the Army Corps of Engineers in 1935. In the heat of summer this deeper channel is an especially good area to try. Trolling is an effective means of covering a lot of water to determine where the fish are holding.

During one memorable trip to Headwaters I stumbled across a large school of crappies. For a crazed 20 minutes or so I pulled in these feisty panfish as fast as I could hook and release them—minus, of course, just enough for that evening's meal. Minnows suspended below a bobber can be very effective for crappie, especially in the deeper water near the dam.

There are three fishing piers at Headwaters for non-boat anglers, but unfortunately shoreline fishing is prohibited because of water quality concerns. The small amount of shoreline access makes Headwaters best accessed by boat.

Anglers should be aware that water levels can fluctuate quite drastically at times when Akron draws off water. In the fall, after the water has been drawn down, forget about fishing from the designated fishing piers. The low water levels might also prevent boaters from being able to launch their boats. Call the Park District to check on water levels.

Because the reservoir is still a vital part of Akron's water supply, water quality is of the utmost importance. There is very limited shoreline fishing due to concerns about erosion, and gasoline engines are a no-no. Trolling motors of 1.5 horsepower or less are all the power that's allowed—except, of course, good old-fashioned human-powered oar locomotion.

Hiking trails, including a section of the Buckeye Trail, wind around the reservoir and offer great wildlife viewing opportunities. In the fall, the reservoir itself is a favorite stopover for migrating waterfowl, including tundra swans, hooded mergansers, and loons, to name just a few. Bald eagles frequent the area, as do ospreys.

Picnic shelters and restrooms are available. A bait shop, located on US Route 322 just west of the causeway, sells night crawlers and tackle.

Nearby bait shop(s): Country Style Drive-In. (See Directory section for details.)

Farther East

Farther East

21

Helen Hazen Wyman Park
Grand River, Big Creek, Kellogg Creek
State Route 86, Painesville

Recreational | Intermediate | Challenging

Water Type: River, stream **Acreage:** N/A

Access: Shoreline, wading

What's Biting: Bluegill, rock bass, smallmouth bass, carp, catfish, muskie, steelhead, sunfish

Season: Year-round **Hours:** Dawn to one-half hour after sunset

Fee: Free **Permission:** Not required

Facilities: Restrooms, picnic area, food nearby, ranger

Administered by: Lake Metroparks

Directions: I-90 east to Exit 200 (SR 44); north on SR 44 to SR 84/Mentor/Painesville exit; right (east) on SR 84 to 5-way intersection of SR 84, SR 86, Bank St., State St., and Cummings Rd; turn sharply onto SR 86 (south); park on left (east) side of road.

Description As any angler who fishes the Grand River can tell you, a good rainfall or snowmelt can make the river swell nearly out of its banks and turn it into a muddy, powerful torrent. At times like these I head to the tributaries. One of my favorites is Big Creek in Helen Hazen Wyman Park, located in Painesville.

Helen Hazen Wyman Park offers excellent fishing opportunities on the Grand River, Big Creek, and Kellogg Creek. In situations where the Grand is running too high or muddy, I can usually find some fishable water on Big Creek, which clears up much quicker than the Grand. Access the creek from the parking lot and follow it downstream. There are numerous holes to hit, and where it feeds into the Grand River there is a very nice pool that often holds fish. Small-mouths congregate in the deeper pools and around structure, and although they tend to be on the small side, their fight makes them exciting quarry.

Lake Metroparks

Kellogg Creek is a small stream that enters Big Creek right next to the parking lot. Only a small section of it is actually in the park, so be careful not to trespass when fishing it. Kellogg Creek can offer some productive steelhead fishing, especially in the spring. However, I have never done very well on it, preferring instead to fish Big Creek or the Grand.

The Grand River at Helen Hazen is a very exciting and productive place to fish in all seasons. It's wide open with plenty of fighting room. There are long, slow flats, fast riffles, and deep pools—all of which are likely fish hangouts. Smallmouth bass fishing, especially around any downed trees or deeper pools, can be excellent. Many of the fish are larger than the ones in the tributaries. Buzzbaits retrieved over deep pools often elicit strikes, and nothing is more fun than seeing your buzzbait disappear in a frenzied bronze splash.

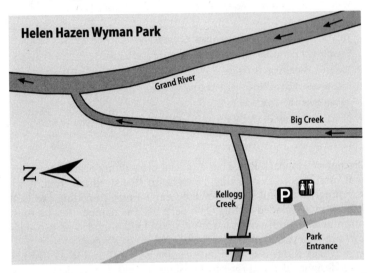

Steelhead fishermen can do very well at Helen Hazen in the Grand River, Big Creek, and Kellogg Creek. Rooster Tails and spawn both produce, as do spawn patterns and Woolly Buggers for the fly fishermen. There is a deep pool on the Grand right where Big Creek enters which often holds steelhead.

The park receives quite a bit of fishing pressure during the steelhead season, but I have never had a problem staking out a pool to myself—although it may have required a short hike upstream. In the summer it is not uncommon to be alone on the river, a situation perfect for enjoying the natural beauty of the Grand River corridor.

The park is open from dawn to one-half hour after sunset. An Ohio fishing license is required to fish the Grand River and its tributaries.

For a real treat, try George's Dinner Bell Restaurant, located at the corner of State Route 84 and Auburn Rd. The atmosphere is casual, the prices reasonable, and if there is a restaurant that serves larger portions than George's, I have yet to find it.

Nearby bait shop(s): D&W Bait & Tackle; Grand River Tackle. (See Directory section for details.)

22

Hogback Ridge Park
Grand River and Mill Creek
Emerson Rd., Madison

Recreational | **Intermediate** | Challenging

Water Type: River, stream **Acreage:** N/A

Access: Shoreline

What's Biting: Bluegill, smallmouth bass, rock bass, muskie, steelhead, suckers, sunfish

Season: Year-round **Hours:** Dawn to one-half hour after sunset

Fee: Free **Permission:** Not required

Facilities: Restrooms, picnic area, hiking trails, ranger

Administered by: Lake Metroparks

Directions: I-90 to Exit 212 (SR 528); south on SR 528; left (east) on Griswold Rd.; left (north) on Emerson Rd. to entrance.

Description Hogback Ridge has a special place in my heart. It was here that, after two years of trying, I caught my first steelhead trout. It is a stunningly beautiful section of the Grand River, providing excellent fishing in a secluded setting. The park itself is named after its most prominent feature: a high, narrow ridge of land bounded on two sides by steep valleys that resembles the bony spine of a hog.

Hogback Ridge is located on a section of the Grand River that has been designated a wild river by the State of Ohio. This indicates that it has received minimal human impact. Mill Creek, a tributary of the Grand, also flows through the park. This creek is a twisting, meandering waterway chock full of riffles, runs, deep pools, and structure. After many trips here, I have yet to discover all the holding spots where fish congregate. It is a very exciting stretch of water to fish. It is also very quick to clear after heavy rains, making it quite fishable even when the Grand River is flowing high and muddy.

From the parking lot, you will see a gravel road. This is the Old Emerson Road Trail. From the early 1800s until the beginning of this century, local residents followed Emerson Road across the river and creek at shallow fords because there were no bridges across the Grand River. The Emerson family operated a mill near the junction of Mill Creek and the Grand River.

About one-half mile down Old Emerson Road Trail you will run into Mill Creek. A deep pool right at the end of the trail is overlooked by many but can produce some nice fish. From this point you can fish upstream on Mill Creek, or head downstream to the Grand River.

Anglers can also take the Bluebell Valley Trail, accessed off the Hemlock Ridge Loop, down to Mill Creek. It is a longer walk but traverses some striking forested areas. From here you should concentrate on the water downstream—a waterfall immediately upstream stops steelhead migration.

Perhaps because I have always done well on Mill Creek I tend to overlook hitting the Grand while I'm there. This is a mistake I intend to rectify in the future, because there are some interesting riffles and pools to fish on this section of the river, and certainly many large fish. If you elect to fish the Grand River, and I recommend it if the water level is suitable, you can reach it at the mouth of Mill Creek or by hiking due north from where the Old Emerson Trail meets Mill Creek. The Grand is a decent hike away across terrain that can be difficult.

Farther East

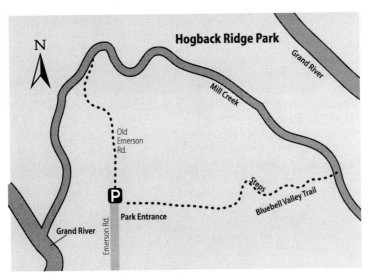

During the warmer months anglers can hook into smallmouth bass in both Mill Creek and the Grand River, which also produces some largemouth bass. Bluegill, suckers, carp, and rock bass can also be caught in both waterways. Buzzbaits and spinnerbaits can be effective, as can live bait, especially crayfish hooked through the tail and hellgrammites.

In the fall, the word of the day is "steelhead." If the Grand River is fishable, give it a try. After a rainfall, however, when the river is running too high and muddy, Mill Creek can be much more accessible—it clears up much more quickly than the main river. I have witnessed large pods of nearly ten steelhead nervously swimming around some of the deeper holes on Mill Creek.

Located in the rural vineyard region of Madison Township, Hogback Ridge is a pleasure to visit and fish. If you can go on a weekday, chances are good that you might have the river to yourself. For local entertainment, Ferrante Winery and Chalet Debonne are both within a couple of miles of the park, and the historic community of Geneva-on-the-Lake can be reached by continuing east on Griswold Rd. to State Route 534 and heading north.

23

Indian Point Park
Grand River and Paine Creek
Seeley Rd., Painesville

Recreational | **Intermediate** | Challenging

Water Type: River, stream **Acreage:** N/A

Access: Shoreline, wading

What's Biting: Bluegill, smallmouth bass, rock bass, carp, catfish, muskie, steelhead, sunfish

Season: Year-round **Hours:** Dawn to one-half hour after sunset

Fee: Free **Permission:** Not required

Facilities: Restrooms, picnic area, hiking trails, ranger

Administered by: Lake Metroparks

Directions: I-90 east to Exit 205 (Vrooman Rd.); north on Vrooman; right (east) on Seeley Rd. for one-half mile to lot on left (north) side of road.

Description At the end of one-half mile of what must be the worst road in Lake County lies Indian Point, a park that may be one of the county's most scenic. Indian Point Park, so named because of a Native American settlement here many years ago, provides wonderful access to both the Grand River and Paine Creek, a tributary of the Grand.

Anglers can access Paine Creek about a quarter mile upstream from its rendezvous with the Grand River by walking about 20 paces north from the Seeley Rd. parking lot. Be careful if you plan to follow Paine Creek to the Grand; it is all too easy to get distracted by the creek's offerings, and before you know it you have passed an entire day on this small creek. From where it enters the Grand River to about two miles upstream, Paine Creek is loaded with enough deep pools, undercut banks, downed trees, and boulders to make a fisherman drool.

The creek is normally very low in the summer, so concentrate on the deeper sections. The water is clear in Paine Creek, so some stealth is required. Carefully observe any deep pools before getting too close, and chances are you will see smallmouth bass, bluegill, rock bass, and suckers swimming about. Polarized sunglasses help locate and identify fish and are therefore a worthwhile investment. The fish are skittish in the low, clear water, so proceed carefully. The smallmouth in Paine Creek are a little smaller on average than their brethren in the Grand River, but once hooked the fish seem unaware of this fact and commonly put on quite an aerial display.

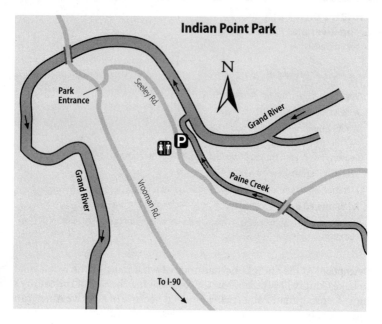

Part of the fun of fishing in clear waters is figuring out what the fish will bite. On one trip, several smallmouth bass had repeatedly ignored my offerings of a black Woolly Bugger, a large black stonefly, and a Muddler Minnow. But as soon as I flicked a grasshopper pattern over the pool I had been working for 20 minutes, the same smallmouth that had given the cold shoulder to all the other flies attacked this one. The bluegill seemed equally intent on this and other terrestrial patterns. In the clearer water, a delicate presentation of whatever lure or bait you are using will prove to be more effective.

If it is larger smallmouth you are after, follow Paine Creek to the Grand River, where you stand a great chance of hooking into football-sized fish. You can travel quite a distance up- or downstream and find an abundance of riffles, deep pools, and runs, all of which can harbor nice fish. Crayfish work well for the smallmouth, as do jigs and buzzbaits. There are also decent populations of panfish and suckers, and some absolutely behemoth-like carp rooting through the mud. As is true almost anywhere on the Grand, it is not out of the question for your next strike to be a muskie, reinforcing the fact that the Grand truly offers a grab bag of exciting angling opportunities.

In the spring and fall look to Indian Point Park for its steelhead action. Right where Paine Creek enters the Grand River is a deep pool that can be very productive. The Grand River will often be flowing fairly strong, so the steelhead will be looking for shelter from the current.

Anglers should concentrate on the larger rocks littering the river, flipping a lure in front of and behind them. Also look for any fluctuations in the current flow that might indicate either some structure or a depression in the river bottom, both of which are likely steelhead hangouts. The same principles hold true when fishing Paine Creek. Concentrate on the pools and any obstructions you see. Sometimes, even in impossibly low water conditions, anglers pull steelhead out from the deep cutouts in front of and behind larger rocks. A waterfall on Paine Creek, roughly two miles upstream from its meeting with the Grand, stops all migration of steelhead.

Lake Metroparks

It is not a writer's embellishment when I say that Seeley Rd. is terrible. I have seen one of its mammoth potholes almost completely swallow a Honda. Even in a truck, the ride proves to be a real kidney-jostler. Keep this in mind when planning a trip to Indian Point. If you or a fishing partner has a truck, it would be in your best interest to drive that.

Indian Point Park is open from sunrise to one-half hour after sunset. A fishing license is required.

Farther East

24

LaDue Reservoir
Shoreline and Boat Fishing
17759 Washington St., Auburn

Recreational | Intermediate | Challenging

Water Type: Inland lake **Acreage:** 1,500 acres

Access: Canoe, boat

What's Biting: Bluegill, largemouth bass, carp, catfish, crappies, perch, sunfish, walleye

Season: Year-round **Hours:** Open 24 hrs.

Fee: Free; fee for boat launch, boat rental, and camping **Permission:** Required

Facilities: Boat rental, boat launch, restrooms, food nearby, ranger

Administered by: City of Akron

Directions: I-480/I-271 to US 422; east on US 422; left (north) on SR 44; immediate right on Washington St. (becomes Valley Rd.) to reservoir.

Description

Ahh, minnows! I'd come to LaDue in hopes of probing the reservoir's depths in search of at least enough crappies for the evening's dinner, and minnows are about the best bait for these tasty panfish. I stopped at Bobbers Bait Shop just up the road, got to talking about the fishing, bought a cold beverage, and promptly headed out to LaDue. Minus, of course, the minnows.

Unfazed by my forgetfulness (I've gotten used to it), I pointed my boat out to deeper waters near the causeway that bisects the reservoir and proceeded to bounce a twister-tail jig off the bottom, raising it about a foot and then letting it drop. Nothing doing. Change colors, change depth, retrieve—still nothing. After about two hours of this, with nothing to show for it but one little crappie that wouldn't be enough for a fish stick, I decided to head into shallower water and work the shoreline for some bass.

The weather called for hot and hazy conditions, but at 10 a.m. it was still tolerable, and I couldn't have asked for more beautiful surroundings than LaDue Reservoir. Constructed in 1963 on a tributary of the Cuyahoga River, the reservoir is a component of the City of Akron's water supply system. Under agreement with the city, the Division of Wildlife began managing the fish populations in the reservoir in 1983. Management includes annually stocking fingerling walleyes, which have little to no natural reproduction, and carefully monitoring catches of other species to ensure fishable populations through natural reproduction. In 1997, for example, 215,521 walleye measuring just over an inch were stocked in the reservoir.

A good time to cash in on LaDue walleye is in June, when the fish are patrolling the weed beds located in the shallow waters. Your first tendency might be to search only the deep water, but in the early summer these weed beds can be very productive. A jig tipped with a night crawler or minnow is a tried-and-true method for hooking into these glossy-eyed predators, with morning and evening being their prime feeding times. The walleye population remains healthy at LaDue, with a good number of 15-inch-plus fish available. Each year the Division of Wildlife stocks more than 100,000 walleye fingerlings, helping ensure a steady supply for area anglers.

Now, however, having struck out on crappie and walleye, I turned my attention to largemouth bass. Just west of the boathouse is a series of small islands. I anchored the boat on the west side, where the water was sheltered a bit from the wind blowing in from the east, and proceeded to work the area with a white spinnerbait. Patches of water milfoil reached up to within about five to six inches of the waterline, and with a fairly quick, steady retrieve, that spinnerbait would cruise just above the weed bed. The first bass rose after about 10 casts.

No matter how many fish I catch, their ability to appear from out of nowhere never fails to amaze me. As I watched my spinner being retrieved, I would have bet anything that there was not a fish in the area. But just as my attention started to latch into an orbit around Venus, it materialized. First the mouth, then brown eyes, then body. It was as if the weeds had somehow melted together and formed this fantastic animal. And then it was gone, turning from something visible into raw energy pulling at the end of my line. This is the scene, the feeling that fishermen live for.

Four more bass were to follow this one's lead, and not one of them was under 14 inches. They were all healthy, strong brutes, and all representative of the overall largemouth bass population at LaDue.

For a day that started out so miserably, this one had definitely turned itself around.

Three roadways—US Route 422, State Route 44, and Auburn Rd.— cross LaDue Reservoir, offering access to shore fishermen. According to several anglers I interviewed who fish the causeways frequently, fishing can be fairly productive at these locations. In the spring, fishermen do quite well there for crappie and perch. Channel catfish can also be caught from the causeways. Unfortunately, both the access and parking are extremely limited at all three roadway crossings. If you do decide to visit any of the causeways, exercise extreme caution at all times when walking the roadway. Nothing can spoil a day of fishing faster than getting hit by a car. Also keep in mind that fishing is allowed only within the right-of-way of the road in all three areas, and anglers are not to use the roadway to gain access to LaDue's shoreline.

If you're planning a trip to LaDue Reservoir, keep in mind that as at all City of Akron Watershed reservoirs, there is no shoreline fishing because of concerns about water quality. Bring your boat or rent one there. A full day will cost you $19.50, and rental for half a day will set you back $12.50 (seniors $11). If you will be launching your own boat, a launch permit, for $10 per day or $40 annually, is required.

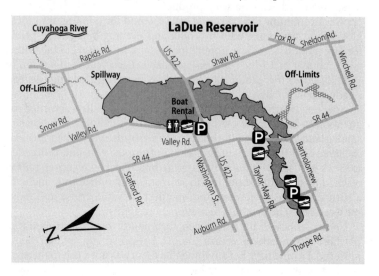

As with all City of Akron impoundments, the water level of LaDue can fluctuate wildly, making it extremely difficult to predict where the fish will be located. Spots that hold fish one day might be completely worthless when the reservoir water level drops a couple of feet. The fluctuation can also make it very difficult, or even impossible, to launch a boat. When the water level is lowered for winter or for shoreline work, the boat launches located west of State Route 44 will usually be inoperable. The main launch, located off Valley Rd., will remain usable longer than the others, but even this one is open only as water conditions permit.

You can reach the LaDue boathouse at (440) 834-4939, and the LaDue Ranger at (440) 834-0830. Anglers can also receive information on LaDue by calling the City of Akron Water Supply at (440) 678-0077. The boathouse usually opens for the season in March, but the reservoir itself is open year round for ice fishing. Bobbers Tackle Shop is located just down the road from the boathouse on Washington St. It generally opens up by April.

Nearby bait shop(s): Bobber's; One Stop Fishing Shop. (See Directory section for details.)

25

Mosquito Lake State Park
Boat, Causeway, and Shoreline Fishing
1439 State Route 305, Cortland

Recreational | Intermediate | Challenging

Water Type: Inland lake **Acreage:** 7,850 acres

Access: Shoreline, causeway, canoe, boat

What's Biting: Bluegill, carp, catfish, crappies, perch, pike, sunfish, walleye, white bass

Season: Year-round **Hours:** Open 24 hrs.

Fee: Free; fee for boat rental and camping **Permission:** Not required

Facilities: Bait shop, boat rental, boat launch, restrooms, picnic area, food nearby, hiking trails, camping, ranger

Administered by: Ohio Department of Natural Resources

Directions: I-480/I-271 to US 422; east on US 422; north on SR 528/SR 88; right (east) on SR 88 to causeway bisecting Mosquito Lake.

Description I'm not normally superstitious. I do not have set routines I must follow before fishing, nor do I blame the fishing deities when my angling success sours. But I do not know of any other explanation for the bad luck that seems to form over our heads whenever Kevin, one of my best friends, and I get together to fish. We have named it the Barbo/Durkin Curse.

The curse was in full force when we decided to hit Mosquito Lake for an August evening of walleye fishing. We put the boat in at a launch off Denman Rd., in the northwest section of the reservoir. At least 30 feet of the shoreline was exposed, turning the area around the launch into one big mud flat. Undaunted, we used our oars to push into deeper water. The stern of the boat carved a canal through the mud, which lay mere inches below the water level, and we finally reached fishable waters. After about one hour of fruitless casting, with neither of us looking forward to the struggle back to the boat launch, we called it quits.

The lesson here is that if you're planning to launch a boat anytime near the end of August, call one of the numbers listed at the end of this description to check on water levels. The fall drawdown of our local reservoirs is a necessary evil. Just don't let it catch you off guard.

Mosquito Lake was created in 1944 by the U.S. Army Corps of Engineers when they dammed Mosquito Creek nine miles upstream from Niles. The project was intended to control flooding, increase the local water supply, and regulate the discharge of pollutants. One other result: it is now one hell of a fishing lake, with walleye getting the top billing among anglers.

The lucky anglers' photos hanging on the wall of Causeway Sporting Goods, located on the eastern side of the State Route 88 causeway, show that walleye is indeed the catch of the day. Mid-April through June is a hot time for walleye, and the cool waters of fall also make for some pretty good fishing. For walleye, a popular and successful technique for boaters is to set up on the southern portion of the lake, just below the causeway, and drift. If the wind is right, it will blow you southeast, right through a section of deeper water that runs down the middle.

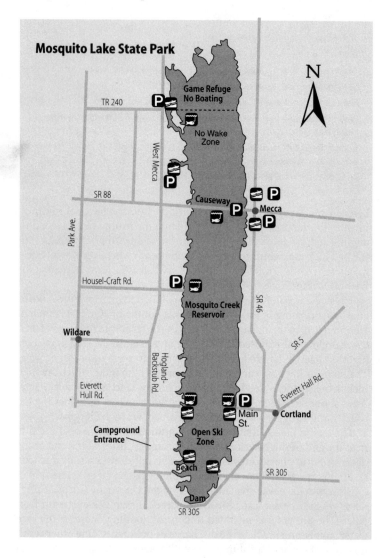

If you look at a topographical map of Mosquito, you'll see that most of the western half shows very little fluctuation in depth. The eastern side, however, has more contour and is deeper. The people I talked to indicated that for walleye, you'll hook into more fish by concentrating on the deeper areas at the middle and eastern half of the reservoir. For bass, you will have more success on the western half.

The dam and spillway are popular spots for shore fishing. Take State Route 305 to the south end of the reservoir, where you'll find public parking. You can fish from the dam into the deeper waters or tackle the spillway, which often remains ice-free throughout much of the winter.

Mosquito Lake is a great place to catch stringers of healthy-sized crappie. On one visit, I observed an elderly man who was fishing next to me off the south side of the State Route 88 causeway. He was using a $\frac{1}{16}$-ounce tube jig, working it along the bottom and raising it about a foot or two. After about 20 minutes he had brought in three fish, which he promptly threw back. "In May and June the crappie fishing is great," my new friend told me. He warned, however, that it can sometimes be tough to find a parking spot along the causeway. Boat fishermen also report good catches of crappie south of the State Route 88 causeway.

If you are planning to bring a boat to Mosquito Lake during the regular fishing season, the summer pool level of the reservoir should make launching at any of the public launches no problem. Near Labor Day, however, you might have problems, as the water is lowered to its winter pool level. The west side of the reservoir is generally shallower; launching from this side becomes difficult to impossible. Choose instead the main park area, located on the southeast side of the reservoir off State Route 305. This area is deep enough to allow launches after the fall drawdown. There is no limit on horsepower.

Ice fishing is allowed on Mosquito when conditions permit. Anglers often park in the lots available on the causeway and then fish the ice to the north.

Causeway Sporting Goods is the place to stop for an up-to-date fishing report. They've got a very thorough selection of tackle and live bait. They also run a boat rental with prices that, compared to those at other lakes and reservoirs, are not too bad. For current prices and fishing conditions, give them a call (330-637-7076).

A state-run campground (330-638-5700) is located off State Route 305 at the south end of the reservoir, making it extremely convenient and cheap to spend a couple of days exploring this vast fishing hole. It's open year round, although there are reduced facilities during the fall and winter months. A boat launch, navigable even at low water, is available for campers' use only.

Nearby bait shop(s): Causeway Sporting Goods; Monty's Mosquito Lake Restaurant and Carryout. (See Directory section for details.)

26

Painesville Kiwanis Park
Grand River and Children's Pond
Main St., Painesville

Recreational | Intermediate | Challenging

Water Type: River, ponds **Acreage:** N/A

Access: Shoreline, wading

What's Biting: Bluegill, rock bass, smallmouth bass, carp, catfish, steelhead, suckers, sunfish, walleye

Season: Year-round **Hours:** Dawn–dusk

Fee: Free **Permission:** Not required

Facilities: Restrooms, picnic area, food nearby

Administered by: Painesville Parks and Recreation

Directions: SR 2 to the Fairport Harbor/Richmond St. exit (SR 283); left on Richmond to Painesville Square; follow Main St. to park entrance (east of square).

Description I'd heard a lot of good things about Painesville Kiwanis Park, located on the Grand River just off Painesville Square. It was the site of the old Painesville Dam, an obstruction that would hold steelhead for at least a short time before they continued their journey upstream. Notice, however, that I said it *was* the site of the Painesville dam. Apparently, sometime during a recent winter a combination of high water and age swept most of the dam downriver. The large chunks of concrete and rebar left behind are the bane of many fishermen who tire of losing expensive lures to this rubble.

This doesn't, however, detract anything from the spot in regards to fish. It has a good number of riffles and runs, and numerous deep pools, all of which provide excellent hold-ing areas. Underneath the Main Street Bridge, near where the dam used to sit, there are some very deep holes. On my first trip to the park there were several steelhead surfacing periodically; none, however, would take my fly nor the spawn my fishing companions were offering. If you venture upstream a bit you will be blessed with several more excellent deep holding areas for fish. One angler I spoke with swears by this tech-nique—he drifts a slightly weighted night crawler along the river bot-tom under these holes and sets the hook at the slightest hesitation. This rather ascetic fishing rig is surprisingly effective for almost any of the fish that inhabit the Grand River, including walleye, which migrate upriver in the spring.

Steelhead are not the only reason to visit the Painesville Kiwanis Park. The deep pools are home to some very nice-sized smallmouth bass, which are readily caught using standard smallmouth techniques. Jigs worked along the bottom produce well, as do small spinnerbaits and buzzbaits. It's not impossible to hook into a walleye in this stretch of the river, either.

Also located in the park is a small pond for the exclusive use of children. Bluegill and bass can be caught here, along with catfish. Each summer a catfish fishing derby is held at the pond, providing youngsters with a rewarding and fun fishing experience. If you are interested in the derby, call the Painesville Recreation Department (440-639-4925) for a specific date and time.

Painesville Kiwanis Park is open from dawn to dusk. As with any river destination, the fishing can be good as long as the river remains free from ice and you've got an insulated pair of waders. Exercise caution when wading the river, especially if the water is running high.

Downtown Painesville, located just a couple of minutes from Kiwanis Park, has numerous fast-food eateries and sit-down restaurants.

Nearby bait shop(s): D&W Bait & Tackle; Grand River Tackle. (See Directory section for details.)

Farther East

27

Punderson State Park
Pine, Punderson, and Stump Lakes
11755 Kinsman Rd., Newbury

Farther East

| Recreational | Intermediate | Challenging |

Water Type: Inland lake   **Acreage:** 150 acres

Access: Shoreline, canoe, boat

What's Biting: Bluegill, smallmouth bass, catfish, sunfish, golden trout, rainbow trout

Season: Year-round   **Hours:** Open 24 hrs.

Fee: Free   **Permission:** Not required

Facilities: Bait shop, boat rental, boat launch, restrooms, picnic area, food onsite, food nearby, hiking trails, camping, ranger

Administered by: Ohio Department of Natural Resources

Directions: I-271 to Exit 29 (Chagrin Blvd./SR 87); east on SR 87 through Newbury; entrance on right (south) side.

Description Anglers can thank the last glacier to enter Ohio's boundaries, the Wisconsinan, for the creation of Punderson Lake. When the glacier receded some 12,000 years ago, it left what would later become one of Ohio's few natural lakes. Punderson is a kettle lake, formed when a large block of ice broke off the glacier, creating a depression that filled with meltwater. It is the largest and deepest kettle lake in Ohio.

Punderson State Park consists of Punderson Lake, Pine Lake, and Stump Lake, together totaling 150 acres. The majority of fishing occurs in Punderson Lake, which has the best access.

Anglers can choose to fish from a boat, the shore, or fishing piers and have success at any of the three. A free boat launch is located at the north end of Punderson Lake, but remember the electric-motor-only restriction. Boat rentals are available at the marina, which can be reached by following the signs upon entering the park. The boat concessions, managed by Newman Outfitters, open in April for weekend business and are open seven days a week from Memorial Day to Labor Day. Boats cost about $7 for the first hour or $18 for the whole day, while electric motor boats will run about $12 for the first hour and $28 for the day. If you decide to rent a boat with a trolling motor, be sure to request a battery with a full charge so you're not caught in the middle of the lake without juice.

There is also ample shoreline fishing if you don't own a boat and don't feel like paying a small fortune to rent one. A fishing pier on the west side of the lake and a concrete fishing area on the east side by the camping area provide good access and productive fishing due partly to the underwater structure strategically placed in front of them. In one morning of fishing, an acquaintance of mine caught four golden trout from the pier on the west side, with one weighing in at over four pounds. Bluegill fishing can also be very good off these points. Shoreline anglers can also do well at the marina and along the shoreline just north of the beach.

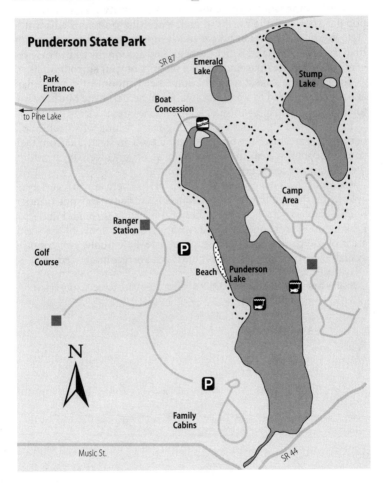

Punderson State Park

SR 87

Park Entrance

to Pine Lake

Emerald Lake

Stump Lake

Boat Concession

Camp Area

Ranger Station

Golf Course

Beach Punderson Lake

N

Family Cabins

Music St.

SR 44

Farther East

Twice per year the Ohio Division of Wildlife stocks Punderson with rainbow and golden trout—many of substantial size. These fish, some of which are monsters exceeding several pounds, are often breeders that can no longer perform their duties. The stockings are well publicized and are therefore heavily attended by eager fishermen who line up two- and three-deep. As the fish are put in, they're just as quickly snatched up.

I always thought they might as well skip the whole formality of fishing and just hand the trout out to the fishermen. But I digress.

One look at Stump Lake and it is easy to see where it got its name. Most of the perimeter of this shallow lake is ringed with tree stumps. To get to Stump Lake, either take the Erie Trail from the road just east of the marina or park at the campgrounds and access it from there. The Erie Trail circles the whole lake, allowing anglers pretty good access. One popular spot is at the northern end, where the trail runs adjacent to State Route 87. The water here is much more open and free of stumps than the rest of the lake. Benches are located around the lake in case you get tired or just feel like enjoying the serenity of your surroundings.

To get to Pine Lake, turn right immediately upon entering the park and follow this road to a parking area. From here take the Mushers Trail to the lake.

Punderson is a popular destination for ice fishing when conditions permit. The area near the beach is a good place to start, and from there you can scout the areas that are productive on any given day by noting the greatest concentration of ice fishermen.

Camping is a great way to enjoy this park. There are 201 sites available, with shower houses, flush toilets, electricity, and pet camping offered for campers. Fourteen miles of trails wind through Punderson Park, taking hikers on a naturally exciting tour of some of the scenic areas of the park. A championship-rated 18-hole public golf course is available; reservations are not required but are recommended.

Nearby bait shop(s): Punderson Marina Bait Shop. (See Directory section for details.)

28

Pymatuning State Park
Lake Pymatuning
Andover

Farther East

Recreational | **Intermediate** | **Challenging**

Water Type: Inland lake **Acreage:** 14,650 acres

Access: Shoreline, causeway, pier, canoe, boat

What's Biting: Bluegill, smallmouth bass, carp, catfish, crappies, muskie, perch, largemouth bass, sunfish, walleye, white bass

Season: Year-round **Hours:** Open 24 hrs.

Fee: Free; fees for camping and boat rental **Permission:** Not required

Facilities: Bait shop, boat rental, boat launch, restrooms, picnic area, food nearby, hiking trails, camping, ranger

Administered by: Ohio Department of Natural Resources

Directions: I-90 east to Exit 193 (SR 306); south on SR 306; east on US 6 through Chardon to Ashtabula County; east on SR 85 in Andover; proceed over causeway, or take Pymatuning Lake Rd. north to the Padanarum Area Boat Launch or south to Pymatuning State Park.

Description Sometimes the fishing gods can be downright cruel. While fishing Pymatuning one summer morning with my good friend Frank Meyerholtz, I had a black cloud of bad luck settle on my side of the boat. After an hour or so without catching a fish, Frank finally hooked into a nice 15-inch walleye, followed shortly thereafter by a second one. Alright, I thought to myself, we must be right over a small school. My first fish should be forthcoming.

About one hour later, we had five walleye on the boat—all caught by Frank. Despite the fact that we were using exactly the same minnow-tipped jigs and were fishing only several feet from each other, I failed to hook into even one fish. "John, you're welcome to a couple of my walleyes," Frank offered on the ride home. Tempting, very tempting. But I've got my pride. If I don't catch it, I don't eat it.

Pymatuning Reservoir, straddling the Ohio–Pennsylvania border in Ashtabula County, is a little more than an hour from Cleveland, but because of the large number of recreational opportunities this park offers, it is a must for inclusion in any Cleveland fishing guide. It is an enormous body of water that offers exceptional angling opportunities for both shore and boat fishermen, who can find a variety of fish species. It is arguably one of the best lakes in Ohio for walleye and muskie and is not bad for largemouth and smallmouth bass, bluegill, and crappie.

Frank and I had launched his boat from the Padanarum Boat Launch in the northern section of the lake. This area held pretty consistently at between 9 and 10 feet, and the lake bottom was covered with tree stumps. It is an area that can produce both walleye and crappie, especially in the spring when the walleye move there to spawn. On this day, however, all it produced were snags.

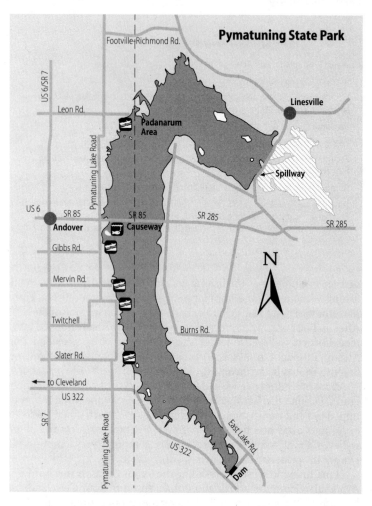

The walleye fishing is good here just about any time of the year. In the spring, the walleye are concentrated in the northern half of the lake. This water is shallower and provides plentiful structure, which the walleye need for spawning. Walleye fishing can be very productive in early March, especially just after ice-out, when these predators come in close to shore to feed. Fishermen can do very well from shore or wading in the shallows, using Rapala-type crankbaits, Hot-n-Tots, or minnows. If you are fishing from a boat, you will want to concentrate on points and sandbars.

At the end of March the walleye leave their spawning grounds, which by now have begun to warm up a little more than they like it, and head south of the causeway. The water here is deeper and much more comfortable for the fish during the heat of the summer. Trolling or drifting with minnow-tipped lead-head jigs, or night crawlers fished just off the bottom, are common methods that produce fish. With so much water to cover, a fishfinder is a valuable piece of equipment. Trolling is an effective way to cover a lot of water when searching for schools of walleye.

In October and November the walleye fishing heats up off the causeway, with Rapala-type crankbaits, Hot-n-Tots, and minnows again producing well. After dark is the most productive time for walleye in the fall. It's also a great time to catch plenty of crappie. The causeway provides easy access and plentiful parking for anglers.

Pymatuning's primary claim to fame might be its walleye, but an overlooked resource is its bluegill population. A 1995 Division of Wildlife angler survey indicated that the average size of these bluegills was 7.7 inches, the largest average size of any Northeast Ohio lake surveyed. Anglers have good success using $1/32$ or $1/64$ ounce jigs tipped with waxworms, redworms, garden worms, or the old reliable maggot. Fly-fishing with nymphs is also an exciting way to catch these aggressive and tasty panfish. Look for these fish to be in relatively deep water, holding around structure.

The muskie population is also on the rise at Pymatuning, after being almost decimated several years ago by a fish disease called Redspot. In 1997 the Ohio Huskie Muskie Club had their tournament here, and several "Huskie Muskies" of 40-plus inches were caught. The lake received a healthy stocking of fingerling muskies the same year. Look for this fishery to keep improving in upcoming years, with population levels hopefully rising to their 1950 and 1960 levels.If you do not have a boat, the causeway, which bisects the lake, is your best bet for walleye, crappie, and catfish. It provides access to deep water, and fish structures placed there by park workers provide excellent fish habitat. It is also handicapped accessible, with parking areas and restrooms located near the fishing access points. It's a great place for anglers to take advantage of Pymatuning's fisheries. Shore anglers can also be effective around boat launches. Unfortunately, the walleye do tend to be located in deeper water during the heat of the summer, so shoreline anglers will normally experience slow walleye fishing during this season.

A vast number of inlets and back bays offer wonderful opportunities for seclusion and enjoyment of the natural beauty of the park. They can also provide some exciting action for both smallmouth and largemouth bass, both of which are fairly plentiful throughout the lake. Smallmouth bass seem to have a stronger population.

There are five free boat launches located on the Ohio side of

Pymatuning, providing access to much of the lake. There is a 10-horse-power limit on the lake. If you would like to rent a boat, there are boat concessions located around the lake, including one near the camp-grounds and one at the Padanarum Area.

If ice fishing is your thing, Pymatuning should be on your list of des-tinations this winter. Ice fishermen can have decent success with walleye and panfish such as crappies and bluegill during the winter months. A popular access point is near the cabins and camping facility, off Pymatuning Lake Rd.

There are 27 recently refurbished family cabins for rent. These sleep six and are heated for year-round use. There are also 33 standard cabins available from May 1 through November 1. A large, modern camp-ground suitable for tents and trailer camping is available for those who prefer roughing it over the luxuries of a modern cabin. Several miles of hiking trails extend throughout the park, and a swimming beach is located just south of the causeway and includes a bathhouse, showers, and a snack bar.

Several local tackle and bait shops are located close to the park. Gate-way Bait & Tackle (440-293-7227) is located on State Route 85 in Andover, while Fisherman's (440-293-5779) can be found on Lake Rd. in Andover, and the Tangled Angler is located just east of the causeway on Pennsylvania State Route 285. Call them for fishing and weather reports (888-627-2490).

An Ohio fishing license is required to fish from the Ohio shore, but ice fishermen can fish anywhere on the lake. Boaters should exercise caution on Pymatuning during inclement weather, as the lake's waters can become very hostile to small boats. (For information on the Penn-sylvania side of Pymatuning, call 724-932-3141.)

While you are at Pymatuning State Park, be sure to allow enough time before or after fishing to visit the Linesville Spillway, located on US Route 6 just across the Pennsylvania Border. You've heard the biblical story of Jesus walking on water, but here you can witness ducks walking on water. Of course, they are helped along by literally hundreds of mon-strous carp that gather here to feast on stale bread tossed into the water by tourists who have traveled here to witness this strange phenomenon. If you have never seen ducks walk on the backs of carp, this will cer-tainly be a stop worth your while.

Nearby bait shop(s): Fisherman's; Gateway Bait & Tackle; Hot Spot Bait & Tackle; Jamestown Boat Livery. (See Directory section for details.)

29

Swine Creek Reservation
Killdeer and Lodge Ponds
16004 Hayes Rd., Middlefield

Recreational | Intermediate | Challenging

Water Type: Inland lake **Acreage:** N/A
Access: Shoreline, pier
What's Biting: Bluegill, largemouth bass, sunfish
Season: Spring/Summer/Fall **Hours:** 6 a.m.–11 p.m.
Fee: Free **Permission:** Not required
Facilities: Restrooms, picnic area, food nearby, hiking trails, ranger
Administered by: Geauga Park District
Directions: I-480/I-271 to US 422; east on US 422 into Parkman; left (north) on SR 528; right (east) on Swine Creek Rd.; left (north) on Hayes Rd.; entrance on left.

Description There are two ponds suitable for fishing at Swine Creek Reservation; both can be accessed from the main entrance off Hayes Road. Killdeer Pond can be reached by taking a right upon entering, and the Lodge Pond can be reached by heading left. Both offer decent fishing for largemouth bass and bluegill.

Many people use natural baits on these ponds with decent success. Smaller twister-tail jigs and spinners can be effective for bluegill, but suspending small red worms or maggots with a bobber is still one of the most popular methods for catching panfish. Bass will often fall for a rubber worm, spinnerbait, or crankbait, especially when fished along the edge of the ponds early in the morning.

The park district has no stocking program, so catch-and-release is strongly encouraged to ensure catchable populations of fish for future generations. More than six miles of hiking trails wind through the park, offering visitors the opportunity to see some of the park's most interesting areas. Naturalist-led programs, such as monarch butterfly tagging, stargazing, bird walks, and a music festival, are held year round. Call the park office to find out more about these.

Middlefield is known for its Amish community, a feature that has helped it become a major tourist destination. Restaurants, gifts shops, and other tourist facilities have sprouted around the area's main attraction—the Amish farms and rural setting that give visitors a glimpse of its culture and natural history. If you decide to visit Swine Creek Reservation, please be aware of the horse-drawn buggies on the road. Drive cautiously around these slow-moving vehicles.

30

Farther East

Veterans Park
Granger Pond
Hopkins Rd., Mentor

Recreational | **Intermediate** | Challenging

Water Type: Pond **Acreage:** 33 acres
Access: Shoreline, pier
What's Biting: Bluegill, largemouth bass, catfish, sunfish, trout
Season: Year-round **Hours:** Dawn–dusk
Fee: Free **Permission:** Not required
Facilities: Restrooms, picnic area, food nearby, hiking trails
Administered by: Lake Metroparks
Directions: SR 2 to SR 615; north on SR 615; north on Center St. at Munson Rd. intersection; left on Hopkins Rd. to park, on left.

Description In the middle of Mentor, a city that seems to get more crowded every time I try to drive through it, is an oasis known as Veterans Park, a 92-acre facility with numerous amenities, including the 33-acre Granger Pond. Veterans Park offers quality fishing for largemouth bass, bluegill, and, occasionally, rainbow trout in a comfortable setting, making this a worthwhile fishing destination for a serious bass angler or a family outing, or just a no-nonsense, easy place to get your line wet after a hard day at work.

There are several fishing piers on Granger Pond that provide great access to some of the deeper water. The pier closest to the parking lot is wheelchair accessible. There is also good shoreline fishing access in case the fishing piers are too crowded or you just prefer shoreline fishing.

During the summer, be prepared to work the weeds if you want to succeed in landing bass. Granger Pond is relatively shallow, and the weed cover can be extreme during the height of

Lake Metroparks

the summer season. Weedless lures are a must, especially Texas-rigged rubber worms and Sluggos. Both of these, dropped into holes in the weed canopy or dragged enticingly across the weeds, can produce strikes. Also, if you arrive before other anglers have taken their positions on the fishing piers, try to put a few casts along these structures. Bass do hang out here, but they are hard to catch after a hundred feet have pounded the piers over their heads.

Bluegill—like most other fish species residing in water that receives a lot of pressure—can be selective at times. They have raced up to my hand-tied nymph, given it a quick once-over, and ignored it. Natural baits can often open up tight-mouthed bluegill. Stay away from heavy 10-lb. test line and hooks large enough to catch a shark. These fish are not that stupid. Instead, use lighter line and thinner hooks.

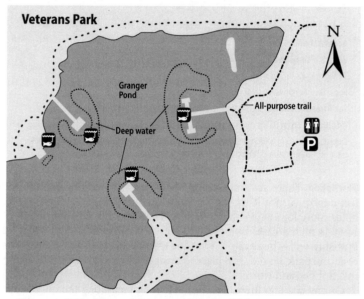

Veterans Park does receive a good deal of fishing pressure, and the park is a popular one. Yet in spite of this, the fishing is consistently productive. The Lake Metroparks staff does a great job of keeping the park extremely clean and aesthetically appealing.

Granger Pond is occasionally stocked with rainbow trout, causing anglers to flock to the park like moths to a porch light. Immediately following the stocking, the fishing piers get crowded pretty early, so try and get out of bed early enough to stake a claim on one. These hatchery-raised stocked trout are not the most finicky of fish, so worms and spinners will both work pretty well. I've seen one fisherman pull in trout in rapid succession using PowerBait.

Picnic areas, hiking trails, great fishing, and a playground make this a great place for a family fishing expedition. There is plenty here to keep the kids occupied in case the fishing is slow. Veterans Park is open from one-half hour before sunrise to sunset. A current Ohio fishing license is required.

Nearby bait shop(s): The Minnow Bucket. (See Directory section for details.)

31

Farther East

Walter C. Best Wildlife Preserve
Best Lake
11620 Ravenna Rd., Chardon

| Recreational | Intermediate | Challenging |

Water Type: Inland lake **Acreage:** 31 acres

Access: Shoreline, pier

What's Biting: Bluegill, largemouth bass, perch, pike, sunfish

Season: Spring/Summer/Fall **Hours:** 6 a.m.–11 p.m.

Fee: Free **Permission:** Not required

Facilities: Restrooms, picnic area, food nearby, hiking trails, ranger

Administered by: Geauga Park District

Directions: I-90 to Exit 200 (SR 44); south on SR 44 through Chardon Square; SR 44 becomes S. Ravenna Rd.; Best Preserve is two miles past square on right.

Description There are some places that I recommend not because the fishing experience itself will overwhelm, but because the destination holds more for anglers than just fish. The Walter C. Best Wildlife Preserve is such a case. It's not that you won't catch fish—you can, and probably will—but even if you don't, you'll be glad you visited this beautiful park. It's the ideal place to bring a young angler, equipped with rod, bobber, and worm.

On my last trip there, I was on a fishing pier along the north edge when I saw a school of about seven largemouth bass cruising along menacingly in front of the pier. If I'd been a demure little bluegill, I would have amscrayed for the next county. I thought I even heard the ominous cello music from *Jaws*. I looked at them, then at the Woolly Bugger I had just clipped from my line, and frantically tried to rejoin lure and tippet. By the time my trembling hands finally managed to complete what looked something like a clinch knot, the fish were out of sight. They did come back later, and my fly was attacked by a 12-inch largemouth bass, which happened to be the smallest one in the school.

There are some feisty largemouth bass in these waters, along with a good population of bluegill and sunfish. Some of the bluegill reach decent sizes, although they are generally the tougher ones to catch. They are very skittish and generally prefer deeper water. There are reportedly some yellow perch and northern pike, although I have never seen either of these species pulled out. Maybe nobody's caught them yet, or I have not been there on a day when they have. The panfish and bass have seen a lot of lures in their time, so getting them to bite can be tough. Live bait—crickets, worms, and maggots—work well for the bluegill.

There are six fishing piers spaced along the lake. One is handicapped accessible and can be reached by taking a left off the access trail leading from the north parking area. There is also some shoreline fishing, but by midsummer most of the shore is inaccessible due to the thick phragmites which grows around most of the lake's perimeter.

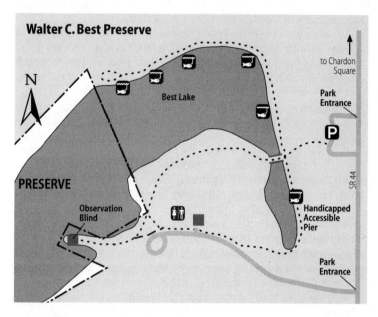

Walter C. Best Preserve

N

Best Lake

PRESERVE

Observation
Blind

to Chardon
Square

Park
Entrance

P

SR 44

Handicapped
Accessible
Pier

Park
Entrance

Farther East

Walter C. Best is a waterfowl and songbird cornucopia, so be sure to bring binoculars to get a close-up view of the migratory songbirds and waterfowl that make the preserve a stopover on their annual migrations. There is a wildlife observation blind, and several short hiking trails wind through woodland, meadow, and prairie habitats, offering great opportunities to see the wildlife that make the preserve their home.

Historic Chardon Square, just a few miles from Best Preserve, offers quaint antique shops, a coffeehouse, and several restaurants. There are several fast-food establishments located on State Route 44 and Water St. in Chardon.

Nature's Fisherman—The Great Blue Heron

When it comes to patient fishing, nothing can top the painfully slow stalking technique of the great blue heron.

Early one fall morning I found myself alone on the Grand River with one of these majestic birds. I settled back on a comfortable spot on the bank and watched as it searched the shallows for breakfast.

If Speedy Gonzalez is the fastest member of the animal world, then this comical bird with the black pompadour must be the slowest. Patiently it made its way in the river, carefully moving one leg, setting it down, then moving the other, never making even the slightest ripple on the surface of the water. It remained motionless for several seconds. Then a few more labored, silent steps forward. Then, with lightning speed it struck, its head like a harpoon cutting through the water and coming up with a chunky creek chub. Two gulps later, the fish was gone.

There's much to be learned from the fishing style of the great blue heron. Not once did I hear him yell out to his buddy, "Hey Bob, did you remember the beer?" Great blue herons understand the importance of stealth when fishing. Boom boxes, yelling kids, oars slamming against boats, fishermen splashing through the water—all of these disturbances can send fish swimming for cover. Although fish do have somewhat limited vision of what's outside their watery world, they are adept at noticing when danger lurks. After all, that shadow stretching over the water could be a great blue heron.

When wading, always try to approach a likely fish-holding spot from downstream. Walk slowly and deliberately (remember our friend the heron), making as little noise, and as few waves, as possible. Stay low, out of the fish's window of vision.

When stalking the shoreline of a lake or pond, stay low. Kneel down and search the shallows for fish or movement before getting too close to the edge of the water. If you see a fish, cast from farther up on the shore. Also, before moving to a fresh shoreline spot, make a couple of casts along the section of the shore where you are heading. Very often a large bass will be lurking in shallow water and will strike the second the lure hits the water near it.

Next time you're wading a shallow shoreline or probing the perimeter of a lake, keep in mind the lessons of the great blue heron. Patience, stealth, and a quiet approach will help you see and catch more fish.

West

32

Bradley Woods Reservation
Bunns Lake
White Oak Ln., Westlake

| Recreational | Intermediate | Challenging |

Water Type: Pond **Acreage:** 5.5 acres

Access: Shoreline, pier

What's Biting: Bluegill, largemouth bass, catfish, crappies, sunfish, trout

Season: Year-round **Hours:** 6 a.m.–11 p.m.

Fee: Free **Permission:** Not required

Facilities: Restrooms, picnic area, food nearby, hiking trails, ranger

Administered by: Cleveland Metroparks

Directions: I-90 to Exit 156 (Crocker/Bassett Rds.); south on Crocker; right (west) on Detroit Rd. (SR 254); left (south) on Bradley past Center Ridge Rd. (US 20); on left; follow White Oak Ln. to the end. OR, I-480 to Lorain Rd./SR 10 exit; east on Lorain; left at Barton Rd.; right (north) on Bradley Rd.; on right; follow White Oak Ln. to the end.

Description The moon had just cleared the trees, and the day's heat was giving way to the coolness of evening. Bats performed aerial acrobatics in the evening sky, often coming alarmingly close to my head. Other than the crickets, the only noise to break the evening stillness was that of my Hula Popper, chugging its way across the surface of Bunns Lake.

Cleveland Metroparks

When your lure is hidden by the darkness of night, your other senses seem to be heightened. So when a bass breaks free of the water, engulfs the topwater lure, and slams back into the murky depths, to your sensitive ears it can sound like an Orca splashing in the small pond. This night was no different. The largemouth bass striking my Hula Popper sent my heart racing faster than the hooked fish. This night, I was to land two bass, both around 12 inches.

Bunns Lake was created relatively recently, in 1985, and opened to the public in 1986. It serves the dual purpose of providing waterfowl nesting habitat and fishing opportunities for area anglers. It is not a huge body of water, but it can provide exciting fishing for beginners and veterans alike.

In order to provide productive fishing, Cleveland Metroparks personnel have strategically sunk old Christmas trees, sapling/brush piles, and gravel-filled structures throughout the lake to improve fish habitat. Despite the large number of anglers this lake might see throughout the course of a year, the structure provided by Cleveland Metroparks helps keep fish numbers up. A lakeside trail (featuring informative signs describing the many natural features of the area) encircles the lake; fishing platforms provide convenient fishing access.

The panfish in Bunns Lake can be taken with nothing more fancy than a bobber, hook, and your choice of bait. Small worms certainly work well, as do maggots, mealworms, and crickets. These panfish can provide exciting action on a lightweight fly rod. For this, try small Woolly Buggers, nymphs, terrestrial patterns, and poppers.

Bass can be taken by any number of common methods, including spinnerbaits, buzzbaits, jigs, or rubber worms. I had a decent night using topwater lures. These fish can be lure-wary, so presentation should be as natural as possible. Also, anglers should try to fish during the early morning or evening and avoid midday. Try to hit the lake when most other fishermen are at home, tucked in bed.

Please be aware that more than half of Bunns Lake is designated as a waterfowl refuge and as such is off-limits to fishing. The refuge provides valuable nesting habitat for several different species. Also, because of the boggy nature of Bradley Woods, mosquitoes can indeed be a major nuisance—depending on the weather—from late spring to early fall. Bring insect repellent unless you like being a human pin cushion.

The minimum legal size for largemouth bass is 12 inches, and fishermen can take two bass per day. The daily harvest limit for rainbow trout is three fish per angler.

West

33

Bradstreet's Landing
Lake Erie Shoreline
22464 Lake Rd., Rocky River

Recreational | Intermediate | Challenging

Water Type: Lake Erie
Access: Pier
What's Biting: Smallmouth bass, carp, catfish, perch, sheephead
Season: Spring/Summer/Fall **Hours:** Dawn–midnight (Apr–Nov)
Fee: $.50 for adults; free for children under 16 **Permission:** Not required
Facilities: Bait shop, restrooms, picnic area, food onsite, food nearby
Administered by: Rocky River Parks and Recreation
Directions: I-90 westbound to Clague Rd. exit; north on Clague; right (east) on Lake Rd.; entrance on left. OR, I-90 eastbound to Exit 161 (SR 254/Detroit Rd.); left (east) on Detroit; left (north) on Elmwood Rd.; left (west) on Lake Rd.; entrance on right.

West

Description Operated by the city of Rocky River, Bradstreet's Landing is a small facility tucked away off Lake Rd. that offers some great access for anglers seeking nearby Lake Erie fishing action. Consisting of one large fishing pier that juts out into Lake Erie, it is a very popular fishing spot during the spring and summer months.

Bradstreet's Landing has a fascinating history that gives some insight into Cleveland at a time when the word "Indians" referred to the Native Americans who occupied the forested lands of America, not the over-paid baseball players who occupy Jacobs Field. This fishing pier is the site of Bradstreet's Disaster, an event that occurred on October 18, 1764, during Cleveland's presettlement history. The story begins with British colonel John Bradstreet being dispatched from Fort Niagara with 2,300 men. His mission: travel to Fort Detroit to help put down Pontiac's Rebellion. On the return trip, his entourage found that the darkness made it too treacherous for their mini-armada to navigate the Rocky River inlet. Determined, Bradstreet aimed his 60 boats, 9 canoes, and 1,500 men toward what is now Bradstreet's Landing.

Lake Erie, unfortunately, had other plans. A surprise storm struck the party, and high waves sent 25 boats to their final resting place on the bottom. After three days, the boats that could be salvaged set sail with as many men as could fit. The rest of the men were forced to travel back to Fort Niagara by land. Despite the destruction of their boats, inclement weather, and a lack of supplies, only one death was confirmed on this treacherous return trip.

I try to imagine the shore of Lake Erie as Colonel Bradstreet and his men must have seen it. The undeveloped, hazardous, rocky shoreline. Mile upon mile of uninhabited forest. The overwhelming sense of wilderness isolation that must have greeted the unfortunate foot travelers from Bradstreet's party. After a century of development, alteration, and abuse, perhaps the only element that has remained constant is the unpredictable and unforgiving nature of Lake Erie.

Today anglers visiting Bradstreet's Landing will not have to face the same dangers as Colonel Bradstreet. But they will have to pay a small fee at the pier office, which also doubles as a bait shop and concession stand. For 50 cents a day, however, it's a bargain. A dry-erase board inside the office/bait store lists some of the recent catches at the pier, and let me tell you, I was impressed by the size of some of the fish that had been hauled in. It is encouraging that anglers without boats can still have productive days fishing Lake Erie, although that success is dependent on whether the fish are around the pier or not. Shore anglers do not have the benefit of being able to chase schools of fish around the lake like boaters do.

According to the man running the bait shop, smallmouth bass fishing from the pier has been very hot during the past couple of summers. This seemed to be the case for a lot of locations along the lakeshore, an indication of the ever-changing Lake Erie ecosystem, and welcome news for Cleveland fishermen, as these fish put up a good fight and are a whole lot of fun to catch. Anglers going for other species, including white bass, perch, smallmouth bass, sheephead, and catfish, had also been successful at Bradstreet's Landing. Several of the fishermen I spoke with said that they have the best luck with minnows, followed by worms. Of course, jigs bounced along the bottom will certainly take their share of smallmouth bass, as will crayfish.

The fishing pier is open from dawn to midnight, April 15 through November 3. The Treasure Cove, a deli located right next door, sells bait (live worms only), food, and beverages. The phone number at the fishing pier is (440) 356-5650.

Nearby bait shop(s): Bradstreet's Landing Bait Shop. (See Directory section for details.)

34

Edgewater Park, Cleveland Lakefront State Park
Lake Erie Shoreline
Memorial Shoreway West (State Route 2), Cleveland

Recreational | **Intermediate** | Challenging

Water Type: Lake Erie

Access: Shoreline, breakwall, pier

What's Biting: Bluegill, smallmouth bass, carp, catfish, perch, steelhead, sunfish, walleye

Season: Year-round   **Hours:** Open 24 hrs.

Fee: Free **Permission:** Not required

Facilities: Bait shop, restrooms, picnic area, food onsite, hiking trails, ranger

Administered by: Ohio Department of Natural Resources

Directions: I-90 to SR 2 west (in downtown Cleveland); west on SR 2 over Main Ave. Bridge; exit at Edgewater Park/Edgewater Marina.

Description The cat prowling around the breakwall at Edgewater Park looked to be the fattest wild feline I had ever seen. And I soon found out why, as a fisherman angrily took a goby off his hook and tossed it to the cat. Within seconds the fish was gone and the cat was licking its lips.

The goby is an introduced exotic species that measures about an inch long, has a fat head, and has the annoying habit of eating minnows that have been cast out for more desirable species like perch or walleye. This pesky little fish has become the nemesis of Lake Erie fishermen. Walk along any breakwall or fishing pier and you will usually see several of these fish flopping around, left to die after stealing an angler's minnow. "They've got tough heads," one man

Michael McElroy/Cleveland Lakefront State Park

told me. "I tried to crush one with my pliers, you know, to kill it, but the pliers just kept sliding off."

There is a lot of lake access at Edgewater Park, which, combined with its proximity to downtown Cleveland, makes it a popular fishing destination for area fishermen.

The fishing pier next to the bait shop seems to attract quite a few anglers. The pier, which is wheelchair accessible, sits high above the surface of the lake, so be sure you've got strong enough line to hoist your

West

fish. There is also a breakwall along this shoreline and extending east into the water, which provides plenty of access to the lake. Bring a folding chair or bucket to sit on, and it can be quite comfortable here.

Smallmouth bass fishing has really picked up at Edgewater Park, as it has elsewhere along the lakeshore. Near the fishing pier you'll see the remains of a concrete platform that used to run parallel to the shore. Only the support structures still stand—the rest lies at the bottom of the lake. The debris from this old fishing pier provides excellent habitat for smallmouth bass. Several anglers confided to me that crayfish can be an absolute killer bait in this area. Most other smallmouth techniques should also work.

One colorful fisherman I met there who fishes Edgewater seven days a week relies primarily on a small jig tipped with a maggot, a combination that has proven effective for perch, smallmouth bass, an occasional bluegill, and steelhead. Hot-n-Tots and Rapala-type plugs are very effective for steelhead and walleye. Along the breakwall the most popular method seemed to be fishing the bottom with a perch spreader baited with minnows and night crawlers.

According to several of the fishermen I talked to, northern pike, muskie, and sturgeon had all been caught during the two weeks before my visit. Edgewater Park can truly give up some nice fish if you've got the patience to get through the days when they refuse to cooperate.

Early morning and night are the most effective times for catching steelhead and walleye, and most of these fish are caught during the early spring and late fall.

A bait shop (216-281-4800) located adjacent to the fishing pier is open from the beginning of April through November, depending on the weather. Anglers can fish at Edgewater Park 24 hours a day.

Nearby bait shop(s): Frank's Edgewater Tackle; Ketchmore Rod & Tackle. (See Directory section for details.)

35

Huntington Reservation
Lake Erie Shoreline
Lake Rd., Bay Village

Recreational | Intermediate | Challenging

Water Type: Lake Erie

Access: Shoreline, breakwall

What's Biting: Bluegill, smallmouth bass, carp, catfish, sheephead, perch, steelhead, sunfish, walleye, white bass

Season: Year-round **Hours:** 6 a.m.–11 p.m.

Fee: Free **Permission:** Not required

Facilities: Restrooms, picnic area, food nearby, hiking trails, ranger, guides

Administered by: Cleveland Metroparks

Directions: I-90 to Exit 159 (Columbia Rd./SR 252); north on Columbia; left (west) on Lake Rd.; enter park on north side of Lake Rd. to access fishing area.

West

Description The monarch butterfly's annual migration is an amazing one. Successive generations journey north from their wintering grounds in Mexico for the summer. As the winds begin to get colder in the fall, they start their perilous and tiring journey back. Unfortunately, many cannot complete the journey. On a recent brisk fall day, with a chilly wind pushing in from the north, the beach and shoreline of Huntington Reservation were littered with the unfortunate ones for whom the trip across Lake Erie from Canada was too much.

The observant fisherman is often witness to nature's drama during a fishing trip. It is important to take time out and observe your surroundings when fishing, because there is always something to be learned about our natural world. Lakeshore fishing destinations in particular offer wonderful lessons about the lake's ecology and natural history for those willing to learn.

Such is the case with Huntington Reservation. Located in Bay Village approximately six miles west of the Rocky River, Huntington offers great fishing amid the splendor of the Lake Erie shoreline. During the summer months, you might encounter some decent crowds using the park's swimming area, but the off-season can offer solitude and very relaxing fishing. Four breakwalls stretch out from the shoreline into Lake Erie and provide angling opportunities in all seasons. The breakwalls are only a couple feet above the water level; waves can easily wash over the top and drench unsuspecting anglers. Be sure of your footing and keep an eye on your tackle box.

As with most lakeshore fishing, the common technique is to still fish live bait such as minnows, night crawlers, or shiners at or near the bottom. Anglers can catch a mixed bag of most of Lake Erie's fish species, including walleye, perch, white bass, smallmouth bass, channel catfish, sheephead, and steelhead. The water clarity here is remarkable: I was able to see several large schools of minnows darting erratically back and forth between the rocks. I also caught occasional glimpses of larger fish chasing them—with the irregular rock outcroppings from the breakwall I wouldn't be surprised if this was a favorite hunting ground for predatory fish like walleye and smallmouth bass.

Small white jigs and twister-tail-type spinners can provide a great deal of excitement when a school of white bass moves in close to shore. This opportunity might not present itself very often, but when it does, be prepared.

For walleye, Rapalas, Hot-n-Tots, and spoons fished from the breakwalls or shoreline can be effective, especially during spring and fall. As always, nighttime is the right time for these predators, when they move in closer to shore to feed on baitfish. Steelhead can also be caught here in the spring and fall, and for that you will want to drift spawn bags around the breakwalls or cast spinners and spoons. Maggot-tipped jigs can also be effective.

Huntington Reservation's swimming beach is popular during the swimming season. Swimmers and razor-sharp treble hooks not being a good combination, the two inside breakwalls nearest the swimming area have been designated off-limits during the swimming season, which runs from Memorial Day through Labor Day. The two outer breakwalls are open to fishing during this time. Outside of the swimming season, anglers can take advantage of all four breakwalls.

A large white tower, known as the Huntington Water Tower, is a focal point of Huntington Reservation. A very picturesque local landmark, this tower was historically used by the reservation's namesake, John Huntington, to pump water from Lake Erie to irrigate his fields of grapes. The Lake Erie Nature and Science Center/Schuele Planetarium and the Huntington Playhouse are located in the southern portion of the park, on the south side of Lake Rd. There is also an all-purpose trail that leads to the Bay Village Bike Trail.

36

Mill Stream Run Reservation
Wallace Lake & Ranger Lake
Valley Pkwy., Berea

Recreational | Intermediate | Challenging

Water Type: Inland lake   **Acreage:** 16 Acres

Access: Shoreline, pier

What's Biting: Bluegill, largemouth bass, bullhead, carp, catfish, crappies, sunfish, trout

Season: Year-round   **Hours:** 6 a.m.–11 p.m.

Fee: Free   **Permission:** Not required

Facilities: Bait shop, restrooms, picnic area, food onsite, food nearby, hiking trails, ranger, guides

Administered by: Cleveland Metroparks

Directions: I-71 to Bagley Rd.; west on Bagley into Berea; left (south) on Valley Pkwy.; Wallace Lake on right.

West

Description Wallace Lake, located in Mill Stream Run Reservation, was created in 1941 when a pill-box structure was constructed at the northern lake outlet. This unusual body of water is composed of two former stone quarries connected by a shallow connecting channel. The former quarries offer the greatest depths in the lake.

A large area of Wallace Lake is easily accessible for shoreline fishing, making it very appropriate for younger anglers. A fishing pier and stone walkway offer additional access.

The largemouth bass population at Wallace Lake is healthy in number and size; some surprisingly large fish are caught each year despite the moderate fishing pressure this lake receives. There is a great deal of habitat diversity at Wallace Lake, including rock and rubble piles, fallen trees, and brushy shoreline overhangs. It is a good idea for anglers to explore the lake to take advantage of these fish-holding structures. Standard bass techniques work well for Wallace

Casey Batule / Cleveland Metroparks

Lake's largemouth bass, but remember that you'll have the most success in the early morning and evening when the bass are hungry and the crowds are at a minimum.

Trout are periodically stocked and seem to attract the greatest attention. Anglers do well with a worm or maggots suspended below a bobber or by fishing the worm off the bottom. PowerBait also seems to be an effective way of hooking into trout, bluegill, and catfish. Small spinners work well for the crappie, trout, panfish, and even an occasional largemouth bass, which seem to fall for spinners, rubber worms, and crankbaits more often than anything else.

Wallace Lake is the West Side site for Cleveland Metroparks' annual Children's Spring Fishing Derby, which is held on the third weekend in May. For specifics on this event, contact the Natural Resources Office at (440) 234-9597.

When the swimmers have long since retired their suits and the surface of the lake has frozen over in a sheet of thick ice, the fishing can still be very good—you just do it through a small, circular hole. Wallace Lake is a popular ice-fishing destination, and those brave souls who tolerate subzero temperatures are often rewarded with good catches of trout and panfish. Winter trout stockings by Cleveland Metroparks help assure some hot action through the ice. Wallace Lake is also the site of one of two ice fishing derbies held annually by Cleveland Metroparks, which also feature ice-fishing clinics presented by a Metroparks staff member.

In the summertime, Wallace Lake abounds with outdoor recreation opportunities. A sand beach and swimming area are available for swimmers and sunbathers, and the Quarry Rock Cafe, a snack bar, bait concession, and paddleboat rental, is in operation at the bathhouse (440-826-1682) from Memorial Day to Labor Day. Of course the rest of Mill Stream Run Reservation offers a multitude of recreation possibilities, including hiking, roller-blading, picnicking, nature exploration, and cycling.

The minimum legal size for largemouth bass is 12 inches, and anglers may take two bass and three rainbow trout per day.

Ranger Lake is also located in Mill Stream Run Reservation, and although it is much smaller than Wallace Lake, it can offer exciting fishing opportunities. To get to Ranger Lake, take Valley Parkway south from Wallace Lake and turn left on Pearl Rd. Follow the directions for the Turnpike. Ranger Lake is located off the entrance to the Ohio Turnpike. Park in the Ranger Headquarters.

The 2.5-acre lake has been stocked with largemouth bass, bluegill, pumpkinseed sunfish, crappie, channel catfish, and rainbow trout. The west side of the lake can be very productive because tree and brush cover was left standing when the lake was flooded, providing good fish habitat. There is also plenty of weed cover along most of the pond's shoreline. Work this cover thoroughly, especially in the early morning, and there's a good chance of hooking into some largemouth bass.

Ranger Lake is stocked with trout to bolster its winter ice fishing, making it popular among ice fishermen.

The same catch restrictions as at Wallace Lake apply at Ranger Lake.

37

Rocky River Reservation
Ford Tour
Valley Pkwy., Lakewood to North Olmsted

Recreational | Intermediate | Challenging

Water Type: River **Acreage:** N/A

Access: Shoreline, wading

What's Biting: Bluegill, largemouth bass, smallmouth bass, carp, catfish, sheephead, steelhead, suckers, sunfish, walleye

Season: Year-round **Hours:** 6 a.m.–11 p.m.

Fee: Free **Permission:** Not required

Facilities: Bait shop, restrooms, picnic area, food nearby, hiking trails, ranger

Administered by: Cleveland Metroparks

Directions: I-90 westbound to Exit 162 (Hilliard Blvd.); left at first light on Hilliard; left (north) on Wooster Rd.; right (east) on Rockcliff Ln. downhill to Valley Pkwy. Fords are all accessible from Valley Pkwy. OR, I-90 eastbound to Exit 161 (SR 254/Detroit Rd.); east on Detroit; right (south) on Wooster Rd. past Hilliard Blvd.; left (east) on Rockcliff Ln.; downhill to Valley Pkwy.

West

Description The Rocky River meanders throughout the Rocky River Reservation, so it would seem to offer many angling opportunities. Those who have fished the Rocky before, however, know that much of this river is rather shallow with a very moderate gradient. Other than the deep water near Scenic Park, which is close to the mouth of the river, there are relatively few deep sections for fish to hold in.

The spots that attract the most attention from anglers are the fords that cross the river at periodic intervals. These fords are cement crossings, remnants from the late 1930s. The water at or near these abandoned fords is generally deeper than the rest of the river, and the fish find it more hospitable than the slower, shallower sections. It is here that fishermen have the best chance for hooking into some of the river denizens they pursue, including smallmouth bass, suckers, sheephead, steelhead, carp, and channel catfish.

These fords are really quite conducive to angling. The water around them can generally be easily waded. In fact, during the height of steelhead season, anglers can sometimes be seen wading shoulder to shoulder. The fords themselves provide a safe, relatively dry platform from which to fish, except during highwater conditions. Parking is decent at all of them, and restrooms and picnic shelters are not far away.

While researching this book, I was not able to determine from the fishermen I spoke with whether any one of the fords was more productive than the others, and they all seemed to receive about the same fishing pressure. The Rockcliff Pool, located at Rockcliff Springs just past the I-90 bridge, did seem to be one of the more popular, and certainly more scenic, pools. A small section of the cement ford has collapsed recently, creating a water column where the river funnels through (as do the fish). Much of the water adjacent to the Rockcliff Pool is productive for wading fishermen, also.

Casey Batule / Cleveland Metroparks

If you are going after steelhead, however, it is a good idea to start at the fords farthest downstream and work your way upstream, away from the lake. As the fish migrate upstream, you will be able to better track where they are in the river. If you start too far upstream, you might be fishing a hole which the fish have not yet reached.

Although these pools are the most popular fishing destinations among Rocky River anglers and consistently produce better than most other areas of the river, it would be a shame to overlook the numerous other potentially productive pools found throughout the river. Many miles of the Rocky are accessible via the Rocky River Reservation, and those anglers willing to do a little exploring away from the roadside access areas will be treated to some very isolated and potentially productive fishing.

Consult the map for exact locations of the individual fords and their accompanying pools. Fishing is allowed in the Rocky River Reservation from 6 a.m. to 11 p.m. daily.

All fords are accessible off Valley Pkwy.

Nearby bait shop(s): L&D Bait & Tackle; Emerald Necklace Marina Bait Shop. (See Directory section for details.)

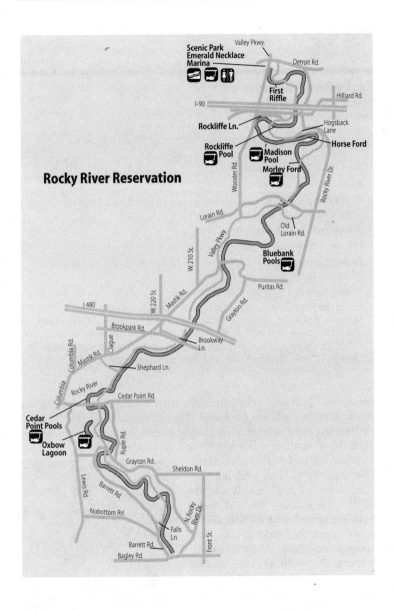

38

Rocky River Reservation
Scenic Park and Marina
Valley Pkwy., Lakewood/Rocky River

Recreational | Intermediate | Challenging

Water Type: River **Acreage:** N/A

Access: Shoreline, wading

What's Biting: Bluegill, smallmouth bass, largemouth bass, bullhead, carp, catfish, sheephead, perch, steelhead, sunfish, walleye

Season: Year-round **Hours:** 6 a.m.–11 p.m.

Fee: Free **Permission:** Not required

Facilities: Bait shop, boat launch, restrooms, picnic area, food onsite, food nearby, hiking trails, ranger, guides

Administered by: Cleveland Metroparks

Directions: I-90 westbound to Exit 162 (Hilliard Blvd.); left on Hilliard at first light; left (north) on Wooster Rd.; right (east) on Detroit over bridge; right on Valley Pkwy. (just after bridge) downhill to Scenic Park entrance on right. OR, I-90 eastbound to Exit 161 (SR 254/Detroit Rd.); east on Detroit, crossing Rocky River bridge; right on Valley Pkwy. (just after bridge) downhill to Scenic Park entrance, on right.

Description "Fish on!" yelled the fisherman wading waist deep in the Rocky River at the Scenic Park area. If anything can come close to actually landing a steelhead, it is watching someone else do it. And I was psyched about watching this struggle between man and fish.

What ensued was your classic steelhead fight, with reel-burning runs and aerobatic leaps. Slowly the angler shortened the distance between himself and the fish, all the while carefully making his way toward the shore. After about 10 minutes the battle was over, and he sat victorious, holding what appeared to be about a six-pound hen steelhead. "Not bad for seven hours," he said with a grin, and then released the fish back into the Rocky River.

Such is the case with steelhead fishing. Long, interminable waiting periods, punctuated by frantic, frenzied bursts of excitement, as a steelhead grabs your bait and heads back to Lake Erie with the force of a freight train.

The Rocky River is one of several Northeast Ohio streams that are stocked annually with approximately 50,000 Manistee strain steelhead by the Ohio Division of Wildlife. Recently, anglers were having better luck for steelies in the lower portion of this river, especially from Scenic Park to the first set of riffles. There is abundant shoreline access here, and at normal water levels wading is also possible.

The Rocky is a relatively flat river that provides fewer deep water pockets for productive fishing than most rivers. The deepest section of the river is a deepwater channel that extends from the boat launches at Scenic Park to the mouth of the river. It is here that the fishing action is usually most consistent, especially for steelhead.

There are six free boat launches available at Scenic Park and the adjacent Emerald Necklace Marina (216-226-3030). The marina also offers boat dockage, gas, and storage facilities. It is a good place to fill up on bait, tackle, boating accessories, and food. Anglers launching from the park or marina have the option of fishing the deepwater section of the Rocky River, or they can head to the open waters of Lake Erie. During my summer visits to Scenic Park, these launches were very busy. Part of the problem is the lack of public boat launches available on the West Side of Cleveland. If you plan on launching a boat here, you'd best be good at maneuvering your trailer.

Besides steelhead, anglers can catch a mixed bag of fish out of the Rocky River, including suckers, carp, sheephead, walleye, and smallmouth bass. These fish are primarily caught during the spring as they migrate upriver to spawn. Surprisingly, there are also the occasional catches of coho and pink salmon and even brown trout. Apparently, the Rocky River is well known for attracting wayward fish from other states' stocking programs.

L&D Bait & Tackle offers a good selection of fishing tackle, live bait, and beverages for anglers fishing the Rocky River. The store is located at 18508 Detroit Ave. in Lakewood.

Nearby bait shop(s): L&D Bait & Tackle; Emerald Necklace Marina Bait Shop. (See Directory section for details.)

39

Rocky River Reservation
Oxbow Lagoon
Valley Pkwy., North Olmsted

Recreational | Intermediate | Challenging

Water Type: Pond   **Acreage:** 5 acres

Access: Shoreline, pier

What's Biting: Bluegill, largemouth bass, bullhead, catfish, crappies, sunfish

Season: Year-round   **Hours:** 6 a.m.–11 p.m.

Fee: Free   **Permission:** Not required

Facilities: Restrooms, picnic area, hiking trails, ranger

Administered by: Cleveland Metroparks

Directions: I-480 to Exit 6 (Great Northern Blvd./SR 252); south on Great Northern; left (east) on Butternut Ridge Rd.; left on Columbia Rd.; right on Cedar Point Rd.; right on Valley Pkwy. to Lagoon Picnic Area, on right.

Description An oxbow is a U-shaped bend in a river, and the Oxbow Lagoon is a remnant of an oxbow that has long since lost its connection with the Rocky River. Although it once flowed freely, it now resembles a small farm pond.

Rocky River Oxbow Lagoon, located near the southern terminus of the Rocky River Reservation, has a very brushy shoreline with abundant tree deadfalls that provide plenty of cover for panfish and bass, which are periodically restocked in the oxbow by Metroparks personnel. All these deadfalls and weeds, unfortunately, also create a very challenging situation for anglers hoping to catch the bass, bluegill, sunfish, and crappie that can be found here. As most fishermen know, however, fish need cover, and learning to fish around

Casey Batule / Cleveland Metroparks

potential snags is a valuable skill to have if you hope to be a successful angler.

Ice fishing is allowed when conditions permit.

West

The Story of the Steelhead

It is not uncommon for fishermen to feel an allegiance to a specific fish species. Perhaps we can somehow relate to a characteristic of our favorite piscatorial prize—the feistiness of a bluegill; the aggressiveness of muskie; or the predatory instincts of bass.

But few fish species enjoy as unbridled a commitment from their pursuers as the steelhead trout.

As the autumn days grow shorter and the leaves begin to blaze, local fishermen start to speculate on this year's run. The run they speak of is the migration of steelhead, which begins each fall and continues throughout the winter. It is an amazing annual phenomenon as thousands of these fish make an annual pilgrimage from Lake Erie back upstream to where their journey began as smolts stocked by the Ohio Division of Wildlife.

Before the steelhead, the Division of Wildlife had stocked other species. They experienced a poor return rate from their brown trout stocking program, and although the coho salmon stocking program might have been a hit with local fishermen, the fish had problems with disease and, unlike steelhead, died after spawning. Now, the Division of Wildlife relies on the Little Manistee strain of steelhead for its stocking program. The strain of a species refers to its place of origin, in this case the Little Manistee River in Michigan.

Steelhead trout are the same genus and species as rainbow trout. The difference is that steelhead migrate out of the rivers in which they were stocked and can spend an extraordinarily long time (up to three years) in Lake Erie before returning to their own stream.

The Division of Wildlife releases 200,000 yearling steelhead between six and nine inches long annually into the Rocky River, the Chagrin River, the Grand River, and Conneaut Creek. (These numbers may increase, however, due to the recent purchase of the Castalia Fish Hatchery by the Ohio Division of Wildlife. After major improvements have been completed on this new facility, the Division of Wildlife should substantially increase the numbers of steelhead stocked each year.) These young trout, or smolts, then begin their journey downriver to Lake Erie, usually reaching the lake during late spring. Once they enter the lake, they begin to grow very rapidly, spurred on by a change in diet from primarily insects to several species of baitfish, including smelt, emerald shiners, and gizzard shad. Steelhead may gain between two and three pounds per year spent in Lake Erie.

Steelhead will normally spend two or three years in Lake Erie before returning to the stream where they were stocked. Although these fish have a fair degree of imprinting regarding this stream, occasionally wayward fish do show up in streams that are not part of the stocking program.

Steelhead begin their spawning runs in the fall. They first congregate near the shoreline by river mouths; and then, usually responding to rains and higher water levels, they enter the rivers. They continue their upstream migration throughout winter, and by the end of November they have usually reached most sections of the rivers and tributaries. There they will wait out the winter months in the deeper pools.

In spring the steelhead prepare to spawn by leaving the deep pools and moving to their ideal spawning areas, usually shallow or riffle areas characterized by a moderate current and a gravel bottom. Spawning takes place from March through mid-April. Unlike salmon, most steelhead do not die after spawning but rather drop to the deeper pools, eventually working their way back to Lake Erie.

Central Basin boat anglers frequently catch steelhead during the summer months in water between 50 and 70 feet deep with spoons or Rapala-type plugs. As fall approaches, boaters should move into the shallow areas near the shore of the Central Basin.

River fishermen can have great success using spawn bags or jigs tipped with maggots for steelhead once they enter the river. Spinners, such as Rooster Tails, and Rapala-type lures can also be effective. Fly fishermen can use any number of patterns, including an egg pattern, sucker spawn, egg-sucking leech, or Woolly Bugger, which can be very effective. Nymph patterns are a good choice when the water is extremely clear and steelhead are skittish. Most fly fishermen have a favorite pattern that they swear by. It's just a matter of discovering which one works best for you.

Good bets for steelheading success:

Grand River—Helen Hazen Wyman Park; Painesville Kiwanis Park; Indian Point; Hogback Ridge.

Chagrin River—Daniels Park; Gilson Park; Todd Field; Chagrin River Park.

Rocky River—Scenic Park in the Rocky River Reservation; Rocky River Fords in Rocky River Reservation.

Smaller Tributaries—Arcola Creek (Arcola Creek Metropark); Wheeler Creek & Cowles Creek (Geneva State Park); Euclid Creek (Wildwood State Park).

Conneaut Creek is a wide open river that receives excellent runs of steelhead and draws anglers not only from Ohio but from surrounding states. Conneaut Creek Boat Launch is located at the north end of Woodworth Rd. in Conneaut.

Farther West

40

Carlisle Reservation
Black River (West Branch)
Nickel Plate-Diagonal Rd., Carlisle

Recreational | Intermediate | Challenging

Water Type: River, pond **Acreage:** N/A

Access: Shoreline, pier

What's Biting: Bluegill, largemouth bass, sunfish

Season: Spring/Summer/Fall **Hours:** 8 a.m.–9:30 p.m.

Fee: Free **Permission:** Not required

Facilities: Restrooms, picnic area, hiking trails, ranger

Administered by: Lorain County Metro Parks

Directions: I-480 to SR 10 (west); west on US 20/SR 10; south on SR 301 (Lagrange Rd.); right (west) on SR 27/Nickel Plate-Diagonal Rd.; on right.

Description Carlisle Reservation is the largest reservation in the Lorain County Metro Parks system, encompassing more than 1,500 acres. The park is cut in half by the West Branch of the Black River and offers a diverse assortment of habitats, including floodplain, upland meadow, mature forests, and wetlands. Three ponds within the park offer convenient, enjoyable, and safe access for local fishermen.

These ponds are ideal places for kids to fish, as there are very few trees in which to cast lures, the shoreline is all well kept and easy to fish from, and there are hiking trails and open fields to keep them busy in case they tire of fishing. A handicapped-accessible fishing pier located on one of the ponds in the Duck Pond Picnic Area is a popular spot for anglers. There is also ample shoreline access available on all the ponds.

Carlisle Reservation's ponds are also fine for anglers more intent on relaxing and enjoying the great outdoors than on busting through brush, fording rivers, and rowing boats. Sometimes even the most intense, gung-ho fishermen find it refreshing to rig up a bobber and hook combination, bait it with a small worm, cast it into the barely rippling water, and relax, the only movement an occasional hook-set when the bobber dips below the surface.

There is no stocking program in place, and there is very little structure. Yet people do pull fish from these ponds fairly consistently.

41

Findley State Park
Findley Lake
25381 State Route 58, Wellington

Recreational | Intermediate | Challenging

Water Type: Inland lake **Acreage:** 93 acres

Access: Shoreline, canoe, boat

What's Biting: Bluegill, largemouth bass, crappies, sunfish

Season: Year-round **Hours:** Open 24 hrs.

Fee: Permission: Not required

Facilities: Boat rental, boat launch, restrooms, picnic area, food nearby, concessions, hiking trails, camping, ranger

Administered by: Ohio Department of Natural Resources

Directions: I-480 to SR 10 (west); follow US 20/SR 10 to SR 58/Oberlin exit; left (south) on SR 58; on left, past the town of Wellington (about 9 miles).

Description Findley State Park's roots can be traced back to 1936, when Guy B. Findley, Lorain County Common Pleas Judge, purchased a large tract of agricultural land. Judge Findley donated the land to the state of Ohio in the hopes that it would be maintained in perpetuity as a state forest to be used for timber production and forest product experiments.

With the help of the Civilian Conservation Corps, the Division of Forestry planted nearly half a million trees, including many varieties of pine and hardwoods, creating Findley Forest. The forest was transferred to the Division of Parks and Recreation in 1950 to be maintained as a state park. In 1956 an earthen dam was constructed, and thus Findley Lake was created.

Never let it be said that a single person cannot have a significant impact on society. Because of Judge Findley's generous donation, hikers, bird-watchers, swimmers, fishermen, and other outdoor enthusiasts have the opportunity to enjoy themselves and seek refuge amid the natural beauty found in this rolling former farmland.

Findley State Park

Among those who should be thankful for this historic act of generosity are fishermen, who now have the opportunity to catch bluegill, largemouth bass, and crappie from Findley Lake. The bluegill popula-

Farther West

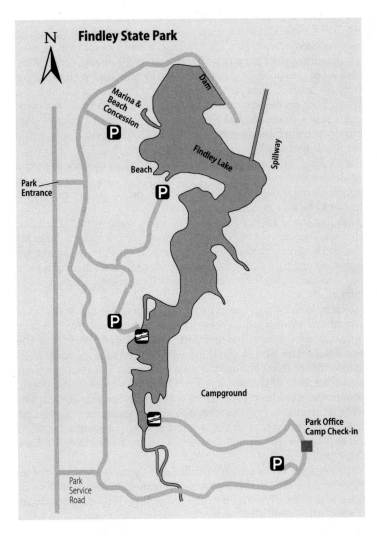

Findley State Park

N

Marina & Beach Concession

P

Dam

Beach

Findley Lake

Spillway

Park Entrance

P

P

P

Campground

Park Office
Camp Check-in

P

Park Service Road

Farther West

largemouth bass, and crappie from Findley Lake. The bluegill population is quite healthy in terms of size and numbers; in fact, fish averaging between six and nine inches are not uncommon. There is a 12-to-15-inch protected slot-length limit in place for largemouth bass at Findley Lake, which means that only fish under 12 inches and greater than 15 inches are allowed to be harvested. This management practice was instituted because the growth rate for bass is very slow here, resulting in too many fish under 12 inches. Thinning out the number of bass will help decrease the competition for food in the lake. More food per bass equals one thing—bigger bass. Therefore, do not be afraid of harvesting a couple of bass from Findley Lake, because doing so will actually help the Division of Wildlife achieve its goal of increasing the average length of the lake's bass. For those who just like to catch fish and are not overly concerned with size, Findley Lake remains a great fishing destination and is a great place to teach youngsters the nuances of angling.

Much of the shoreline is not accessible by foot, making it prime territory for boaters. There are two public boat launches available free of charge, both on the west side of the lake. For those who do not own a boat, canoes, rowboats, and paddleboats can be rented at the marina during the main fishing season. There is an electric-motor-only restriction for all watercraft on Findley Lake.

Ice fishing is allowed at Findley State Park when conditions permit. Hardwater anglers can be treated to a fun, productive day of pulling in bluegill through the ice. The water off the picnic area near the State Route 58 entrance is a good place to start.

Findley State Park is a great place to set up camp, with 272 nonelectric sites. There are showers, flush toilets, laundry facilities, a dump station, and a fully stocked camp commissary. Three Rent-A-Camp units, consisting of a tent, dining fly, cooler, cookstove, and other equipment, can be rented during the summer months. Reservations are required for these.

Nearby Wellington, located two miles north of Findley State Park, is a community with a rich heritage, and worth a visit. Nearly 75 percent of the downtown district is included on the National Register of Historic Places. The New England influence can be seen in much of the architecture of the community. A little farther north is the quaint, cosmopolitan town of Oberlin, home of Oberlin College and the Oberlin Conservatory of Music. I felt like I was entering Mayberry the first time I visited this charming community. Oberlin is a great place to grab a bite to eat, window-shop, or just enjoy the fine details, beautiful buildings, and well-kept landscaping that make this such a comfortable, habitable community.

Findley Lake is not a lunker-producing fishery by any stretch of the imagination, although there are certainly some decent-sized fish swimming in its waters. What it offers as a whole, however—the opportunity to catch fish, camp, hike, swim, and observe a great variety of Ohio's native flora and fauna—makes this quiet, peaceful park a very worthwhile fishing destination.

Nearby bait shop(s): Findley Lake Bait Shop. (See Directory section for details.)

42

Lakeside Landing
Lake Erie and Lake Erie Shoreline
Lakeside Ave., Lorain

Recreational | Intermediate | Challenging

Water Type: Lake Erie   **Acreage:** N/A

Access: Shoreline, breakwall, canoe, boat

What's Biting: Bluegill, smallmouth bass, carp, catfish, crappies, perch, pike, sheephead, steelhead, suckers, sunfish, walleye

Season: Year-round   **Hours:** Open 24 hrs.

Fee: Free; fee for boat launch   **Permission:** Not required

Facilities: Bait shop, boat launch, restrooms, picnic area, food onsite, food nearby, concessions

Administered by: Lorain Port Authority

Directions: I-90 to Exit 151 (Colorado Ave./SR 611); west on Colorado into Lorain to Lakeside Ave.; left on Lakeside to boat basin.

Farther West

Description My arms ached from reeling in fish, but it was one of those good kinds of hurts, and I did not mind it as we unloaded our gear from the charter boat and set it on the docks. The heaviest items were two large coolers loaded with fish. It was a successful outing, and we would all be leaving with enough walleye to keep our bellies full for quite some time. There were also a couple of "Fish Ohio" walleyes in the coolers. Every one of them was caught within sight of land, only a couple miles from where our charter, the *Y-Knot,* had departed Lakeside Landing. We all felt pretty pleased with ourselves as we lugged our fish from the boat and carried them onto the breakwall that led back to the parking lot, and the attention our catch received from some of the other fishermen was appreciated. The fact that our captain had done most of the work seemed an insignificant detail at this point. We were all too proud of our catch to ponder such things.

The evening sun was bidding us farewell as we unloaded the fish, yet the breakwall was still occupied by a handful of fishermen who did not look like they were leaving any time soon. Upon questioning, one of them informed me that they were having some decent luck with walleye at night—nothing great, but good enough to entice the dedicated. There are certainly worse ways to spend a spring evening.

Lakeside Landing is located in the city of Lorain, where the East Branch of the Black River joins Lake Erie. A walkway extending from the Spitzer Marina Clubhouse along the marina ends in a circular fishing wall. It is handicapped-accessible and provides a clean, comfortable place to fish. It is open year round, 24 hours a day, and is lit for night anglers. After 11 p.m., anglers 18 years and older are required to show a valid I.D. From the parking lot, however, it is at least a quarter mile to the end, so you will want to either keep your gear to a minimum or bring a cart.

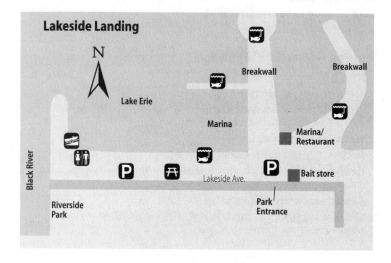

Farther West

Anglers can also fish along the grass shoreline located just west of the parking lot. This area is decent for panfish and bass, and, according to a fisherman I spoke with, has produced more than one northern pike.

There is a second breakwall at the eastern extreme of the park, extending from the parking lot closest to the bait shop. This breakwall is make up entirely of large rocks, resulting in an incredibly uneven, jagged walkway. Exercise extreme caution, especially if night fishing. A flashlight is a necessity.

Shoreline fishing is most productive here during the spring. Very large crappies move in early in the spring, and fishermen along the grassy shoreline can enjoy some pretty productive days fishing for these tasty panfish. Minnows suspended below a bobber are the most effective bait, although jigs—the smaller the better—can also produce some fish.

Perch can be caught from either of the breakwalls during May and June, before they head out into much deeper water. Again, minnows are probably your best bet in bait, and perch spreaders the most efficient way of fishing them.

In May, walleye anglers brave the chilly spring nights casting plugs and crankbaits from the east breakwall, hoping to hook one of the predators that have moved into the shallows to spawn. Rat-L-Traps and Rapalas are good bets for this time of year.

There are two public boat launches available at Lakeside Landing, with a daily launching charge of $4. The launches are found by following Lakeside Ave. just west of the park. For boat fishermen, these launches are a wonderful resource. During the early summer limits of walleye can be caught just a couple miles offshore, and Lakeside Landing provides a very convenient means of reaching these fish.

A walk-on charter service departs daily from Lakeside Landing, with trips leaving at 7 a.m. and returning at 1 p.m. No reservations are necessary for these trips. The Jackalope Restaurant, located on the second floor of the Spitzer Marina Clubhouse, is open to the public. Riverside Park, located on the Black River just west of Lakeside Landing, offers a playground, picnic shelters, and a picturesque walkway along the river. The park closes at 11 p.m.

If you need live bait, tackle, or other fishing necessities, Lakeside Bait & Tackle, located on Colorado Ave. a mile or so away, offers a great selection of fishing and trolling gear. Lakeside usually opens around March 1. There is also a bait shop operated at Lakeside Marina during the summer months.

Nearby bait shop(s): Lakeside Bait & Tackle. (See Directory section for details.)

Farther West

43

Vermilion River Reservation
Vermilion River
Vermilion Rd., Vermilion

Recreational | **Intermediate** | Challenging

Water Type: River **Acreage:** N/A

Access: Shoreline

What's Biting: Bluegill, rock bass, smallmouth bass, carp, catfish, crappies, steelhead, sunfish

Season: Year-round **Hours:** 8 a.m.–dusk

Fee: Free **Permission:** Not required

Facilities: Restrooms, picnic area, food nearby, hiking trails, ranger

Administered by: Lorain County Metro Parks

Directions: I-90 west to SR 2 west (stay on SR 2 as it splits off from I-90); exit at Vermilion/Sunnyside Rds.; follow signs to Vermilion Rd. via Jerusalem Rd., south from highway exit; right (west) on Jerusalem; left (south) on Vermilion Rd.; right (downhill) on North Ridge Rd.; entrances on both sides of bridge.

Farther West

Description Tucked away in the northwest corner of Lorain County is a great fishing destination known as the Vermilion River Reservation. A component of the Lorain County Metro Parks, this linear park is named after the river that flows through it. Before my visit, a park representative told me that the Vermilion is a relatively undisturbed waterway. I was not disappointed. It is indeed a magnificent river, its protected waters flowing cold and clear and teeming with aquatic life.

For part of its meanderings through the park, the Vermilion is flanked on one side by towering shale cliffs, barren except for some unique plant species not found in other habitats. On the other side lie floodplain forests of sycamore, maple, oak, and cottonwood.

The river itself has a nice variety of riffles, deep pools, chutes, and slow-moving flats. Be prepared to wade when fishing it. Much of the shoreline has heavy vegetation and provides little room for walking.

The park district has taken great care to protect the riparian habitats around the river. I found this out firsthand when I tried to find the river, which is not visible from the parking lot. After taking several small trails only to dead-end in jumbled thickets of woods and brush, and just missing a very lively hornet's nest, I finally found an easier path to the river. Your best bet is to take the park road all the way to the farthest parking lot. You'll see a restroom at the northeast end of the parking lot, and a picnic shelter at the southwest end. A trailhead just behind the shelter provides easy access to the river.

I decided to leave the spinning gear in the trunk and go solely with my fly rod, a 6-weight Fenwick. On this day the Vermilion River produced three smallmouth bass, all of them falling for an olive Woolly Bugger. I started with a grasshopper imitation, but switched after several smallmouth bass came up, took a close look, and retreated to deeper water. They evidently were not fooled by my hand-tied fly or were not in the mood for grasshoppers. The weighted Woolly Bugger, hopped along the bottom like a crayfish, did the trick. After the third bass, I switched to a dry fly for a few minutes and caught a handful of creek chubs that were slurping insects off the surface of the river like hungry trout. They are not big fish, but it is exciting to see them hungrily attack a dry fly as the current takes it by.

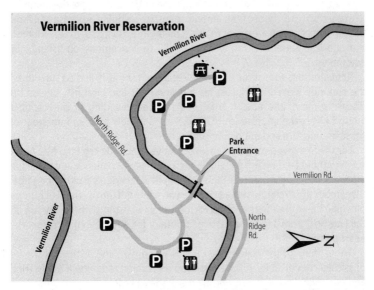

Anglers can catch a mixed bag when fishing the Vermilion River. There are decent populations of smallmouth, rock bass, sunfish, and some crappie. Though not stocked with them, the river does receive some wayward steelhead in the spring and fall. The clarity of the water, especially during the low-water periods of summer, demands a fairly delicate presentation. Use light line, and if the fish seem tight-lipped and uncooperative, scale down your offerings a bit.

The North Ridge Rd. bridge crosses the river as it winds through the park. There were some deep holes underneath it, with several logs that had been carried down the river in past storms. It would be worthwhile to spend some time probing this water, as the deeper water here most likely harbors some decent-sized fish.

Pack a lunch and plan on spending the better part of a day exploring and fishing this river. The scenic natural areas and exciting fishing make this a very worthwhile West Side fishing venture.

Nearby bait shop(s): The Bait Box; Rich's Hook, Line & Sinker. (See Directory section for details.)

Getting Kids Hooked on Fishing

The look on a child's face after catching a fish is priceless. By teaching the sport of fishing to youngsters in a positive way, you are introducing them to something that may become a lifelong pursuit that will provide exercise, knowledge of the outdoors, and great lessons in responsibility. If you want to hook kids on fishing, you've got to make their first few outings enjoyable ones. Here are some suggestions to help you make their earliest angling experiences enjoyable:

Start with equipment a child can handle and use proficiently. It's probably best not to begin with a bait-casting or fly rod outfit, as these are the toughest to master. Instead, choose from among open-face spinning, spincast, or hybrid trigger outfits, which are easier to use. A medium-action, 5 ½- to 6 ½-foot rod is a good beginner rod. You want the child to concentrate on fishing, not equipment.

Acquaint him with some of the essentials of fishing, including how to tie the commonly used knots, cast his rod, and fight and land fish. Be sure to discuss some of the fundamental safety issues, including proper conduct around water, the importance of life jackets, and how to keep hooks out of those around him and out of himself.

For the first few outings, the main objective should be catching fish. A day spent without landing fish will surely tax a youngster's patience and make the prospect of going again less than thrilling. The fish don't have to be large. Remember the excitement the first time you really got into a school of hungry bluegill? These are the formative, exciting years of fishing, where any tug on the line, be it from a four-pound largemouth or four-inch bluegill, can get the heart pumping.

Try to think of the child's other needs when planning a trip. Will she be physically comfortable? Just because you don't mind toughing it out in wind and rain trying to catch bass doesn't mean she'll like it.

Are there other activities she can do if she so chooses? Invariably a child's patience wanes after a while, so try to take her to a place with nature trails, a nature center, or playground. Be ready for more frequent potty stops than you're accustomed to. Pack a lunch, something to drink, and sunblock.

Always be on your best behavior when fishing with youngsters. Remember, whatever values they learn will be from you. Always demonstrate proper ethics and respect for the outdoors, and instill in youngsters a love and respect for natural resources that they will incorporate into their outdoor pursuits.

Don't get mad if they catch more—or bigger—fish than you do.

HAVE FUN! Your young fishing buddy will have more line tangles and questions, and will cast more lures into trees than you would like. Don't yell. Take a step back (unless you're on a boat), count to ten, and then help. With a little patience and instruction, you can work through these problems.

Fishing can provide a lifetime of rich memories when done correctly and with respect for the environment. So take a kid fishing and pass on some of your expertise. You'll be happy you did.

South

44

Cuyahoga River Dam/Ohio & Erie Canal Towpath, CVNRA
Shoreline and Wading
Chippewa Creek Dr., Brecksville

Recreational | **Intermediate** | **Challenging**

Water Type: River **Acreage:** N/A

Access: Shoreline, wading

What's Biting: Bluegill, smallmouth bass, carp, catfish, steelhead, suckers, sunfish

Season: Year-round **Hours:** 6 a.m.–11 p.m.

Fee: Free **Permission:** Not required

Facilities: Restrooms, picnic area, food nearby, hiking trails, ranger

Administered by: Cleveland Metroparks

Directions: I-77 to SR 82 (N. Royalton Rd.); east on SR 82 to Riverview Rd.; right on Riverview downhill to Chippewa Creek Dr.; parking area on left.

Description The Ohio & Erie Canal was built between 1825 and 1832, and it provided a vital transportation route from Cleveland and Lake Erie to Portsmouth, on the Ohio River. For good or bad, by the time the canal ceased to operate in 1913 it had proved to be a key component in opening up Ohio for permanent settlement, turning a sparsely settled wilderness into a populous state with a thriving economy.

There may not be mules trudging along the canal towpath today, but there are plenty of cyclists, walkers, and other recreationists, including fishermen, who enjoy this historically significant trail.

If you want to experience what one fisherman claimed to be the best smallmouth bass fishing in the area, and get a unique perspective on Ohio's history and heritage, then the dam located on the Cuyahoga River at State Route 82 in Brecksville should be on your list of destinations. The area, a relatively unknown angling destination, is accessed through the Brecksville Reservation, but it is actually part of the Cuyahoga Valley National Recreation Area.

To get to the fishing area, park at the Chippewa Creek Drive/Towpath Trail parking lot. From here, follow the trail across the bridge and take a left when you hit the towpath trail. Follow this to the dam. Anglers here can hook into carp, suckers, steelhead, smallmouth bass, catfish, and panfish. The area is especially productive from May through July. After a heavy rainfall, it is usually a good idea to let the water settle for a day or two before heading to the river.

The river bottom here is literally crawling with hellgramites and crayfish, offering a smorgasbord to the resident smallmouth bass. The wise fisherman will therefore use jigs that match the color of these two food sources and crawl them along the bottom of the river. Fly fishermen should tie on a black or olive Woolly Bugger or crayfish pattern, weight it just enough to get it to the bottom, and hang on! Either of these techniques can prove to be quite deadly for these river smallmouth. For smallmouth, as with all fish, you'll need to keep the lure in their strike zone for as long as possible to be successful, which means basically keeping your lure right at the bottom. If your lure is not occasionally getting snagged on the bottom, you will want to add a split shot or two to keep it down where the hellgramites and crayfish crawl about.

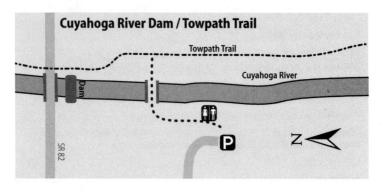

Live bait, of course, such as the crayfish and hellgramites that occur naturally here, are also extremely effective at tempting the fish to bite. As a rule, you will have the most success fishing when you can match the food source that the fish are used to eating. A tail-hooked crayfish drifted along the bottom can be deadly.

If you're going to the State Route 82 bridge dam, why not bring along the bikes and spend a couple of leisurely hours pedaling along the remnants of the Ohio & Erie Canal Towpath? Not only will you and your family get plenty of exercise, but you will also get to enjoy the forest, fields, and wetlands that flank the path as it meanders through the Cuyahoga Valley National Recreation Area.

You might also want to visit the Brecksville Nature Center, located off Chippewa Creek Drive, or hike any of the well-maintained trails that wind through the park to really enjoy the natural beauty of the Brecksville Reservation. Fishing is allowed in the Brecksville Reservation from 6 a.m. to 11 p.m. daily.

Nearby bait shop(s): Atlantic Gun & Tackle. (See Directory section for details.)

45

Hinckley Reservation
Hinckley Lake
West Dr., Hinckley Township

Recreational | Intermediate | Challenging

Water Type: Inland lake   **Acreage:** 87 acres

Access: Shoreline, pier, canoe, boat

What's Biting: Bluegill, largemouth bass, bullhead, catfish, crappies, pike, sunfish, trout

Season: Year-round   **Hours:** 6 a.m.–11 p.m.

Fee: Free; fee for boat rental   **Permission:** Not required

Facilities: Bait shop, boat rental, boat launch, restrooms, picnic area, food nearby, hiking trails, ranger, guides

Administered by: Cleveland Metroparks

Directions: I-271 to Exit 3 (Ridge Rd./SR 94); north on Ridge Rd.; right (east) on Hinckley Hills Rd./SR 606; right (east) on Bellus Rd.; right (south) on West Dr. to boathouse entrance, on left.

Description Fishing can be as active or leisurely a sport as you want to make it. On a day when I preferred the latter of these choices, I could not have found a better companion than the gentleman who was reclining peacefully on a lawn chair dug into the sandy beach near the Hinckley Lake Boathouse. He had one fishing rod leaning against his tackle box, the line taut from the sinker at the other end, and a steaming thermos of coffee. It was just past 6:30 a.m., and the morning mist was beginning to burn off the lake. I could just start making out the forms of numerous Canada geese and other waterfowl on the lake.

Casey Batule/Cleveland Metroparks

"Usually I do real well here," he told me. "But sometimes I just feed the fish. Either way, I just enjoy being here." A good attitude to have.

I, too, was more interested in enjoying the perfect morning than in knocking myself out trying to catch fish. So with that in mind, I took off down one of the well-maintained trails that parallel the lake and parked my butt on the first fishing pier I came to. Casually I flipped a white twister-tail jig into the lake, paying more attention to the waterfowl, which by now had fully awakened and were making a hell of a racket. I

South

was jolted out of my daydreaming by the tug at the end of my line, which I soon discovered was a nice-sized crappie. Twenty minutes later I had caught and released two more without once hurrying a cast. It was truly relaxing fishing. May is the best time to take advantage of Hinckley Lake's crappie fishery, with the rocky areas near the dam producing well. There's good fishing from the fishing piers, too.

Hinckley Lake was impounded in 1926 and currently holds back about 87 acres of the East Branch of the Rocky River. Adult channel catfish are stocked annually by Cleveland Metroparks personnel, and every two years the lake receives adult northern pike to maintain a catchable population of this predatory gamefish. Other fish species that might pique an angler's interest are largemouth bass, black and white crappie, brown bullhead, and rainbow trout.

Hinckley Lake has really built a reputation for its channel catfish, which often stretch more than two feet. The Cleveland Metroparks hosts a Catfish Derby and Fishing Day at Hinckley Lake each summer. Although the lake has a good population, several hundred pounds of adult catfish are stocked for the derby. A catfish clinic presented by Cleveland Metroparks personnel is held the morning of the event. For specific information regarding this year's Catfish Derby and Fishing Day, call the Cleveland Metroparks (440-234-9597).

In addition to catfish, Hinckley Lake also has a good largemouth bass population. Each year there are several "Fish Ohio" largemouth registered from Hinckley Lake.

A boat launch, suitable for canoes and small boats, is available at the south end of the lake on State Rd. Electric-powered motors are permitted on the lake provided the owner obtains an operating permit, available for free at the boathouse. You can also rent a boat at the Hinckley Lake Boathouse, which is open from April until mid-October and located off West Dr., between Bellus and State Rds. A rowboat costs $7 for the first hour and $18 for the entire day, while a boat with electric motor costs $22 for two hours and $30 for the day. There is also a complete bait and tackle shop. For current boat rental rates, or for a Hinckley Lake fishing report, call the boathouse (330-278-2122).

Hinckley Lake is also a popular ice fishing destination when conditions permit, and it can provide a surefire cure for the cabin fever blues. Ice fishing is allowed near the boathouse and away from the ice-skating area.

(*See the Hinckley map in Chapter 47.*)

46

Hinckley Reservation
Ledge Lake
Ledge Rd., Hinckley Township

Recreational | Intermediate | Challenging

Water Type: Inland lake **Acreage:** 4.5 acres

Access: Shoreline

What's Biting: Bluegill, largemouth bass, catfish, crappies, sunfish, trout

Season: Year-round **Hours:** 6 a.m.–11 p.m.

Fee: Free; fee for swimming and recreation area **Permission:** Not required

Facilities: Restrooms, picnic area, food onsite, hiking trails, ranger

Administered by: Cleveland Metroparks

Directions: I-271 to Exit 3 (Ridge Rd./SR 94); north on Ridge Rd.; right (east) on Ledge Rd.; entrance on left.

Description Tucked away in the southwest corner of the Hinckley Reservation in Medina County is Ledge Lake, which, though not impressive in size, does offer some fine fishing. Thanks to the management program carried out by the Cleveland Metroparks Natural Resources Division, which involves periodic fish stocking and fish habitat improvement, anglers can do quite well here.

Ledge Lake, located off Ledge Rd. between Kellogg and State Rds., offers a chance to catch largemouth bass, bluegill, crappie, rainbow trout, and channel catfish. There is also a smaller pond, just under an acre, situated southwest of the lake.

Rainbow trout are stocked in the winter for ice fishing. It might be cold, but it is a wonderful way to experience the quiet winter beauty of Hinckley Reservation.

Ledge Lake is a perfect place for a family outing because in addition to the fishing, there is a pool area, a basketball court, and a game room and concession area. Bring the family and spend a leisurely summer morning fishing and an afternoon swimming.

The minimum legal size for largemouth bass is 12 inches, and the daily harvest limit is two per angler. You can take three rainbow trout daily per angler.

(*See the Hinckley map in Chapter 47.*)

South

47

Hinckley Reservation
Judge's Lake
Ledge Rd., Hinckley Township

Recreational | Intermediate | Challenging

Water Type: Pond   **Acreage:** 2 acres

Access: Shoreline

What's Biting: Bluegill, largemouth bass, catfish, sunfish, trout

Season: Year-round   **Hours:** 6 a.m.–11 p.m.

Fee: Free   **Permission:** Not required

Facilities: Hiking trails

Administered by: Cleveland Metroparks

Directions: I-271 to Exit 3 (Ridge Rd./SR 94); north on Ridge Rd.; right (east) on Ledge Rd.; entrance on left, past Bellus Rd.

Description Sometimes fishermen take the sport just too seriously. I know I do, and I never felt more foolish for it than when I visited Judge's Lake, located in Hinckley Reservation in Medina County. I introduced myself to a fisherman to get some information and noticed some striking differences between us. Here I was, spinning rod in one hand, fly rod in the other, tackle box strapped around my waist, fishing vest with 20 different fully loaded pockets, and a fishing net hanging from the back. He, on the other hand, was lounging in one of those low-riding beach chairs, listening to a local talk show on a small radio, and was sucking on a cheap stogie, and all the while we were talking, he kept a keen eye on his fishing rod. I was ready for the angler's equivalent of World War III, and he was ready to enjoy a morning in the park.

I'm just thankful he held his laughter in until I was out of earshot.

Judge's Lake is the smallest of the three lakes in Hinckley Reservation. But don't let its small size fool you. The gentleman mentioned above did pull in a decent-sized catfish while I was there, and I was successful in landing a largemouth bass, which, though on the small side (about 10 inches), put up a champion fight. To keep the fishing productive at Judge's Lake, Cleveland Metroparks Natural Resources Division periodically stocks the lake and works to improve fish habitat by sinking old Christmas trees and brush/sapling bundles to provide protective cover.

There is a picnic area at this location, but that's about it. There are no restrooms or other amenities. Ledge Lake, located just west of Judge's Lake, does have restrooms and concessions available during the summer.

The minimum legal size for largemouth bass is 12 inches, and the daily harvest limit is two per angler. You can take three rainbow trout daily per angler.

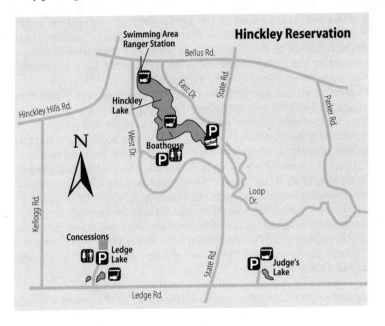

Ice Fishing

If you are one of the special breed that enjoys the sport of ice fishing, there are numerous opportunities for it within the Greater Cleveland area. Cleveland Metroparks lakes and ponds are all open to ice fishing, and ice conditions are monitored by Metroparks personnel. Call the Natural Resources Office at (216) 234-9597 for up-to-date information. Cleveland Metroparks also holds annual ice-fishing derbies that feature ice-fishing clinics presented by Metropark fishing specialists.

Most of the lakes and ponds mentioned in this book are open to ice fishing, although conditions may not be monitored. During an extended cold snap, Lake Erie becomes suitable for ice fishing and can be very productive for perch and walleye. For most ice-fishing destinations, however, it is up to the individual angler to determine whether or not the ice is safe for fishing. Ice fishing is a wonderful way to enjoy the solitude of winter and also keep the cabin-fever blues at bay. For your safety, please keep the following guidelines in mind when venturing out onto the frozen water.

Never fish on ice that is less than three inches thick. Opinions vary on this matter, with some sources saying two-inch ice is safe, and others stating that anything under four is unsafe. The safest ice is clear, blue ice, preferably with no snow cover, which can act as an insulation and weaken the ice. Avoid cloudy ice formed from slush.

Fish with a buddy or two and walk at least a couple yards apart in case one of your party should fall through the ice. Carry a length of rope with you to use as a rescue aid.

Avoid rivers and creeks, and any other body of water that has a flowing current or feeder creek beneath the ice. Ice conditions are unpredictable in such situations.

Be aware of the symptoms of frostbite and hypothermia and leave the ice immediately if you or someone in your party starts exhibiting signs of either.

Persistence is truly a virtue for ice fishermen. The metabolism of the fish slows down substantially in the winter, so they are not as actively on the prowl for food. If you stay at one spot for longer than 20 or 30 minutes without getting a strike, it's time to move on.

Farther South

48

Hubbard Valley Park
Hubbard Valley Reservoir
Hubbard Valley Rd., Gilford Township

Recreational | Intermediate | Challenging

Water Type: Inland lake **Acreage:** 18 acres

Access: Shoreline, pier, canoe, boat

What's Biting: Bluegill, largemouth bass, catfish, crappies, pike, sunfish

Season: Year-round **Hours:** 7 a.m.–dusk

Fee: Free; permit for boat use required **Permission:** Not required

Facilities: Boat launch, restrooms, picnic area, food nearby, hiking trails, ranger

Administered by: Medina County Park District

Directions: I-71 to Exit 209 for I-76 east; east on I-76 to Exit 2 for SR 3; north on SR 3 (Wooster Pike); right (east) on Blake Rd.; right (south) on Hubbard Valley Rd.; on right.

Description Medina County Park District's ponds offer a number of wonderful fishing opportunities, but if you yearn to fish a place where you can really let loose with a cast and not worry about hitting the opposite shore, then the 18-acre reservoir located in Hubbard Valley Park is the place you seek.

A trail completely circling the reservoir provides decent access for shore fishermen, although a large portion of the shore is off-limits, mostly for safety reasons. There is also a small dock located near the entrance, from which anglers may cast a line.

Northern pike were stocked in the past and have since been able to maintain a healthy population through natural reproduction. Not overwhelming numbers, but enough to make it interesting.

The reservoir's size, together with the fact that there is little boat traffic on it, means that there is much water not regularly pounded by lures, bobbers, sinkers, and worms. These areas provide ideal, relatively undisturbed habitat for largemouth bass, whose average size has increased since the park's boat rental was closed down.

In the spring, anglers will do well from the shore, as the fish come in close to spawn. Fall will also prove productive, especially for largemouth, which feed heavily in the shallows in preparation for the winter. During the summer, morning and evening will see fish move into the shallows, but they will spend the majority of the day in the deeper, cooler sections of the reservoir. If you are on a boat equipped with a fishfinder, look for brush and rock piles and other structure along the bottom of the reservoir, as these are likely holding spots.

Park district personnel annually place submerged tree trunks, Christmas trees, and rock piles throughout the fishing areas of the lake in an attempt to enhance fish habitat and thus improve the overall fishing. Good news for anglers.

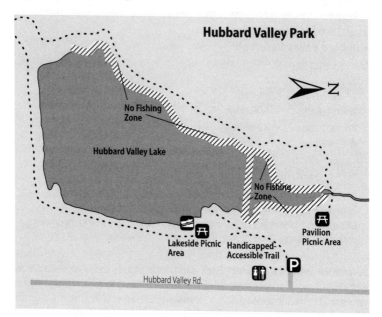

Despite the termination of the boat rental service, boating is still allowed on the reservoir, although there is an electric-motor-only restriction in place. Also, there is no improved boat launch available, so visitors must carry their craft from the parking lot to the lake. This puts somewhat of a natural restriction on the size of watercraft you might want to bring to Hubbard Valley Lake. If you do decide to launch your private fishing vessel on the waters of Hubbard Valley Lake, you are required to obtain a permit from the park district.

If you can swing it, boat fishing allows you to take advantage of the many areas of the lake that cannot be reached by shore fishermen.

A handicapped-accessible trail leads to a shoreline fishing area, a picnic shelter, picnic tables, restrooms, and a play structure.

There is a 13-inch limit for largemouth bass, with a daily bag limit of four fish. Northern pike must be more than 20 inches; there is no daily limit on them.

49

Medina Fish Hatchery
3148 Sharon-Copley Rd., Medina

Recreational | Intermediate | Challenging

Water Type: Pond   **Acreage:** N/A
Access: Shoreline
What's Biting: Bluegill, largemouth bass, catfish, pike, sunfish, trout
Season: Year-round   **Hours:** Fri–Mon 7:30 a.m.–5 p.m.; closed Tue, Wed, Thu
Fee: $10 per day adults; $9 seniors; $5 children   **Permission:** Required
Facilities: Bait shop, restrooms, food onsite, food nearby
Administered by: Medina Fish Hatchery
Directions: I-71 to Exit 218 (SR 18); right (west) on SR 18; left (south) on River Styx Rd.; left (east) on Sharon-Copley Rd. (SR 162); on right.

Description Some anglers, especially those who like to take more of an active role in fishing, might find the Medina Fish Hatchery to be a little bit on the dull side. The ponds are all rectangularly shaped, with no observable structure or interesting features. There are no woodland trails to hike in order to get to the ponds, and as far as wildlife or aquatic diversity, forget about it. But there is one thing the Medina Fish Hatchery does provide, and that is the opportunity to catch fish, including some extremely large catfish.

Most anglers fish the bottom or use bobbers with minnows and night crawlers, PowerBait, or some other bait. Basically, any type of catfish rig will produce. Others are successful using small spinners or Rapala-type lures. The fishing at the hatchery is not technically complex. In fact, anglers using less sophisticated approaches and strategies seemed to have the most success. Go figure.

The people who fish the hatchery certainly seem to enjoy it. "I have fished here for 25 years," one angler said, "and I usually catch a lot of trout." A sly glance into his tackle box revealed nothing more than a couple of the standard red-and-white bobbers, a tangled mess of assorted hooks, and a jar of pink PowerBait. Ascetic, perhaps, but effective, and his stringer bore the proof—three trout. Several of the people I spoke with claimed that they have been fishing there for years and consistently have successful days.

There are some jumbo catfish stocked in the ponds, with some weighing in at more than 40 pounds. That's a nice fish by anyone's standards. Moreover, there are almost always trout and catfish stocked in the ponds, although the species that are stocked do vary to some degree by season, as do the fish's tolerance of different water temperatures. Pike

Farther South

and panfish are stocked in the spring. Stocking switches to trout and catfish in the summer. Trout are the primary stockings during the colder months of early and late fall. You might want to call ahead to check on what has been stocked before venturing out.

It would be an exaggeration to say that the Medina Fish Hatchery provides the scenic qualities that draw many anglers to the sport. It would not, however, be an exaggeration to say that the patient fisherman can do quite well here for a variety of species. And for many anglers, that's what it's all about—catching fish.

Nearby bait shop(s): Medina Fish Hatchery. (See Directory section for details.)

50

Plum Creek Park

Plum Creek Pkwy., Brunswick Hills Township

Recreational | Intermediate | Challenging

Water Type: Pond **Acreage:** N/A

Access: Shoreline

What's Biting: Bluegill, largemouth bass, catfish, sunfish

Season: Year-round **Hours:** 7 a.m.–dusk

Fee: Free **Permission:** Not required

Facilities: Restrooms, picnic area, food nearby, hiking trails, ranger

Administered by: Medina County Park District

Directions: I-71 to Exit 222 (Medina/SR 3); west on SR 3; immediate right on Hamilton Rd.; right (north) on Plum Creek Pkwy.; on left.

Description You may not be able to tell when you are there, but part of Plum Creek Park was once a township landfill that has since been covered over and reclaimed. The results are impressive, and Medina County residents, and anyone else for that matter, can now enjoy an area that not too many years ago was covered in refuse from neighboring communities.

Plum Creek Park, located in the northern half of Medina County, boasts two fishing ponds that both offer fine fishing. It is truly a wonderful park, and a great place to spend a few hours casting a line for the ponds' largemouth bass, bluegill, and catfish.

There is a lot of access around both ponds, and kids will be able to cast and, hopefully, catch fish without too much trouble. The fishing pressure can make the fish in both ponds tough to catch at times, but one way to overcome this problem is to start your fishing excursion either early in the morning or later in the evening. As with most fishing situations, fish usually stay low and stop feeding during midday.

The park district stocks the ponds with rainbow trout each fall, opening up an exciting fishing opportunity for those who normally do not get much opportunity to catch these tasty fish. Natural baits, such as worms, mealworms, and maggots, work well for these hatchery-raised fish, as will PowerBait, small spinners, and even small Rapalas.

There is a 13-inch limit for largemouth bass, with a daily bag limit of four fish.

Farther South

51

River Styx Park

Blake and River Styx Rds., Gilford Township

Recreational | **Intermediate** | Challenging

Water Type: Pond **Acreage:** 3.5 acres

Access: Shoreline

What's Biting: Bluegill, largemouth bass, catfish, sunfish, trout

Season: Year-round **Hours:** 7 a.m.–dusk

Fee: Free **Permission:** Not required

Facilities: Restrooms, picnic area, food nearby, hiking trails, ranger

Administered by: Medina County Metroparks

Directions: I-71 to Exit 218 (SR 18); right (west) on SR 18; left (south) on River Styx Rd. (merges with SR 57; stay on River Styx); on right, before Blake Rd.

Description As I understand it, the River Styx is a legendary river of fire located in the bowels of hell. River Styx Park, located in more temperate southern Medina County, bears the same name as the underworld waterway, but the resemblence stops there. This 83-acre park, operated by Medina County Park District, is a haven for a wide array of plants and animals, and offers a place where visitors can go to relax and take in the natural beauty of the River Styx Valley. It is also a great place to wet a line, with a 3.5-acre pond that boasts a decent population of largemouth bass, bluegill, catfish, and, in the fall and winter, rainbow trout.

Access is good around this fishing hole, with few trees to snag a backcast. I would certainly not hesitate to bring a young angler here. As with most public ponds, fishing pressure can make the fish tight-lipped. You'll have the best results if you hit the water early in the morning or in the evening, and by all means avoid the heat of the midday. Also, fish can become conditioned to seeing the same lures and same presentations day in and day out. Try different lures and baits, and vary your presentations and retrieves.

Each fall, when water temperatures drop, the park district stocks the pond with rainbow trout weighing from one to a few pounds. Remember, these are not the ultrafinicky trout that inhabit cold Colorado spring creeks. These are hatchery-raised fish that lack the refinement of their wild brethren. Natural baits, such as worms, mealworms, and maggots, will entice them into biting, as will PowerBait, small spinners, and even small Rapalas. There is a 13-inch limit for largemouth bass, with a daily bag limit of four fish.

The Politics of Fishing

How long have politicians used environmental protection to pull at the heartstrings of the public? It's not a new phenomenon, as illustrated in this 1986 article by Cleveland's legendary "tell-it-like-it-is" columnist, Dick Feagler, who recounts an environmental publicity stunt gone awry.

Unfortunately, when the environmental success for which a political leader claims responsibility proves to be nothing but smoke and mirrors, the illusion is lost, and, along with it, the public's trust. If contemporary politicians hope to win votes through natural resource protection, there must be more than a quick-fix solution. True environmental protection means more than mass-stocking non-native fish into stagnant, polluted waterways. It means preserving and restoring all the pieces of the natural resource puzzle.

Jim Rhodes Goes Fishing

Last week somebody sent Governor Dick Celeste an envelope with a newspaper clipping in it. The clipping was yellowed and old, which didn't make me feel so hot because I wrote it.

Celeste handed it to me with a grin.

"Thanks," he said. "Here's another vote for me."

It was a story written in 1969 about a day in the life of then-governor Jim Rhodes. A day he went fishing.

Let me set the scene for you ...

It is early morning somewhere on the Chagrin River. The only sounds are of birds twittering in the trees and the babbling of the flowing water ...

Whoops! Wait a minute. That isn't the river babbling. That babbling is coming from a crowd of people who now appear from over the horizon. There are a couple of state troopers in the crowd and a gaggle of officials from the state wildlife commission. A few politicians are there, sticking close to a younger Jim Rhodes, and a couple of newspaper reporters, including a younger me.

We have gathered at the river to watch the governor catch a fish. The fish he is after is a fish he more or less invented. The coho salmon.

This is a year when Lake Erie is a stagnant pond. Its fish have died in it or left town. Rhodes is trying to show that all is not lost. He has stocked the river with coho salmon—a new kind of fish to most of us who are only used to salmon in cans. Now he has come to pull one of his fish out of the water and regard it and call it good.

So the governor and his troopers and the crowd of state officials and the political hangers-on all struggle into waders. They enter the water. And the governor begins to fish.

Nothing's biting.

The wildlife people begin to eye each other nervously. Finally, one of them splashes out of the water and squishes, in his waders, upstream. Bored, I follow him.

Around the bend, a man crouches next to some kind of electrical device. The wildlife man marches up to him.

"The governor hasn't gotten a nibble," he says, sternly. "Did you shock the fish to stun them like you were supposed to?"

"Yeah," says the crouching electrician.

"Well, do it again," says the wildlife man.

Then he marches back to the fishing party and I follow him. Everybody gets out of the water. Around the bend the electric man zaps the river. And soon some groggy coho salmon come floating around the bend, resting on their sides.

Jim Rhodes hops back into the river. He hoists a fish by the gills and turns, grinning, to the cameras. He addresses the reporters.

"Here boys," he says. "Have some feesh ..."

I finished reading the story. I remembered it all. Attached to the clipping was a note from a voter. The voter said she was writing to tell Dick Celeste that she had come across the story in a drawer and, after reading it, was certainly not going to vote for Jim Rhodes.

I handed the clipping to Celeste.

"Why don't you ever do anything like that?" I said.

"Like what?" he said.

"Stun fish," I said. "It probably would never occur to you, that's your trouble!"

Celeste looked puzzled. And I guess I don't blame him.

But the truth is, I'm going to miss Jim Rhodes. I can see that some of you want to argue about that, but I'm not interested. I didn't say I'd vote for him.

But miss him ... hell, yes.

Worth the Drive

52

American Electric Power ReCreation Land
Lake and Pond Fishing
State Route 83, McConnelsville, Ohio

> Recreational | Intermediate | Challenging
>
> **Water Type:** Inland lakes, ponds **Acreage:** 2,000 total
> **Access:** Shoreline, wading, canoe, boat
> **What's Biting:** Bluegill, largemouth bass, bullhead, catfish, sunfish
> **Season:** Year-round **Hours:** Open 24 hrs.
> **Fee:** Free **Permission:** Required
> **Facilities:** Boat launch, restrooms, picnic area, hiking trails, camping, ranger
> **Administered by:** American Electric Power
> **Directions:** I-77 south through Akron, Canton, and Cambridge; take Exit 25 (SR 78); west on SR 78 to SR 83; north on SR 83 into recreation area.

Description What visions come to mind when you think of coal mining? Deep, gaping holes in the earth. Streams polluted from runoff. Mountainous piles of dirt and coal. Well, pay a visit to the American Electric Power ReCreation Land, and you might form a different opinion.

Located in southern Ohio about 28 miles north of Marietta, the ReCreation Land is a 30,000-acre tract of forest, meadows, rolling hills, and ponds and lakes, all situated on land reclaimed from coal mining.

The rolling land just north of Marietta might not be the most productive farmland, but there is one thing that it is rich in—coal. Underneath layers of limestone, clay, and shale, lies an abundant seam of coal, some 3 ½ to 4 feet thick. The coal

American Electric Power

deposits found in this area most likely originated more than 300 million years ago in the Paleozoic or Carboniferous eras, when shallow seas or extensive swamps covered the surrounding lowlands and organic matter became partially decomposed. It probably took 12,000 to 15,000 years for the coal to form.

It is this coal that American Electric Power, through its affiliate, Central Ohio Coal Company, surface mines. When they are through mining the land, the company is responsible for restoring it back to something like its original condition. Fortunately, this is a responsibility that American Electric Power takes seriously. Since the utility started the surface mining operation back in the mid-1940s, it has planted more than 50 million trees and created more than 500 lakes and ponds in the ReCreation Land and in two other, smaller public wildlife areas.

Visitors to ReCreation Land are rewarded with a relaxing camping experience in a beautiful setting of woods and gently rolling hills. They are also rewarded with abundant fishing opportunities in any of the hundreds of lakes and ponds that dot the landscape. Many of the lakes are located adjacent to campgrounds and roads, offering easy access. Kids can have a great time catching panfish, bass, and catfish with nothing more complicated than a hook and bobber.

If solitude is what you are after, however, adventurous anglers can fish any of the numerous ponds and lakes located far off the beaten path and accessible only by trail. The hike to these ponds through woodland and meadow is reason enough to pay them a visit, but the fishing potential of some of these remote bodies of water is icing on the cake.

Fishermen will catch primarily largemouth bass, panfish, catfish, and carp from ReCreation Land ponds. The Ohio Division of Wildlife stocks selected ponds with yearling channel catfish averaging between 10 and 14 inches, although they will occasionally stock brood fish weighing in at a hefty eight pounds or so. The stocking is not substantial, with only two to four ponds per year receiving fish. The lakes in proximity to campgrounds, especially Campground C, are stocked most frequently, offering campers a convenient, productive fishing opportunity close to base camp.

Largemouth bass and bluegill, found in most of the other ponds and lakes, were stocked at one time but have since been able to maintain healthy populations through natural reproduction.

According to a representative from the Ohio Division of Wildlife District 4 office, some surprisingly large fish are pulled from ReCreation Land water, with a few 8-to-10-pound lunkers landed every year. The lakes and ponds have good, fertile soil, and their water has good alkalinity. Thanks to both of these factors, they can produce above-average amounts of phytoplankton and zooplankton and thus support a high concentration of bluegill and the other baitfish that feed on them. More bluegill and baitfish means one thing—more and bigger bass. In fact, the pounds-per-acre carrying capacity of ReCreation Land ponds and lakes exceeds that of most other reclamation ponds. This is good news for ReCreation Land anglers.

Standard bass tactics will work on ReCreation Land ponds, including spinner- and buzzbaits. Texas-rigged rubber worms are also effective, especially on the smaller, weed-filled ponds. For bluegill, small spinners, twister-tail-type spinners, and live bait all work. Worms and maggots on thin bait hooks will get you some frenzied panfish action.

Fishing is wonderful when combined with camping, because there is not the sense of urgency to get through the fishing trip and return home to the commitments that invariably await you there. You can spend the entire morning fishing, go back to camp for a short lunch, and then spend the rest of the day exploring new places to fish. Nighttime is spent huddled around a campfire, swapping stories of the one that got away.

It is estimated that ReCreation Land receives an average of 100,000 visitors per year. It costs about $300,000 per year to manage and maintain the land and the camping and picnic facilities, a tab picked up entirely by American Electric Power. Sure, they are the ones who mined the land in the first place. And, yeah, the positive publicity these public lands generate will certainly come in handy when deregulation hits the power industry. But how many other power companies have demonstrated such a commitment not only to the public, but to the environment? None. And for that reason alone the company should be given credit. They are providing the public with an opportunity to enjoy the outdoors in a wilderness setting uncharacteristic of much of Ohio's landscape.

There are nine campsites situated throughout this sprawling 30,000-acre recreation area, with a total of 380 designated camping sites available free of charge on a first-come, first-served basis. All of the campsites offer running water, latrines, and picnic tables.

The campsites are open year round. Ice fishing is permitted, depending on the weather and the condition of the ice. ReCreation Land's ponds and lakes often thaw earlier in the spring than ponds and lakes in Northeast Ohio, offering an excellent opportunity for those anglers champing at the bit to get their lines wet after a long, cold winter season. An important note: winter anglers will be sharing the woods with hunters, so exercise caution.

A permit is required for visiting ReCreation Land, as well camping there. The free permits and map are available through any of the following sources:

American Electric Power
P.O. Box 328, McConnelsville, OH 43756

Ohio Department of Natural Resources
Public Information Center
Fountain Square, 1952 Belcher Dr., Bldg. C-1
Columbus, OH 43224-1386

Permits can also be obtained from any Ohio Division of Wildlife office.

Worth the Drive

53

Chapman State Park
Chapman Lake, Tionesta River
Chapman State Park, Clarendon, PA

Recreational | Intermediate | Challenging

Water Type: River, inland lake **Acreage:** 68 acres

Access: Shoreline, canoe, boat

What's Biting: Bluegill, largemouth bass, smallmouth bass, sunfish, trout

Season: Year-round **Hours:**

Fee: Free; fee for camping and boat rental **Permission:** Not required

Facilities: Bait shop, boat rental, boat launch, restrooms, picnic area, food nearby, hiking trails, camping, ranger

Administered by: Pennsylvania Department of Conservation and Natural Resources

Directions: I-90 to Exit 1 in PA (US 6N); route becomes US 6; east on US 6 to Clarendon, PA; right at stoplight in Clarendon to Railroad St. (becomes Chapman Dam Rd.); road deadends at park (about 5 miles).

Description It's a liberating feeling when you are fishing and you realize that past that ridge of trees in the distance lies not an interstate highway or housing development, as is so often the case in Ohio, but even more forestland. And in the case of Chapman State Park, the 500,000 acres of trees that surround the park offer a sense of isolation that is rare in Ohio.

Situated in the northwest corner of the Allegheny National Forest, Chapman State Park (805 acres) offers extraordinary opportunities for outdoor recreation, including fishing, hiking, swimming, boating, cycling, and hunting. The park itself is kept in immaculate condition. There are more than 80 camping sites, several of which are walk-in sites, offering a bit more seclusion than the others.

Chapman State Park

Chapman State Park offers some wonderful fishing opportunities for trout, bluegill, and smallmouth bass in Chapman Lake (68 acres) and the West Branch of the Tionesta, which feeds into the lake at its southwest end.

Chapman Lake receives regular stockings of brook and brown trout, usually at least a couple thousand per stocking. Rainbow trout had his-

Worth the Drive

torically been stocked, but these fish could not tolerate the acid rain that fell on the lakes a couple decades ago, thanks to the industry in Youngstown, Pittsburgh, and Cleveland. Officials switched to brook and browns because of their tolerance for more acidic waters.

"The day I first came to this park in 1970," the park's manager told me, "we stocked 3,000 rainbow trout. That night it rained, and the next morning we collected 3,000 dead rainbow trout."

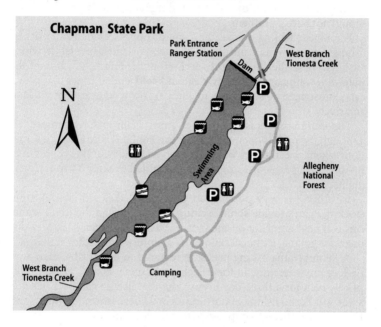

Chapman State Park

The lake's pH is currently close to the level it should be, but old habits die hard, and brookies and browns continue to be the species stocked at Chapman Lake. That's fine, because these fish fight hard and taste great. Anglers can also expect to catch smallmouth bass, bluegill, and crappie.

Maggots floated beneath a small bobber work well enough to fill an angler's creel with trout, and spinners and minnows can also be effective. June is the ideal time for fly fishermen because as the lake water begins to warm, the trout move closer to where the stream enters the lake. Fly fishermen flock to this area during June, pulling in trout which, according to the park's manager, are often released.

A boat rental is available and is a great way to access the lake. An aluminum rowboat costs $5 per hour to rent. Registered campers, however, have a special deal. They can rent a boat for $10 and keep it from 7 p.m. to 11 a.m. the next day, thereby taking advantage of great evening and morning fishing. There is a boat launch on Chapman Lake, but a free permit, available at the campground office, is required.

The West Branch of the Tionesta River, which feeds into the lake at its

Worth the Drive

northwest end, also provides some wonderful fishing for brook and brown trout. It is slightly more difficult fishing because the river flows through forested country, and much of its shoreline is tree-lined or brushy. Fly fishermen need to watch their backcasts, or they are destined to spend much of their time untangling their flies from trees and bushes. Anglers must be able to hike along the river, which, at times, can require navigating some fairly tricky terrain. However, there's really nothing too strenuous or difficult, and if you are in decent shape you should not have a problem.

For anglers willing to hike, the Tionesta offers secluded and pristine fishing conditions as it meanders through the state game lands, which are adjacent to the Chapman Park. Even in the middle of summer the water flows almost impossibly clear and cold, and at times the fishing can almost become secondary to enjoying the wild beauty of the land and river.

The campground is open from April 1 through December 15, although the park is open for fishing year round. There are no reservations taken for campsites, but other than on holiday weekends this does not present a problem. Campers are permitted to camp 14 consecutive nights.

Ice fishing is very popular on Chapman Lake, and late fall trout stockings can provide some exciting fishing through the ice. A winter carnival held annually on the first weekend in February features dog races, ice golfing, ice bocce ball, snow sculptures, and other activities.

A Pennsylvania fishing license is required to fish at Chapman State Park or anywhere else in the Allegheny National Forest. These can be pricey, even for a three-day license, but that license can be a ticket to some wonderful fishing opportunities in wilderness settings that, quite frankly, are difficult to impossible to find closer to home.

Worth the Drive

54

Lake La Su An
6901 County Rd. R, Montpelier, Ohio

Recreational | **Intermediate** | Challenging

Water Type: Inland lake **Acreage:** N/A

Access: Shoreline, pier, canoe, boat

What's Biting: Bluegill, largemouth bass, sunfish

Season: Year-round **Hours:** N/A

Fee: Free **Permission:** Required

Facilities: Boat launch, restrooms, food nearby, hiking trails

Administered by: Ohio Department of Natural Resources

Directions: I-80/I-90 west (Ohio Turnpike) past Toledo to Exit 2; north on SR 5; west on Alt-US 20 to County Rd. 7; right (north) for 3 miles to County Rd. "R"; left (west) on County Rd. "R" for one-quarter mile to the Lake La Su An checking station.

Description It can't be denied that bluegills are fun fish to catch. They are usually not too finicky, they fight well, and they taste great. Unfortunately, however, many anglers turn their backs on these scrappy panfish in search of the bigger-name sport fish, leaving bluegill to the amateurs.

Perhaps they've never hooked into a true trophy-sized bluegill, like one in the neighborhood of eight or nine inches. These fish are much more difficult to trick into biting, fight like small bulldogs, and can convert even the most loyal bass fisherman into a bluegill fan. Spend a day catching fish like these, and we'll see where your allegiances lie.

There might not be a better spot in the state to catch broiler-sized panfish than the Lake La Su An Wildlife Area, located about an hour west of Toledo in the northwest corner of Ohio. For a long day trip or weekend getaway, the beauty, seclusion, and fishing found in this wildlife area make it more than worth the trip.

The Lake La Su An Wildlife Area consists of more than 2,200 acres, and sprawled throughout it are 12 lakes that are managed strictly for the production of large bluegill. Size and bag-limit restrictions, combined with a reservation system that keeps angling pressure relatively low, are tactics employed to maintain this wonderful fishery. The limited number of anglers per lake helps with fish management but also ensures a relatively quiet, peaceful angling experience. All anglers must report to the main office before departing to check in the fish they've kept or report the number and sizes of the fish released.

The fishery of the Lake La Su An Wildlife Area is intensively managed to maintain a healthy, naturally reproducing population of large bluegills. Fishing with live bait is allowed during the early part of the

Worth the Drive

fishing season (except for minnows, which are verboten), and the daily size limit is 8 ½ inches. Every fish that is kept is checked in, and once a preset cutoff is reached, angling is restricted to artificial bait only and the minimum size is increased to 9 ½ inches. These measures make it harder to catch and keep the larger bluegill, thereby protecting the following season's population of large fish. I would therefore recommend visiting this area as early as possible to avoid these tighter restrictions. When it comes to catching bluegill, it is hard to beat the effectiveness of live bait.

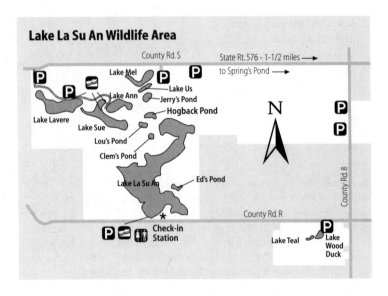

My trip to the Lake La Su An left a very positive impression. Although I did not catch any of the infamous pan-sized bluegill, I did land four broad-shouldered bass, ranging in size from 12 to 16 inches. Judging from the photos taken in 1997 of five- and six-pound bass taken from the area, I have no doubt that there are many bigger than the four I landed that day.

But it was the natural beauty of the area that most impressed me. If you are the type of fisherman who relishes fishing for its inherent fun but also appreciates the solitude it can provide, then this is a trip worth your while. I went the whole day and saw only two other people on the trail that circles Lake La Su An. The feeling of isolation was almost overwhelming.

Shoreline access is more than adequate on the lakes, and much of the shoreline is open for wading. If you plan to attack Lake La Su An from the shore, it is a good idea to bring some water and a small lunch, especially if you intend to hike around the entire lake on the gravel access road that rings it. I did it, and the heat and thirst made the last hour of the trip unnecessarily uncomfortable. Hiking fishermen have the added possibility of catching a glimpse of any number of animal species inhabiting the area, including wild turkey, white-tailed deer, ring-necked pheasants, coyotes, hawks, turkey vultures, and countless others. While hiking one section of the trail, I had been lulled into a daze by the heat and the steady rhythm of my hiking boots. I happened to glance up for a second, and found myself staring straight into the eyes of a strikingly brilliant red fox, which quickly scampered off into his forest home.

There are boat launches on the four largest lakes, which certainly opens those up. There is a lot of water that is inaccessible to shoreline fisherman but can prove to be very productive from a boat, especially one armed with a fishfinder. A handicapped-accessible fishing pier is located on the lake.

If you are planning a trip to the Lake La Su An Wildlife Area, be advised that advance reservations are necessary. Reservations are accepted by phone (419-636-6189) one week in advance for the wildlife area's six largest lakes, and they are taken on Monday, from 8 a.m. to noon, for the following Thursday, Friday, Saturday, Sunday, and Monday. All lakes are closed on Tuesdays and Wednesdays. This is such a popular place to fish that during peak times the demand far exceeds the available reservations, which are usually all filled within the first hour on Monday. Reservations will be accepted for no more than two people in each party, except for youth reservations, which can be made for two of the lakes. There are no restrictions on the number of young people in the party.

The lakes open for fishing from April 3 to October 10, although hours vary during this time. A current Ohio fishing license is required to fish any of the lakes. Ice fishing is allowed, but the specifics of when and how many fish can be caught are not available until all the data from the previous season can be assembled and analyzed. Call the park office for up-to-date ice-fishing information.

There are several motels located close to the Lake La Su An Wildlife Area, including the Exit 2 Motel (1-800-453-4511), a Holiday Inn (419-485-5555), and the Rainbow Motel (419-485-3432). If you'd like to rough it a bit more try one of the local campgrounds, such as the Funny Farm Campground (419-737-2467), Harrison Lake State Park (419-237-2593), the Lazy River Resort Campground (419-485-4411), and Shady Shore (419-459-4502).

Worth the Drive

55

Oak Orchard Creek
Point Breeze, NY

Recreational | **Intermediate** | **Challenging**

Water Type: River **Acreage:** N/A

Access: Shoreline, wading, canoe, boat

What's Biting: Smallmouth bass, chinook salmon, coho salmon, steelhead, brown trout, rainbow trout

Season: Year-round **Hours:** N/A

Fee: Free **Permission:** Not required

Facilities: Bait shop, boat launch, picnic area, food onsite, food nearby, hiking trails, camping

Administered by: N/A

Directions: I-90 east through Buffalo, NY, to Exit 48 (SR 98); north on SR 98 through Albion, NY, into Point Breeze.

Description I stood there, frozen, as the chinook salmon swam toward me. It was so huge that it created a wake like an Orca's. Before I could collect myself and move out of the way, it slammed into my leg. I stumbled for a second, and then looked over my shoulder to watch the anadromous brute plow its way upstream. Fish just shouldn't be this big, I thought to myself.

But in the Oak Orchard Creek they do come that big—and even bigger! Chinooks weighing in at 30 pounds, and brown trout tipping the scales at between 8 and 20. And don't forget about the coho salmon and steelhead. For sheer numbers and size, it is tough to beat Oak Orchard Creek.

Located in New York on the shores of Lake Ontario, Oak Orchard is about five hours away from Cleveland and more than worth the drive. I was lucky enough to visit and fish Oak Orchard Creek in the fall with my brother-in-law, Dave, an exceptionally experienced fisherman who has landed more than his share of bass, but never a 30-pound salmon.

I knew we were in trouble when we first reached the wading section of the river. Dead salmon as long as my leg littered the river bottom, having reached the final stop in their life's journey and now becoming food for other creatures. These things were enormous, and Dave and I could hardly speak, both of us thinking about what it might be like to have one of these monsters battling at the end of a fly rod. We found out soon enough—it felt like trying to reel in a locomotive traveling at full speed.

In early spring the steelhead and brown trout move into the river, with the average brown weighing 6 to 10 pounds. In the summer, all the fishing takes place out in the lake, where anglers deepwater troll for chinooks and coho. The fall action heats up early, as the migrating chinook start moving into the river in early September. Brown trout start their run shortly after that, with coho and steelhead not far behind. Depending on water conditions, this exciting fishing can continue right through the winter into May.

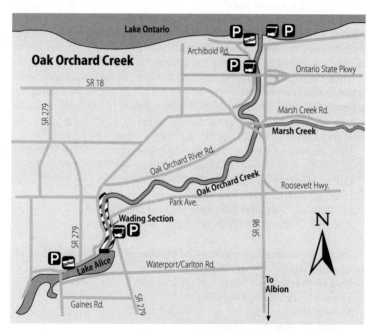

The migrating salmon are usually not very interested in eating, so hooking one is usually a matter of repeatedly sight-casting to a fish until it either gets so annoyed it strikes your fly, or you foul hook it. In the case of the latter, newcomers learn quickly that it is proper fishing etiquette to break off your line as quickly as possible.

Woolly Buggers in brown, purple, or olive are popular on the creek, although spawn patterns are also widely used. The spawn patterns are especially effective for the browns, which like to hang out below the spawning salmon and feast on their eggs. Fool 'em with a little faux caviar. I also came across a large black stonefly nymph that proved to be effective. It is one that I continue to tie today for local steelhead and panfish.

Oak Orchard is truly no place for the faint of heart. A 30-pound chinook salmon can peel your fly line right down to the backing in a matter of seconds, and a brown trout can do it even quicker. When hooked, the browns make a mad dash downstream toward Lake Ontario, usually with a frantic angler in waders sprinting close behind.

Heavy-duty equipment is a must. An 8- or 9-weight fly rod with plenty of backing is required. The incredible weight of these fish (which they will use to their advantage) can make it feel like you are pulling in a log, and battles can be excruciatingly long. A rod with some backbone is essential to provide continuous pressure to tire the fish out.

Dave and I stayed at the Four C's Marina, located right at the mouth of the Oak Orchard River where it dumps into Lake Ontario. For a very modest price we got a comfortable cottage complete with kitchen, showers, and two double beds. Regardless of where you stay, be sure to call early, as many of the hotels and such book up early.

There are more cottages, motels, bed and breakfasts, and campgrounds than can be listed here, so you will want to call for a complete list from the tourism hot line listed below. Before reserving a room, be sure to ask the proximity to the river, and ask if they have a guide service, and a place to freeze any fish you might want to bring home.

Here are some important numbers to know when planning your trip:

Orleans County Tourism Hotline: (800) 724-0314
Fishing Hotline: (716) 589-3220
Harry's Bait Shop and Boat Livery: (716) 682-3970
The Oak Orchard Fly Shop: (716) 682-4546

New York fishing licenses may be purchased at any bait and tackle store in the state, or by writing to:
NYS Department of Environmental Conservation
License Sales Office, Room 111
50 Wolf Road
Albany, New York 12233-4790

Worth the Drive

Fish Consumption

Besides being very delicious, fish are also an important nutritional element in many people's diets. They are very high in protein and low in saturated fat. Including plenty of fish in your diet is a great way to reduce the risk of heart disease and improve your overall health.

Unfortunately, the benefits of eating fish caught in local waters are tempered by risks. Polychlorinated Biphenyls (PCBs), Polycyclic Aromatic Hydrocarbons (PAHs), mercury, lead, and other chemicals one might expect to find in a chemist's lab are now widespread throughout our local waterways and therefore, unfortunately, in the fish we eat. Through decades of industrial pollution, chemical spills, and assorted other mishaps, we have tainted entire watersheds and the animals that live in them.

Every day we are exposed to small amounts of various chemicals found in our environment. At these levels the chemicals are considered safe, and exposure to them is deemed acceptable. Sometimes, though, elevated levels of harmful chemicals are found in the fish we consume, and that is when we need to take notice.

Even when environmental levels of a chemical are below the concentrations considered harmful, these concentrations can slowly increase as the chemicals progressively accumulate through the food chain. The higher we go on the food chain, the more concentrated these chemicals become. As predatory fish, such as walleye, consume smaller prey fish, they ingest harmful chemicals, which then accumulate in their fatty tissue. Over time, these concentrations can rise to dangerous levels.

Although the health effects of eating contaminated fish are not completely known, exposure even to low levels of contaminants is believed to be harmful on a regular basis. If a pregnant woman eats fish contaminated with PCBs, the birth weight of the baby may be affected, and even its behavior at later stages of development. PCBs, PAHs, Mirex, and chlordane do cause cancer in animals, and it is believed they can do the same in humans.

The recommended restrictions on consumption that have been put forth for various fish species are a source of contention between different interest groups, with many people believing that the Ohio Department of Health guidelines tend to be too strict. Well, that's fine by me, because when it comes to eating fish that is potentially contaminated with mercury, lead, or PCBs, I would rather err on the side of caution.

Who needs to be especially careful? According to the Ohio Department of Health's Fish Consumption Fact Sheet, "Groups of people who should be particularly careful include pregnant women because the fetus may have an increased sensitivity to chemicals, people who could become parents, the young, the old, and people having health problems that might be affected by the chemicals."

My only question is, Who's left?

It is troubling that we even need to worry about the presence of such terrible chemicals in the fish we catch from local waterways. But please remember that the benefits of including fish in your diet far outweigh the potential health risks, especially when you follow the recommended restrictions regarding fish consumption. It is very satisfying to dine on a meal of fish that you caught, and local anglers should not be afraid to enjoy the fruits of their angling labors.

Tips to Make Your Fish Safer for Consumption

The highest concentrations of dangerous chemicals are found in the fat of the fish, as opposed to the meat. You can therefore reduce your exposure to these harmful chemicals by removing the fat from the fish. Begin by removing the skin and trimming all the fat from the areas directly underneath it. Additional fat can be trimmed away from the underside of the fish (by cutting off the belly flaps) and along the sides and back. The fatty tissue is usually a different color from the rest of the meat and easily identifiable.

Cooking has no effect on the chemicals themselves, but it does melt away much of the remaining fat, taking the chemicals with it. By broiling, grilling, or baking the fish on a rack, you allow the fat and chemicals to drip away.

Unfortunately, these precautions are not effective in reducing the amount of mercury in the fish, because this nasty chemical is stored in its muscle tissue. To reduce mercury intake you must reduce your consumption of fish you suspect might be contaminated.

Species, age, size, location, and fat content are the factors that affect contaminant levels in fish. A large, old fish that has a high fat content is likely to contain higher levels of dangerous chemicals than a leaner, younger one, because it has had longer to accumulate them.

Following is a short list of some local waterways in which you might fish, and the advisories that are currently in place for them. One meal is considered to be one-half pound of fish (before cooking) for a 150-pound person. For more details on advisories statewide, please contact the Ohio Department of Health.

Fish Consumption Chart

Body of Water	Advisory Area	Species	Meal Frequency	Contaminant
Lake Erie	All Waters	Yellow Perch	No Restrictions	None
		Freshwater Drum	1 meal per week	PCBs
		Walleye		
		Chinook Salmon under 19"		
		White Perch	1 meal per month	PCBs
		Steelhead Trout		
		Coho Salmon		
		Chinook Salmon 19" +		
		Smallmouth Bass		
		White Bass		
		Carp under 20"		
		Carp 20" +	1 meal every 2 months	PCBs
		Channel Catfish		
		Lake Trout		
Conneaut Creek	All Waters	Smallmouth Bass	1 meal per month	Mercury
Ashtabula River	24th St. Bridge to Lake Erie	Rock Bass	No restrictions	None
		Smallmouth Bass	1 meal per week	PCBs
		Largemouth Bass	1 meal per month	Mercury/PCBs
		Walleye		
		Channel Catfish	1 meal every 2 months	PCBs
		Common Carp		
Chagrin River	All Waters	Rock Bass	1 meal per month	Mercury/lead
		Smallmouth Bass		
Cuyahoga River	Upstream of Ohio Edison Dam Pool	Rock Bass	No restrictions	None
		Bluegill		
		Smallmouth Bass		
		Pumpkinseed Sunfish		
	Ohio Edison Dam Pool to Lake Erie	White Sucker under 11"	1 meal per week	PCBs
		Common Carp	1 meal per month	PCBs
		White Sucker 11"+		
		Largemouth Bass	1 meal per month	Mercury
		Brown Bullhead	1 meal every 2 months	PCBs
		Yellow Bullhead		

Keeping a Journal

One sure way to increase your fishing success is to start keeping a fishing log. Experience is a great teacher, but it is the constant reflection on past experiences that makes great anglers. This is where fishing logs come in. They give you the opportunity to reflect on what did or did not work the last time you fished a certain destination, and will give you help in developing a strategy for your next fishing trip. The benefits are many.

Here are a few suggestions for what to keep in your fishing log:

- *Location*
- *Date and time*
- *Weather conditions*
- *Water conditions*
- *Lure or bait used*—include the size, and the presentation used.
- *Specific location*—use reference points so you will be able to locate that exact spot at a later date.
- *Fish caught*—include species, length, weight, and any other physical characteristics you might note.
- *Miscellaneous notes*—list any bird or other wildlife sightings here, along with any other memorable observations from your trip. Short anecdotal notes are wonderful to read during the cold months of winter or any other time you need an uplifting outdoor memory.

Keeping a log will not only make you a better fisherman, it will add depth to each fishing outing. It will compel you to take notice of your surroundings, and perhaps even make you appreciate them more.

Directory

Park Management Organizations

Ohio Department of Natural Resources Division of Wildlife
912 Portage Lakes Dr., Akron • (330) 644-2293

The Ohio Department of Natural Resources Division of Wildlife is responsible for managing many of our local rivers, ponds, and lakes. This is a great resource for learning more about local fishing and hunting opportunities. For a listing of maps and educational brochures, and other information, you can contact the Ohio Department of Natural Resources Public Information Center, Fountain Square, 1952 Belcher Dr., BLDG. C-1Columbus, OH 43224-1386; (614) 265-6605.

Cleveland Metroparks
4101 Fulton Pkwy., Cleveland • (216) 351-6300 (24-hour line)

Cleveland Metroparks, which encompasses more than 19,000 acres in five counties, was established in 1917 and since that time has provided wonderful outdoor recreational opportunities for the residents of Northeast Ohio. Personnel at the Natural Resources Office succeed in providing productive, fun fishing opportunities at their ponds and lakes despite the great amount of pressure they receive. They also sponsor children's fishing derbies and ice-fishing derbies and offer other educational fishing programs. Anglers are encouraged to donate to the Cleveland Metroparks to assist their fish-stocking program. A donation of $25 or more will provide the donor with a one-year membership to Cleveland Metroparks Fishing Fund. As a member, you will receive a window decal and *Fishing Lines*, their quarterly newsletter that includes updates on fishing programs. You can reach the Natural Resources Office at 9485 Eastland Rd., Strongsville, OH, 44136, or by calling (440) 234-9597. A public information hot line, which includes updates on ice conditions for ice fishermen, is available by calling (216) 351-6300 and going through the prompted menu.

Geauga Park District
9160 Robinson Rd., Chardon • (440) 285-2222 ext. 5420

Several of Geauga Park District's holdings offer fishing, and they do offer occasional fishing programs. Although they do not have any type of stocking or fish monitoring program in place yet, their ponds and lakes receive less pressure than those in the more populated counties, and one can still find fairly productive fisheries. Call them to receive the latest park district newsletter or individual park maps.

Lake Metroparks

Concord Woods, 1211 Spear Rd., Concord Township • (440) 639-7275; (800) 227-7275

Lake Metroparks, which currently manages more than 5,000 acres in Lake County, offers many pond, lake, Lake Erie shoreline, and river fishing opportunities in Lake County. The park district also works in conjunction with local and national fishing groups to sponsor fishing tournaments, symposiums, and how-to instructional programs. They have taken a very proactive role in preserving land along the Grand River corridor, helping to maintain the water quality of the river and preserve the unspoiled state of this largely undeveloped land. A free publication called *Parks Plus!* is a great way to learn about the fishing programs they periodically sponsor.

Lorain County Metro Parks

12882 Diagonal Rd., Lagrange • (440) 458-5121; (800) 526-7275.

Beginning with the donation of Mill Hollow in 1958, Lorain County Metro Parks has steadily grown to nine open parks encompassing almost 6,000 acres. Their parks offer an assortment of opportunities for outdoor activities, including hiking, golfing, bird-watching, sledding, and, of course, fishing. There are fishing opportunities along both the Vermilion and Black rivers, along with several small ponds suitable for fishing. Their bimonthly publication, *The Arrowhead*, is available by calling the park office.

Medina County Park District

6364 Deerview Ln., Medina • (330) 722-9364

The Medina County Park District was formed in 1965 with the intention of preserving the natural features of the county. Given the high rate of development in Medina County, their mission is certainly a necessary one. They currently manage 12 open parks, several of which have small ponds on the premises offering potentially productive fishing. They also sponsor a Youth Fishing Derby every spring for kids ages 15 and younger. Call the park district's main office for more information on individual parks or for updated fishing derby information.

Fishing and Conservancy Organizations

Ashtabula County Rod and Reel Association
619 W. 33rd St., Ashtabula • (write for information)

The Ashtabula Rod and Reel Association has been around for about 15 years. There are currently about 60 members in the club, but they are looking to increase this number. Membership is $15 per year; rates are adjusted for seniors and kids. Each year they sponsor a kids' fishing day in July. They are also active in protecting the natural resources in Ashtabula County.

Chagrin River Salmon Association
38375 Tamarac Blvd. #105-2, Willoughby • (440) 269-1759

The Chagrin River Salmon Association was formed in 1973, taking its name from the coho salmon that were being stocked in area rivers at the time. The coho salmon may be long gone, replaced by the steelhead that are currently stocked, but the Chagrin River Salmon Association is still going strong. There are approximately 100 members in the organization, which takes pride in being very active in the community. Activities range from fish fries to a fishing derby held every June at the CEI breakwall. Monthly meetings are held the last Wednesday of the month at the JFK Senior Center in Eastlake, and presentations cover fishing and conservation-related topics. A year's membership will cost you $15.

Cleveland Museum of Natural History Trout Club
Cleveland Museum of Natural History
1 Wade Oval, Cleveland • (216) 231-4600

The Cleveland Museum of Natural History Trout Club is a wonderful opportunity for fly fishers who are passionate about not only the sport of fly-fishing, but the heritage and history behind it. The Trout Club, which boasts more than 300 members, holds dinner meetings the third Wednesday of every month from October to May. These meetings are held at the Cleveland Museum of Natural History and cost around $20, which covers the cost of the meal and the speaker. Monthly speakers include noted fly-fishing personalities, fly tiers, guides, artists, and others. These speakers are normally the heavy hitters of the fly-fishing world, nationally known and very knowledgeable. Museum membership ($35 individual/$55 family) is required to join the Trout Club, which costs $25 for an individual membership and $35 for a family membership. The Outings Committee organizes fly-fishing trips to surrounding states.

Directory

Cool Running Bass Masters

4063 Mooreland Ave., Willoughby • (440) 953-0295

If bass fishing is your game, then Cool Running Bass Masters might be just the group for you. The group consists of 28 dedicated, knowledgeable bass anglers who all share a singular passion for catching largemouth and smallmouth bass. They fish many of the local reservoirs and also hit East and West Side rivers and Lake Erie. Cool Running members participate in Bass Master tournaments, starting first at the local level, and then progressing through the regional, state, divisional, and national tournaments—as far as their talent and luck can take them. There is the possibility of making it all the way to the Bass Masters Classic, the true granddaddy of bass fishing tournaments. Interested anglers must go through an application procedure before joining and can get information on it by calling the number listed above.

Northcoast Fly Fishers

Concord • (800) 227-7275

This is an absolutely great fishing club. Monthly meetings held on the East Side provide a wealth of information on fly-fishing and fly tying. The first hour is spent tying flies, with instruction given so that even a first-time tier can leave with a finished product. In the second hour of each meeting, a presentation is given by a professional fly tier or fly fisherman. The meetings are enjoyable, and there is a great feeling of cooperation among members. Annual membership is $10, which includes a monthly newsletter.

Northeast Ohio Walleye Association

1351 East 357th St. Unit 2, Eastlake • (440) 946-8877

The Northeast Ohio Walleye Association is a great source of fishing information but also takes pride in being very community oriented. The 50-member group sponsors fishing derbies and contests and makes every effort to work with kids to get them interested in fishing. Conservation plays a large role in this club's activities. They also sponsor a summer walleye fishing contest for Walleye Association members, and several annual ice-fishing trips. Meetings are held on the East Side on the first Tuesday of the month and feature speakers who talk about conservation, fishing methods, equipment, and other fishing-related subjects. Membership is $15 for the first year, $10 every year after that.

Ohio Central Basin Steelheaders

P.O. Box 29577, Parma, OH 44129 • (write for information)

The Ohio Central Basin Steelheaders (OCBS) is an association of fishermen dedicated to the protection and promotion of sportfishing in Ohio. It is a great group that emphasizes preservation of clean water, education, and the fun of fishing. Club activities include monthly meetings, tournaments, raffles, and an annual Kids Day Fishing Derby in cooperation with Cleveland Metroparks. Both novice and experienced

Directory

steelhead fishermen can benefit from the experience of club members and from the information presented at each meeting. New memberships cost $25, and renewals cost $20. For information on meetings, call Grand River Tackle (440-352-7222), L&D Bait & Tackle (216-226-FISH), or Rodmakers Shoppe (440-572-0400).

Ohio Huskie Muskie Club, Inc.
5170 Deer Rd., SW, Bowerston • (740) 269-2122

The Ohio Huskie Muskie Club, Inc., is a statewide organization for those who have been bitten by the muskie bug. Membership is $12 per year for individuals and $20 for families. The club sponsors an outing in the spring and fall, and a summer tournament. Locations vary for both outings and the tournament each year. They also participate in the Ohio Division of Wildlife scale sample program. Club members send in a scale sample of muskies they catch, along with weight, length, date, and location caught. This information gives wildlife officials vital information which they use in their muskie stocking program.

Rod and Reel Association
c/o Grand River Tackle (440-352-7222) or D & W Bait and Tackle (440-354-8473)

The Rod and Reel Association is a nonprofit group that centers primarily around the Lake Erie fishery. They have as their motto "Fishermen for cleaner water" and therefore make it their mission to stay abreast of issues concerning water quality. Like many of the fishing organizations, these anglers work closely with their community. They co-sponsor a kids' fishing tournament in June with the *News Herald*, attracting between 400 and 600 kids. Meetings, which are open to the public, are held on the third Thursday of each month at the Fairport Harbor VFW Hall and usually feature a guest speaker. The gentlemen I spoke with from this club were extremely well informed, making this a very valuable organization for anybody interested in learning more about local fisheries, especially Lake Erie. For more information, please contact Grand River Tackle (440-352-7222), or D & W Bait and Tackle (440-354-8473).

Directory

Bait Shops

Angler's Mail   ☎ (440) 884-7877
6495 Pearl Rd., Parma Hts.   South
Lures, tackle, fly-tying equip., fly-fishing equip., clothing
Hours: Mon 12 p.m.–8 p.m., Tue–Fri 10 a.m.-5:30 p.m., Sat 10 a.m.-4 p.m.; closed Sun
Specializes almost exclusively in fly-fishing equipment. Large selection of books and videos. Free
introductory fly-casting lessons available.

Atlantic Gun & Tackle   ☎ (216) 475-5240
5425 Northfield Rd., Bedford Hts.   East
Live bait, lures, tackle, fly-tying equip., fly-fishing equip., boating supplies, clothing
Hours: Mon–Fri 10 a.m.–9 p.m., Sat–Sun 10 a.m.–6 p.m.
Very large selection of fishing rods and other tackle, plus hunting equipment.

Atlantic Gun & Tackle   ☎ (440) 526-1176
7594 Chippewa Rd. (State Routes 21 & 82), Brecksville   South
Live bait, lures, tackle, fly-tying equip., fly-fishing equip., boating supplies, clothing
Hours: Mon–Fri 10 a.m.–9 p.m., Sat 9 a.m.–6 p.m.; closed Sun
Very large selection of fishing rods and other tackle, plus hunting equipment.

Atwell's Sporting Goods   ☎ (440) 352-0758
205 Chestnut St., Painesville   Farther East
Lures, tackle, clothing
Hours: Mon & Wed–Fri 9 a.m.–5 p.m., Tue 9 a.m.–8 p.m., Sat 9 a.m.–2 p.m.; closed Sun
Primarily a hunting store, but they do carry an assortment of fishing tackle. They also have
outdoor clothing and camping equipment.

Bait Box, The   ☎ (440) 967-5107
3655 Liberty Ave., Vermilion   Farther West
Live bait, lures, tackle, boating supplies
Hours: Daily 6 a.m.–6 p.m.
Formerly known as Wharf Marine Corp.

Bilicic's Country Mall   ☎ (440) 466-9111
5218 Township Rd., Harpersfield   Farther East
Live bait, lures, tackle, clothing
Hours: Daily 7 a.m.–11 p.m.
About a one-quarter mile south of I-90 on State Route 534. They are primarily a convenience/gro-
cery store, but they do carry a decent selection of tackle and live bait.

Bobber's   ☎ N/A
Washington St., Mantua   Farther East
Live bait, lures, tackle
Hours: Dawn–dusk
A small but well stocked bait store with the latest information on fishing conditions at nearby
LaDue Reservoir. Food and beverages also available. Open spring until fall.

Bradstreet's Landing Bait Shop   ☎ (440) 331-3800
22464 Lake Rd., Rocky River   West
Live bait, lures, tackle
Hours: Daily 6 a.m.–11:30 p.m..
Located at Bradstreet's Landing, Rocky River's municipal fishing pier, it's open from April to
November. A convenience store/deli, the Treasure Cove, is located next to the entrance to
Bradstreet's and is open year-round. They sell worms only.

Causeway Sporting Goods
☎ (330) 637-7076
Farther East
2233 Greenville Rd., Cortland
Live bait, lures, tackle, fly-fishing equip.
Hours: Summer: daily ½ hour before sunrise to 10 p.m.; Winter: Mon–Sat 9 a.m.–5 p.m.
On the east side of Mosquito Lake on State Route 88. They have rowboat, boat, and motor rentals and an excellent selection of fishing supplies.

Civitarese's
☎ N/A
East
10 Erie St., Eastlake
Live bait, tackle
Hours: N/A
Housed in a trailer on the CEI breakwall in Eastlake. Selection is limited. Food and beverages available.

Country Style Drive-In
☎ (440) 635-5716
Farther East
15052 Mayfield Rd., East Claridon
Live bait, lures, tackle
Hours: Open year round, but hours vary; call ahead.
Located on US Route 322 about a hundred feet from the East Branch Reservoir causeway in Headwaters Park.

Covered Bridge Bait & Tackle
☎ (440) 466-0476
Farther East
County Rd. 154, Harpersfield
Live bait, lures, tackle, fly-fishing equip.
Hours: Daily 8 a.m.-8 p.m.
Open April through November, depending on the weather and how the fish are running. A small selection of food and beverages. Great access to both the Grand River and Harpersfield Covered Bridge.

D & W Bait & Tackle
☎ (440) 354-8473
Farther East
786 Richmond St., Painesville
Live bait, lures, tackle, fly-fishing equip., boating supplies
Hours: Open daily; off-season: 8 a.m.–6 p.m.; peak season: 5:30 a.m.–9 p.m.
Located close to the Grand River and Lake Erie.

Emerald Necklace Marina Bait Shop
☎ (216) 226-3030
West
Rocky River Scenic Park, 1500 Scenic Park Dr. (off Valley Pkwy.), Lakewood
Live bait, lures, tackle, fly-fishing equip., boating supplies
Hours: Mon–Fri 8:30 a.m.–9 p.m., Sat–Sun 8 a.m.–9 p.m.
Sweetwater Landing Restaurant also located on the premises. Rocky River Reservation Scenic Park boat launch is nearby.

Erieshore Bait & Tackle
☎ (440) 942-3470
East
35608 Lake Shore Blvd., Eastlake
Live bait, lures, tackle
Hours: Summer: Mon–Sat 6 a.m.–9 p.m., Sun 6 a.m.–8 p.m.; Winter: Mon–Fri 6 a.m.–9 p.m., Sat 8 a.m.–9 p.m., Sun 8 a.m.–6 p.m.
Located just down the street from the CEI Breakwall and adjacent to the Chagrin River.

Findley Lake Bait Shop
☎ (440) 647-3322
Farther West
Findley State Park (State Route 58), Wellington
Tackle, live bait, lures, fly-fishing equipment, boat supplies
Hours: Daily 7 a.m.–7 p.m. (Apr–Oct)
Located at the Findley Lake Beach area in Findley State Park

Fisherman's
☎ (440) 293-5779
Farther East
5579 Lake Rd., Andover
Live bait, lures, tackle, boating supplies
Hours: Spring through fall: 6 a.m.–10 p.m.
A stone's throw from Pymatuning State Park.

Directory

Frank's Edgewater Tackle
☎ (216) 281-4900
West
Edgewater Park, Memorial Shoreway West (State Route 2), Cleveland
Live bait, lures, tackle
Hours: Daily 7 a.m.–10 p.m.
Located adjacent to the fishing pier at Edgewater Park.

Frank's Tackle Co.
☎ (216) 961-4000
West
10802 Madison Ave., Cleveland
Live bait, lures, tackle, boating supplies
Hours: Mon–Fri 6 a.m.-8 p.m.; Sat–Sun 6 a.m.-9 p.m.; open thru December (call for winter hours)
Basic terminal tackle with a complete line of live bait. Also a convenience store, so you can stock up on other outing necessities. About 10 minutes from Edgewater Park and Rocky River Metropark.

Gateway Bait & Tackle
☎ (440) 293-7227
Farther East
6517 State Route 85, Andover
Live bait, lures, tackle
Hours: Daily 5 a.m.–10 p.m.
A convenient stop for Pymatuning-bound anglers; open year round.

Geneva Bait & Tackle
☎ (440) 466-7683
Farther East
4140 North Broadway, Geneva
Live bait, lures, tackle, boating supplies
Hours: Vary, but usually by summer they open at sunrise and close in the evening.
For marine supplies, this is the place to go in the Geneva area. Usually opens sometime in spring, but that varies with the weather. Stop by or call to arrange a fishing charter out of Geneva State Park, as they have information on the charters and the fishing conditions.

Geneva State Park Marina
☎ (440) 466-7565
Farther East
Padanarum Rd., Geneva
Live bait, lures, tackle, boating supplies
Hours: Daily 7 a.m.-8 p.m., extended hours on weekends
Open from May 1 through October 31, the marina's bait shop sells gasoline, boating essentials, food and drink, and bait. It has a small selection of fishing and boating gear, and is a good resource for fishing information. Hours are limited at the start and end of the boating season.

George's Bait Shop
☎ (440) 282-2660
Farther West
5150 W. Erie Ave., Lorain
Live bait, lures, tackle, fly-tying equip., fly-fishing equip., boating supplies
Hours: Daily 6 a.m.–8 p.m.
Complete selection of local bait and tackle. Up-to-date area fishing report posted daily.

Grand River Tackle
☎ (440) 352-7222
Farther East
1250 High St., Fairport Harbor
Live bait, lures, tackle, fly-fishing equip.
Hours: Mon–Sat 6 a.m.–8 p.m., Sun 6 a.m.–5 p.m.
Located 500 feet north of the Richmond Street Bridge. Fishermen can call for up-to-date fishing conditions 24 hours a day, year round. Grand River Tackle offers river guides for the Grand, Conneaut, Elk, and Chagrin rivers. Rod and reel repair service available.

Hot-Spot Bait & Tackle
☎ (724) 932-3630
Farther East
1 Gibson St., Jamestown, PA
Live bait, lures, tackle
Hours: Daily 6 a.m.–8 p.m.
Close to Pymatuning State Park.

Hotwaters Bait & Tackle
☎ (440) 244-6301
Farther West
116 W. 1st St., Lorain
Live bait, lures, tackle, fly-tying equip., fly-fishing equip., boating supplies
Hours: Mon–Thu 6 a.m.–9 p.m., Fri–Sun 5 a.m.–9 p.m.
Large selection of gear, with easy access to Lake Erie from Hotwaters Marina. Boat rental available at Findley State Park.

Jamestown Boat Livery
☎ (724) 932-3267
Farther East
281 Orangeville Rd., Greenville, PA
Live bait, lures, tackle, boating supplies
Hours: 6 a.m.–8 p.m. (open until dusk in the summer)
Located at the south end of Pymatuning State Park off US Route 322. Boat rentals begin in early spring. Available watercraft: pontoons, motorboats, rowboats, canoes, and paddleboats.

Karran Shop, Inc.
☎ (440) 466-3561
Farther East
413 South Ridge East, Geneva
Live bait, lures, tackle, fly-fishing equip., boating supplies
Hours: Mon–Fri 9 a.m.–6 p.m., Sat 9 a.m.–5 p.m., Sun 9 a.m.–noon
Easy to pass by because of its small size, but the amount of merchandise stocked inside is incredible. About one-half mile east of SR 534.

Ketchmore Rod & Tackle
☎ (216) 961-1770
West
5405 Detroit Ave., Cleveland
Live bait, lures, tackle, fly-tying equip., fly-fishing equip., boating supplies
Hours: Summer: daily 5:30 a.m.–11 p.m.; Winter: daily 7 a.m.–7:00 p.m.
Good selection of hand-tied flies and other fishing tackle.

L & D Bait & Tackle
☎ (216) 226-3474
West
18508 Detroit Ave., Lakewood
Live bait, lures, tackle
Hours: Mon–Fri 6 a.m.–8 p.m., Sat 5:30 a.m.–8 p.m.; Sun 5:30 a.m.–6 p.m.; Winter hours: daily 6:30 a.m.–6 p.m.
Within walking distance of Scenic Park on the Rocky River. Offers charter services for stripers and walleye and a guide service for the Rocky River. Also features a taxidermy service for fish and deer.

LaDue Reservoir Boathouse
☎ (440) 834-4939
Farther East
17759 Valley Rd., Mantua
Live bait, lures, tackle, fly-fishing equip., boating supplies
Hours: N/A
See main entry for boat rental information.

Lakeside Bait & Tackle
☎ (800) 937-5668; (440) 288-2002
Farther West
925 Colorado Ave., Lorain
Live bait, lures, tackle, boating supplies
Hours: Mon–Fri 6 a.m.–9 p.m.; Sat, Sun 5 a.m.–9 p.m.
A full-service tackle shop for Lake Erie that boasts an excellent selection of trolling equipment, lures, live bait, and other tackle. E-mail address for more info: capteye@centuryinter.net.

LCCAA Bait and Tackle
☎ N/A
Farther West
301 Lakeside Ave., Lorain
Live bait, lures, tackle
Hours: Open during the warm-weather months only
Located near the "mile-long pier" at Marina International in Lorain. Operated by the Lorain County Community Action Agency.

Medina Fish Hatchery
☎ (330) 725-8018
Farther South
3148 Sharon-Copley Rd., Medina
Live bait, lures, tackle
Hours: Fri–Mon 7:30 a.m.–5 p.m.; closed Tue, Wed, Thu
Bait and equipment available on the premises. (Please see main entry.)

Minnow Bucket, The
☎ (440) 257-7046
Farther East
8292 Lake Shore Blvd., Mentor
Live bait, lures, tackle, boating supplies
Hours: Spring: 7 a.m.–6 p.m.; Summer: 5:30 a.m.–10 p.m.
Located less than a quarter-mile from Veterans Park in Mentor, this is a convenient stop for anglers heading to Veterans Park or Lake Erie. A live-bait vending machine is available outside the store.

Directory

Molnar Outdoor
☎ (440) 986-3366
9191 Leavitt Rd., Elyria
Farther West
Live bait, lures, tackle, fly-tying equip., fly-fishing equip., clothing
Hours: Mon–Sat from 10 a.m.–6 p.m., Sun noon–5 p.m.

Monty's Mosquito Lake Restaurant and Carryout
☎ (330) 638-5598
1241 Greenville Rd., Cortland
Farther East
Live bait, lures, tackle, fly-fishing equip.
Hours: Summer: daily 5 a.m.–11 p.m.; Winter: Mon–Sat 6 a.m.–9 p.m., Sun 7 a.m.–9 p.m.
Located on the west side of Mosquito Lake. Full-service restaurant on the premises.

Northfield Gun & Tackle
☎ (330) 468-0676
30 W. Aurora Rd., Northfield
East
Live bait, lures, tackle, fly-fishing equip.
Hours: Mon–Wed 8 a.m.–6 p.m., Thu–Fri 8 a.m.–8 p.m., Sat 9 a.m.–5 p.m.; closed Sun
Sponsors an annual fishing derby at LaDue Reservoir, usually in late May or early June. Charter
service and guide information available.

One Stop Fishing Shop Ltd.
☎ (440) 834-2248
11799 Washington St., Burton
Farther East
Live bait, lures, tackle, boating supplies
Hours: Summer: 6 a.m.–7 p.m.; Winter: 7 a.m.–4 p.m.
Located conveniently close to LaDue Reservoir, open daily. Sponsors one crappie and two walleye
tournaments per year on LaDue Reservoir. Rents trolling motors, and also sells a type of small boat
called Waterbusters—cute little craft ideal for fishing Northeast Ohio's lakes and reservoirs.

Parma Bait and Tackle
☎ (216) 398-9877
5341 Broadview Rd., Parma
Farther East
Wide supply of tackle for bass, walleye, steelhead, and panfish. Also carry live bait. Will be
expanding their fly fishing inventory. They have a 24 hour live bait vending machine.
Hours: Mon–Fri 9 a.m.–6 p.m. During boat season they open around 6 a.m.

Punderson Marina Bait Shop
☎ (440) 564-5246
Punderson State Park 11755 Kinsman Rd., Newbury
Farther East
Live bait, lures, tackle, fly-fishing equip., boating supplies
Hours: Mon–Fri 7 a.m.–8 p.m., Sat–Sun 7 a.m.–9 p.m.
Operated by Newman Outfitters.

Rich's Hook, Line & Sinker
☎ (440) 967-2750
5200 Ohio St., Vermilion
Farther West
Live bait, lures, tackle
Hours: 4:30 a.m.–dusk
Has an efficiency rental that sleeps up to four people located conveniently near a boat ramp and
the Vermilion River.

Rodmakers Shoppe, The
☎ (440) 572-0400
20884 Royalton Rd., Strongsville
South
Live bait, lures, tackle, fly-tying equip., fly-fishing equip., clothing
Hours: Mon, Thu–Fri 10 a.m.–9 p.m., Tue–Wed, Sat 10 a.m.–5 p.m.
Located on the corner of State Route 82 and Prospect in Royalville Plaza. Has one of the largest
selections of fishing tackle in the state. Also sells most kinds of live bait, except minnows.

Shine's Live Bait, Tackle & Beverage
☎ (216) 431-9090
1293 East 55th St., Cleveland
East
Live bait, lures, tackle
Hours: Daily 5:30 a.m.–7 p.m.
Conveniently located near the E. 55th St. Marina and Gordon Park fishing areas. The fish report on
the chalkboard tracks warm-water discharge from the CEI plant on E. 72nd. (The warm water
attracts schools of minnows and other baitfish.)

Sonny Shore's Live Bait
☎ (216) 486-8220
17700 Lake Shore Blvd., Cleveland
East
Live bait, lures, tackle, fly-fishing equip., boating supplies

Hours: Mon–Sat 8 a.m.–8 p.m., Sun 8 a.m.–4 p.m.
Located near Wildwood State Park; open year round.

Tackleshack, The ☎ (330) 929-9977
2769 Front Street (State Route 59), Cuyahoga Falls — **Farther South**
Live bait, lures, tackle, fly-fishing equip., boating supplies, clothing
Hours: Mon–Fri 8 a.m.–8 p.m.; Sat, Sun 7 a.m.–7 p.m.; Winter: Daily 9 a.m.–7 p.m.
Besides having a good selection of live bait, tackle, and lures, this place provides a boat and canoe rental service on the Cuyahoga (after April 1), allowing anglers to try their luck for the pike and bass that inhabit this section of the Cuyahoga. Also rents fishing videos, including six videos that were shot right there on the Cuyahoga and deal with fishing on that stretch of the river. A full-service Bass Pro Shop.

Ted's Bait & Tackle ☎ (216) 651-5321
4417 Detroit Ave., Cleveland — **West**
Live bait, lures, tackle, fly-fishing equip.
Hours: Summer: daily 6 a.m.–10 p.m.; Winter: 9 a.m.–5 p.m.
Near the West Memorial Shoreway (State Route 2) and minutes from Edgewater Park.

Wildwood Marina ☎ (216) 481-5771
Wildwood/Villa Angela State Park, 16975 Wildwood Dr. (Off Lake Shore Blvd.), Euclid — **East**
Live bait, lures, tackle, boating supplies, clothing
Hours: Mon–Fri 6:30 a.m.–9 p.m., 5:30 a.m.-9 p.m.
Located at Wildwood/Villa Angela State Park Marina.

Other Gear Suppliers

American Sportsman Shop ☎ (440) 235-2144
27097 Bagley Rd., Olmsted Township — **West**
Live bait, lures, tackle, clothing
Hours: Mon, Tue, Thu 11 a.m.–7 p.m.; Wed, Fri 10 a.m.–9 p.m.; Sat 10 a.m.–6 p.m.; closed Sun
Specializes in hunting, fishing, and archery equipment.

Angler's Mail ☎ (440) 884-7877
6495 Pearl Rd., Parma Hts. — **South**
Lures, tackle, fly-tying equip., fly-fishing equip., clothing
Hours: Mon 12 p.m.–8 p.m., Tue–Fri 10 a.m.-5:30 p.m., Sat 10 a.m.-4 p.m.; closed Sun
Specializes almost exclusively in fly-fishing equipment. Large selection of books and videos. Free introductory fly-casting lessons available.

Atlantic Gun & Tackle ☎ (216) 475-5240
5425 Northfield Rd., Bedford Hts. — **East**
Live bait, lures, tackle, fly-tying equip., fly-fishing equip., boating supplies, clothing
Hours: Mon–Fri 10 a.m.–9 p.m., Sat–Sun 10 a.m.–6 p.m.
Very large selection of fishing rods and other tackle, plus hunting equipment.

Atlantic Gun & Tackle ☎ (440) 526-1176
7594 Chippewa Rd. (State Routes 21 & 82), Brecksville — **South**
Live bait, lures, tackle, fly-tying equip., fly-fishing equip., boating supplies, clothing
Hours: Mon–Fri 10 a.m.–9 p.m., Sat 9 a.m.–6 p.m.; closed Sun
Very large selection of fishing rods and other tackle, plus hunting equipment.

Directory

Atwell's Sporting Goods
☎ (440) 352-0758
Farther East

205 Chestnut St., Painesville
Lures, tackle, clothing
Hours: Mon & Wed–Fri 9 a.m.–5 p.m., Tue 9 a.m.–8 p.m., Sat 9 a.m.–2 p.m.; closed Sun
Primarily a hunting store, but they do carry an assortment of fishing tackle. They also have outdoor clothing and camping equipment.

Backpackers Shop-Ohio Canoe
☎ (440) 835-0861
Farther West

5128 Colorado Ave., Sheffield Village
Fly-tying equip., fly-fishing equip., clothing
Hours: Mon–Thu 10 a.m.–9 p.m., Fri & Sat 10 a.m.–6 p.m., Sun noon–5 p.m.
The Backpackers Shop-Ohio Canoe offers an excellent selection of outdoor gear, canoes, and miscellaneous recreational equipment. They are also an Orvis dealer, offering a great selection of fly rods, reels, and fly-tying equipment.

Dick's Sporting Goods
Various locations
Lures, tackle, fly fishing equip., boating supplies, clothing
Dick's has a surprisingly large and comprehensive supply of fishing gear, including rods, reels, and most of the brand-name tackle and lures. Fly-fishing equipment also available. Also on hand are boating supplies and other outdoor equipment.

East	North Randall: 21250 Miles Rd., (216) 587-0080
	Highland Hts.: 6235 Wilson Mills Rd., (440) 449-9199
	Mentor: 9565 Mentor Ave., (440) 354-8800
South	Middleburg Hts.: 6875 Southland Dr., (440) 886-2600
	Akron: 4036 Medina Rd., (330) 668-1231

Kmart
Various locations—see below
Lures, tackle, boating supplies, clothing

East	Chagrin Falls: 17625 Chillicothe Rd., (440) 543-1833
	Cleveland: 7701 Broadview Rd., (216) 524-0180
	Eastlake: 33752 Vine St., (440) 946-2906
	Euclid: 26100 Euclid Ave., (216) 261-3117
	Euclid: 1200 Babbitt Rd., (216) 289-4040
	Garfield Hts.: 12501 Rockside Rd., (216) 261-3117
	Maple Hts.: 21000 Libby Rd., (216) 663-0600
	Solon: 6221 SOM Ctr. Rd., (440) 248-3313
Farther East	Mentor: 9200 Mentor Ave., (440) 974-6434
	Warren: 2485 Parkman Rd. NW, (330) 898-4387
Farther South	Akron: 2975 S. Arlington Rd., (330) 644-7113
	Akron: 4040 Medina Rd., (330) 668-2755
	Barberton: 241 Wooster Rd. N., (330) 745-4426
	Brunswick: 3301 Center Rd., (330) 225-0700
	Canton: 3801 Harmont Ave., (330) 453-8418
	Kent: 1830 E. Main St., (330) 673-4903
	Medina: 1105 N. Court St., (330) 722-1127
	North Canton: 1446 N. Main St., (330) 821-3019
	Stow: 4332 Kent Rd., (330) 688-7461
	Streetsboro: 9059 State Route 14, (330) 626-4946
	Tallmadge: 555 South Ave., (330) 630-2990
	Wadsworth: 180 Green Oaks Tr., (330) 336-7644
Farther West	Elyria: 445 Midway Blvd., (440) 324-5757
	Lorain: 5350 Leavitt Rd., (440) 282-3015
South	Macedonia: 500 E. Aurora Rd., (330) 468-0787
	Brooklyn: 7700 Brookpark Rd., (216) 485-9400
	Cleveland: 14901 Lorain Ave., (216) 671-2122

Directory

Cleveland: 3250 W. 65th, (216) 961-0900
Middleburg Hts.: 17840 Bagley Rd., (440) 234-9303
Westlake: 30010 Detroit Rd., (440) 871-8300

Molnar Outdoor
☎ (440) 986-3366
Farther West
9191 Leavitt Rd., Elyria
Live bait, lures, tackle, fly-tying equip., fly-fishing equip., clothing
Hours: Mon–Sat from 10 a.m.–6 p.m., Sun noon–5 p.m.

Pine Lake Fly Shop
☎ (440) 543-8322
Farther East
17021 Chillicothe Rd. P.O. Box 23282, Chagrin Falls
Lures, tackle, fly-tying equip., fly-fishing equip., clothing
Hours: Spring, summer, and fall: Tue–Sun 10 a.m.–6 p.m.
Pine Lake Fly Shop is an open-to-the-public store located on the premises of a private fishing club owned by the same people who run the Valley Angler. It is primarily a fly-fishing shop, offering fly-tying classes and fly-fishing instruction and dealing exclusively in Orvis equipment and clothing. They do sell worms in the summer, but I cannot verify if these are Orvis-certified worms. The merchandise is all very high quality, and both the Pine Lake Fly Shop and the Valley Angler have a sort of Montana-ish feel to them.

Rodmakers Shoppe, The
☎ (440) 572-0400
South
20884 Royalton Rd., Strongsville
Live bait, lures, tackle, fly-tying equip., fly-fishing equip., clothing
Hours: Mon, Thu–Fri 10 a.m.–9 p.m., Tue–Wed, Sat 10 a.m.–5 p.m.
Located on the corner of State Route 82 and Prospect in Royalville Plaza. Has one of the largest selections of fishing tackle in the state. Also sells most kinds of live bait, except minnows.

Sportsman's Outpost
☎ (440) 967-4000
Farther West
4340 Liberty Ave., Vermilion
Lures, tackle, boating supplies
Hours: Mon–Sat 7 a.m.–6 p.m., Sun 7 a.m.–2 p.m.
Seasonal hours may vary by how the fish are biting. (Call ahead if you need to get in early or late.) Charter information available. Also carries a limited selection of hunting equipment.

Wal-Mart
Various locations—see below
Lures, tackle, fly fishing equip., boating supplies, clothing
A very large—if not basic—offering of rods, lures, tackle, and other angling fare. Prices for most items are usually better than at more specialized retailers, but there is less variety of choice.

East	Eastlake: 34440 Vine St., (440) 269-8827
Farther East	Ashtabula: 3551 N. Ridge Rd. NE, (440) 998-4000
	Mentor: 9303 Mentor Ave., (440) 974-3300
	Warren: 2015 Elm Rd. NE, (330) 372-1722
South	Macedonia: 590 E. Aurora Rd., (330) 468-0200
Farther South	Akron: 2887 S. Arlington Rd., (330) 645-9556
	Fairlawn: 3750 W. Market St., (330) 668-1129
	Medina: 4141 Pearl Rd., (330) 723-1122
	Streetsboro: 9440 State Route 14, (330) 626-9998
West	Brooklyn: 10000 Brookpark Rd., (216) 741-7340
	North Olmsted: 25001 Brookpark Rd., (440) 979-9234
	Strongsville: 858 Pearl Rd., (440) 826-0004
Farther West	Elyria: 149 Midway Blvd., (440) 324-4104

Directory

Charters & Guides

1st Pursuit Sport Fishing Charters   ☎ (440) 942-3249
36967 Stevens Blvd., Willoughby   **Farther West**
Main port: Port Clinton; secondary port: Fairport.

Angling Consulting Services   ☎ (440) 846-8877
13098 Tradewinds Dr., Strongsville   **Farther East**
Specializes in providing steelhead guide service on the Conneaut River.

Aqua Fantaseas Fishing Charters   ☎ (440) 257-3231
6076 Walden Court, Mentor   **Farther East**
Main port: Fairport Harbor.

Aqua Holic Charters   ☎ (440) 248-4472
6820 S.O.M. Center Rd., Solon   **East**
Main port: Chagrin River.

Argument Sport Fishing Charters   ☎ (440) 466-3254; (800) 209-6263
3107 S. Myers Rd., Geneva   **Farther East**
The *Argument* takes out from Port Clinton in April and switches to Geneva from May through
September.

Bandit Charters   ☎ (440) 543-9160
10980 Meadow Ln., Auburn   **East**
Main port: Cleveland (Wildwood Park); secondary port: Geneva.

Blue Moon Charters   ☎ (440) 357-8781
10270 Page Dr., Concord   **East**
Main port: Chagrin River; secondary port: Cleveland.

Burns Charters   ☎ (330) 747-1797
978 E. Dewey, Youngstown   **Farther West**
Main port: Port Clinton (Apr–Jun), Geneva (Jul–Sep).

Central Basin Charter Boat Association, Inc.   ☎ (800) 686-4702
C.B.C.B.A. Dept. C7, Box 155, Lorain   **Farther West**
This is a service that can set clients up with individual charter captains who suit their specific
needs, from last-minute, late-day excursions, to all-inclusive, full-day executive fishing charters.
Visit them on the Web at www.walleyecentral.com\cbcba.htm.

Coastal Fishing Adventures   ☎ (440) 585-0774
30621 Crescent Dr., Willowick   **East**
Main port: Chagrin River; secondary port: Cleveland.

Cold Springs Guide Service Inc.   ☎ (440) 466-6618
5412 Cold Springs Rd., Geneva   **Farther East**
Main port: Geneva.

DB Sport Fishing Charters   ☎ (440) 259-2511; (800) 769-1750
4113 Green St., Perry   **Farther East**
Charters depart from Geneva State Park Marina; secondary port: Fairport Harbor.

Dead-eye Sportfishing Charters   ☎ (800) 579-4483
1543 Collier Rd., Akron   **Farther West**
Main port: Lorain; secondary port: Cleveland.

Double J Charters   ☎ (800) 950-4887
14391 Shore Rd., Kent   **Farther West**
Double J Charters are available on the Niagara River (Jan–Mar), Lake Erie from the Port Clinton
area (Apr–Jun), and Lake Ontario (Jul–Oct).

Double-0-Seven Charters   ☎ (440) 974-8970
7324 Case Ave., Mentor   **Farther West**
Main port: Port Clinton; secondary port: Fairport.

Evil Eye Sportfishing   ☎ (440) 636-5663
11630 Clay St., Huntsburg   **Farther East**
Main port: Fairport Harbor.

***EyePopper* Fishing Charters**   ☎ (440) 288-2002; (800) 937-5668
925 Colorado Ave., Lorain   **Farther West**
Main port: Lorain. The *EyePopper* offers full-service charters in the Central Basin area for walleye, perch, smallmouth bass, and steelhead. Contact them on the net for more info at capteye@centuryinter.net. An updated Lake Erie fishing report is available at www.charterfishing.net/eyepopper/.

Fish Man Guide Services   ☎ (412) 269-1285
118 Shippen Dr., Coraopolis, PA   **Farther East**
John Bodner of Fish Man Guide Services offers guided trips for steelhead, smallmouth bass, and trout on Northeast Ohio and Pennsylvania waterways. Trips are spent not only in pursuit of fish, but learning about their habits, hangouts, and life cycles, and learning how to read the water and understand the fishery. John Bodner also offers hand-tied flies and detailed maps of many Ohio and Pennsylvania rivers and streams.

Fish-on-Charters   ☎ (330) 467-1132
9054 McKinley Dr., Northfield   **Farther West**
Main port: Lorain (Jun–Jul); Lake Michigan (Aug–Sep). More info available online at www.FishonCharters.com.

Fishin' Boat Charter Service   ☎ (800) 777-9304
630 Oakmore, Bay Village   **East**
Main port: Cleveland (E. 55th Street Marina); secondary port: Lorain.

Fishmaster Charters   ☎ (440) 428-1938; (800) 879-8025
2729 Burns Rd., Madison   **Farther East**
Main port: Geneva.

Four Aces Fishing & Pleasure Chartering Service   ☎ (800) 998-8888
1133 Warren Rd., Newton Falls   **West**
Charter service for the Western and Central Basins of Lake Erie. All equipment included except lunch and fishing licenses.

Gremlin Charters   ☎ (800) 865-8732
9559 Mentor Rd., Chardon   **Farther East**
Main port: Fairport; secondary port: Geneva. More information available online at www.ncweb.com/biz/gremlin/web page.

Hooker Charter Services   ☎ (440) 417-0101
3420 Dayton Rd., Madison   **Farther East**
Main port: Geneva. Information available online: hooker@ncweb.com

J & L Charters   ☎ (440) 466-4475; (412) 884-4000
4240 White Oak Ct., Pittsburgh   **Farther East**
J & L Charters depart from Geneva during the months of June, July, August, and September. Main port: Geneva.

Key of the Sea Charters   ☎ (440) 466-7297 (May–Oct); (412) 366-0919
8095 Dormar Dr., Pittsburgh   **Farther East**
Main port: Geneva.

L. A. Charters   ☎ (440) 209-0713; (440) 257-1803
5709 Anna Ct., Mentor-on-the-Lake   **Farther East**
Main port: Fairport. More information available via e-mail: jgar@bbs2.rmrc.net

Laid Back Charters   ☎ (330) 343-6887
164 Herbert Rd. NE, Sherrodsville   **Farther East**

Main port: Fairport; secondary port: Port Clinton.

Lake Erie Charters   ☎ (440) 953-1117
905 Mannering, Eastlake   **East**
Main port: Chagrin River.

The Last Unicorn II   ☎ (330) 467-2191
8133 Olde Eight Rd., Northfield Ctr.   **East**
Main port: Cleveland.

Liv'n-Good Sport Fishing Charters   ☎ (330) 296-1234
3124 Robin Dr., Ravenna   **Farther East**
Located at Geneva State Park Marina. Fishes Lake Erie's Central Basin from Mentor to Conneaut.

Magic Moments   ☎ (440) 934-5875; (800) 270-9873
2392 Abbe Rd., Sheffield Village   **Farther West**
Main Port: Lorain.

Marble Eye Charters   ☎ (440) 428-6034
1669 Meadows Rd., Madison   **Farther East**
Main port: Geneva.

Mariner Sport Fishing Charters, The   ☎ (440) 953-8831
36558 Lakehurst Dr., Eastlake   **East**
Charter service for the Central Basin out of the Chagrin River. Secondary ports: Fairport Harbor and
Cleveland.

Memories Charters   ☎ (440) 946-7194
5450 Chestnut Hill, Willoughby   **East**
Main port: Chagrin River; secondary port: Cleveland. More information available via e-mail:
captom@bbs2.rmrc.net.

No Woes Charters   ☎ (440) 942-3570
224 Traymore, Eastlake   **East**
Main port: Chagrin River; secondary port: Cleveland.

One Stop Charters, Inc.   ☎ (216) 481-5771; (440) 942-1909 (24-hour info line)
P.O. Box 5387, Willowick   **East**
One Stop Charters, located at Wildwood State Park in Cleveland, offers private charters for both
walleye and perch to groups as large as 30 or as small as six. They also operate a walk-on boat
called the *Linda Mae* that offers anglers excellent perch-fishing opportunities. Call (440) 942-1909
to hear a 24-hour information tape on One Stop Charters.

Perfecter Sport Fishing Charters   ☎ (440) 354-2239
270 Mill Morr Rd., Painesville   **Farther East**
Main port: Fairport Harbor.

Pooh Bear Sport Fishing   ☎ (888) 698-2381; (440) 559-1636 (boat)
733 East Main St., Apple Creek   **Farther East**
Main ports: Fairport, Port Clinton.

Priority Charters   ☎ (330) 274-3072
3052 Frost Rd., Mantua   **East**
Main port: Cleveland (Wildwood Marina); secondary port: Fairport.

Prowler Charters   ☎ (888) ON-PROWL
1220 Williamsport Rd., Elizabeth, PA   **Farther East**
Main port: Fairport; secondary port: Point Breeze, NY (for salmon).

Reel-Eye-Deal Fishing Charters   ☎ (800) 203-3201
6165 Cedar Wood Rd., Mentor   **Farther East**
Main port: Fairport; secondary port: Geneva.

Reelers Choice Charters   ☎ (330) 337-3371
10880 SR 62, Salem   **Farther East**

Main port: Geneva; secondary port: Ashtabula.

The Release Charter Service ☎ (800) 432-0709; (330) 745-5157
733 E. Tuscarawas Ave., Barberton East
Offers charter trips for walleye and steelhead on Lake Erie, and salmon and trout on Lake Ontario.

Rock-Eye Fishing Charters ☎ (440) 352-3663
2670 Larchview Dr., Painesville Farther East
Main port: Fairport.

Rock-N-Reel Charters ☎ (216) 883-2630
3969 E. 29th St., Newburgh Hts. East
Main port: Cleveland (E. 55th St. Marina).

Royal Charters ☎ (330) 856-1945
7740 Micawber Rd. NE, Warren Farther East
Main port: Ashtabula.

Sara J. Fishing Charters, Inc. ☎ (216) 573-0449
6861 Chadbourne Dr., Valley View East
Main ports: Cleveland and Eastlake; Lorain in May and June.

Schoney Charters ☎ (440) 951-4012
6227 Thunderbird Dr., Mentor Farther East
Charter service offering trips for smallmouth bass during May, June, September, and October. Also can be booked for walleye and steelhead from May through September. Offers a "hands-on charter," on which the customers are taught to set the gear, even if they have little experience. Main port: Fairport.

Shirley B. Charters ☎ (330) 722-0268; (800) 996-4453
7283 Branch Rd., Medina Farther West
Features trips for walleye and perch fishing out of Lorain and Fairport, Ohio, and salmon and trout fishing out of Olcott, New York.

Sportsman Charter Service ☎ (800) 546-FISH; (419) 798-4720
2086 S. Sugar Bush Rd., Marblehead Farther West
Main ports: Marblehead and Geneva.

Stow-A-Way Charters ☎ (330) 688-7928
1960 Bryn Mawr, Stow Farther West
Main port: Port Clinton; secondary port: Fairport.

Sugartime ☎ (440) 543-4856; (440) 834-8406
8423 E. Washington St., Chagrin Falls Farther East
Main port: Geneva State Park Marina; secondary port: Cleveland.

Sunrise Sportfishing ☎ (800) 236-8659
P.O. Box 668, Grand River Farther East
Sunrise Sportfishing offers charters for salmon on Lake Ontario, and for walleye on Lake Erie. Two boats are available for charter, *Sunrise* and *Sunrise II*.

Swetkis, Jay ☎ (216) 476-1406
14626 Orchard Park Ave., Cleveland West
Freelance captain, specializes in western-basin fishing.

Thumper Charter Fishing ☎ (440) 255-3372; (440) 639-0185 (evenings)
7278 Jackson St., Mentor Farther East
Main port: Fairport; secondary port: Port Clinton.

Tibbels Charter Service ☎ (419) 734-1143
6965 E. Harbor Rd., Marblehead Farther West
Charter service offering fishing excursion in the Western Basin of Lake Erie.

Tomasko, Bob ☎ (440) 834-1347
P.O. Box 258, 14569 Hickox St., Burton Farther East

Directory

Bob Tomasko has been a fishing guide since the early 1970s, and in 1992 he was inducted into the National Freshwater Hall of Fame. He offers guide services on Pymatuning, Mosquito, and Conneaut lakes, and West Branch Reservoir, for all species of fish. Bob also developed the "Learn-A-Lake System," a series of map/tape sets that gives detailed information on fishing local waters.

Trophy Charters ☎ (440) 293-7249
7041 Lake Rd. S., Andover **Farther East**

Trophy Charters offers trips out of Port Clinton (Apr–May) and Ashtabula (Jun–Sep).

Twins II Fishing Charters ☎ (216) 391-7032
7502 Lockyear Ave., Cleveland **East**

All trips depart from the Eastbank Marina on the Chagrin River. Secondary port: Cleveland. No alcohol allowed.

Wave Walker Charters ☎ (216) 641-2549
P.O. Box 27382, Cleveland **East**

Departs from the East 55th Marina. Wave Walker was one of the only charter services to specialize in fishing off the Cleveland shoreline back when most fishermen ventured to the Western Basin for walleye fishing charters.

Whitecap Marine Charters ☎ (216) 347-9601
5827 Parkville Dr., Parma Hts. **East**

Main port: Cleveland.

Directory

Selected Reading List

Here are some other sources of information on fishing in Northeast Ohio and on fishing in general that I have found useful:

Of Local Interest:

Cleveland Metroparks Fishing Areas and Fishing Programs, Cleve. Metroparks, 1998.

Lake Erie Fishing Guide, Ohio Department of Natural Resources, 1997.

Ohio Fish Identification Guide, Ohio Department of Natural Resources/Division of Wildlife, 1997.

Great Fishing in Lake Erie & Its Tributaries, Will Elliott, Stackpole Books, 1991.

The Fishes of Ohio, Milton B. Trautman, Ohio State University Press, 1981.

The Plain Dealer (regular colums by D'Arcy Egan).

The News Herald (regular colums by Jeff Frischkorn).

Of General Interest:

Field & Stream magazine.

Fly Fisherman magazine.

Freshwater Fishing Tips & Techniques, Gene Kugach, Stackpole Books, 1997.

Our Native Fishes, John R. Quinn, Countryman Press, 1990.

The Fascinating Fresh Water Fish Book, John Wiley and Sons, Inc., 1994.

Sports Afield magazine.

Steelhead Fly Fishing, Trey Combs, Lyons & Burford, Publishers, 1991.

Pond and Brook, Michael J. Caduto, University Press of New England.

Index

Index

...crapbook / Rare photos, show transcripts, and video captures from "The Main ...veland late-night TV. *Ron Sweed & Mike Olszewski* / $17.95 softcover

...Cleveland / The best from three decades of commentary by Cleveland's top ...Dick Feagler. Witty, insightful, opinionated, thoughtful. / $13.95 softcover

...u Read Feagler Today?" / The most talked about recent columns by Cleveland's most ...en columnist. / $13.95 softcover

...ing Brown / Thoughtful essays and interviews exploring what it means to be a true fan of ...eveland Browns. *Scott Huler* / $18.95 hardcover, $10.95 softcover

...ians Memories / A nostalgic roller coaster ride including laughably bad seasons and two ...iting eras of championship baseball. *Tim Long* / $5.95 softcover

...arnaby and Me / Linn Sheldon, a Cleveland TV legend as "Barnaby", tells the fascinating story of his own extraordinary life. / $20.00 hardcover

The Great Indoors / The first decade of Eric Broder's hilarious weekly "Great Indoors" column. Reread favorites, or get caught up with the ongoing saga. / $13.95 softcover

Cleveland Sports Trivia Quiz / Test your knowledge with these 500 brain-teasing questions and answers on all kinds of Cleveland sports. *Tim Long* / $6.95 softcover

Cleveland TV Memories / Remember when TV was local? A nostalgic collection of 365 favorite local shows, hosts, jingles, bloopers, stunts, and more. *Feran & Heldenfels* / $6.95 softcover

Bed & Breakfast Getaways from Cleveland / 80 charming small inns perfect for an easy weekend or evening away from home. *Doris Larson* / $13.95 softcover

The Cleveland Orchestra Story / How a midwestern orchestra became a titan in the world of classical music. With 102 rare photographs. *Donald Rosenberg* / $40.00 hardcover

Available at your local bookstore.

These books are stocked at Northeast Ohio bookstores, are available through most online book retailers, and can be ordered at any bookstore in the U.S.

Need help finding a retailer near you? Call us: 1-800-915-3609.

Gray & Company, Publishers
1588 E. 40th St., Cleveland, OH 44103 / 216-431-2665
www.grayco.com